Teaching Mathematics in Elementary Schools

By

Prof. Marlow Ediger

Division of Education

Truman State University

Kirksville MO. 63501, Missouri State

USA

&

Dr. Digumarti Bhaskara Rao

M.Sc., M.A., M.A., M.Ed., Ph.D.

R.V.R. College of Education

Guntur–522 006

Andhra Pradesh

DISCOVERY PUBLISHING HOUSE

NEW DELHI-110002

TEACHING MATHEMATICS IN ELEMENTARY SCHOOLS

First Published - 2004

Reprinted - 2017

ISBN: 978-93-5056-516-2 (Set)

ISBN: 978-81-7141-687-5

Teaching Mathematics in Elementary Schools

Published by:

DISCOVERY PUBLISHING HOUSE PVT. LTD.
4383/4B, Ansari Road Darya Ganj
New Delhi - 110 002 (India)
Phone: +91-11-23279245, 43596064-65
Fax: +91-11-23253475
E-mail: discoverypublishinghouse@gmail.com
sales@discoverypublishinggroup.com
web: www.discoverypublishinggroup.com

Printed at:
Infinity Imaging Systems
Delhi

To
A Great Educationist and Philosopher

Maharajasri Babaji
Vidwan Gogineni Kanakaiah
"Founder of Several Educational Institutions"

Preface

Teaching Mathematics in Elementary Schools is written for pre-service and in-service education of elementary teachers. It integrates well in content with science, social studies and languages. The contents will guide teachers to provide for individual differences so that each pupil may achieve as optimally as possible. As teachers need to keep up with the latest in literature pertaining to teaching mathematics in elementary schools, this book will help in teaching mathematics effectively.

–Dr. Marlow Ediger
–Dr. Digumarti Bhaskara Rao

Contents

1

Current Concepts in Teaching Mathematics

A mathematics teacher has to determine what the literature in the teaching of mathematics indicates to be trends in selecting objectives, learning opportunities, and evaluation procedures. Indepth surveying pertaining to literature in teaching mathematics indicates that there are selected concepts that recur rather frequently. A further purpose of this paper is to indicate from a research study of mathematics literature which concepts appear most frequently. By communicating relevant concepts, the mathematics teacher may benefit in upgrading the curriculum. Hopefully, pupil achievement will increase as a result of the teacher's increased knowledge pertaining to the teaching of mathematics.

Providing Equity for All Pupils

A major concern in mathematics is providing equal opportunities to learn for all pupils. There has been much discussion on the pros and cons pertaining to tracking pupils. Davenport (1993) summarizes research studies pertaining to tracking pupils. The results indicated that pupils in lower tracks, in particular, experienced the following:

1. inequities to a strong mathematics curriculum
2. inequities to well qualified mathematics teachers
3. inequities to quality classroom learning opportunities

Devenport then recommends strongly that schools move

away from homogeneous to heterogeneous grouping of pupils in a classroom. The homogeneous-heterogeneous grouping controversy has been in evidence for some time. Shepherd and Ragan (1982) give the following advantages of homogeneous grouping; gifted students may achieve more optimally with this plan of grouping; parents who have sons/daughters in the higher ability groups favor this plan of grouping pupils; teachers find it easier to teach when pupils are of similar abilities in a classroom; and teachers can provide for individual differences better when uniformity of achievement is in evidence in a classroom. Disadvantages given are the following: the plan violates the pupil's right to be different; one trait only is then used for grouping and that is ability, ability grouping is a form of segregation in that high ability pupils come from upper socioeconomic level of income; and parents frequently object to having their child in the slowest group.

Educational literature in mathematics is quite concerned in providing for equity among pupils in ongoing learning opportunities. Pupils should not be discriminated against due to race, creed, and national origin, among other items. Presently, there has been much writing about equality and equity in learning activities and experiences for pupils. Equal access is to be stressed be it in computer use, materials of instruction, quality teachers, school building and classroom, as well as equipment in teaching and learning situations.

Ernst (1991) states that "a teacher working from a multicultural, social-reconstructionist approach attempts to create a learning environment that is 'as democratic and open as the power asymmetries of the classroom allow, but with explicit recognition of this asymmetry." He suggested that genuine discussion between students and the teacher with pedagogical processes that stress the following:

1. Cooperative group work, projects and problem solving to promote engagement and mastery.
2. Autonomous projects, problem posing, and investigative work to afford pupil opportunities for self-directed and personally relevant activities.

In a multicultural social-reconstructionist approach in

teaching, equity and fairness within the framework of democratic tenets should be stressed in mathematics. The subject matter of mathematics is emphasized with critical and creative thinking as well as its use/application in the societal area. Cooperative learning stresses that pupils be grouped heterogeneously so that the talented/gifted as well as slower learners may learn from each other. Quality human relations as well as acquiring vital subject matter in mathematics are being emphasized. Learning to respect each other as well as possess vital knowledge to solve problems is vital. To promote the concept of providing for individual differences, pupils individually may work autonomously on a project, activity, or independent study. There needs to be rational balance between group and individual pupil endeavors in mathematics. Thus pupils need to be able to work within committees effectively and work by the self in aiming toward optimal achievement. Life itself in the real world consists of being with others and with the self. Each person should learn to live abundantly as a member of a committee and profit from being able to achieve and grow as an individual. The National Council Teachers of Mathematics in their publication Professional Standards for Teaching Mathematics (1991) recommends that teachers of mathematics know and use the following:

1. How students' linguistic, ethnic, racial, gender, and socioeconomic backgrounds influence their learning of mathematics.
2. The role of mathematics in society and culture, the contribution of various cultures to the advancement of mathematics, and the relationship to other subjects and realistic applications.

All pupils need to attain optimally in mathematics. African-American, Hispanic and Native Americans, among other minority groups, need to have a mathematics curriculum which harmonizes with preferred personal ways of learning. A pupil not speaking English in a proficient manner may need a mathematics curriculum written in whole or part for use in his/her native language. Racial and linguistic biases of teachers must be eliminated. With peer teaching and coaching, teachers can assist each other to respect all learners in the classroom with fair and conscientious teaching. Care and concern for each pupil is a necessity.

Female pupils need encouragement to develop and achieve optimally. Girls too frequently have not developed their skills in mathematics due to gender bias. They may also have not selected mathematics related careers due to not receiving needed encouragement in the school setting.

Diverse philosophies are in evidence to guide each pupil to attain more optimally. (Ediger, 1994-95) emphasized four philosophies that mathematics teachers may emphasize in the classroom. These are the following:

1. Mathematics as subject matter acquisition. Here, the teacher stresses pupils acquiring relevant facts, concepts and generalizations. A subject centered curriculum is then in evidence. Abstract teaching materials are used largely. Concrete and semiconcrete experiences for pupils are stressed if this assists learners to attain more optimally in symbolic learnings.
2. Measurement driven instruction. Predetermined objectives have been chosen for pupil to achieve. Each objective is stated so that the measurement device in testing used will determine if the learner has/has not achieved the stated ends.
3. Humanism in the mathematics curriculum. There is considerable pupil-teacher planning in selecting objectives, learning opportunities, and evaluation procedures. Input from pupils is welcomed in ongoing learning activities.
4. Mathematics as problem solving. In context as problems are identified, pupils with teacher guidance use subject matter in mathematics to solve the chosen problems. Probem solving is a utilitarian approach in teaching mathematics.

We strongly recommend problem solving procedures in mathematics teaching more so as compared to the other three above-named approaches. There are times when individual decision-making (humanism) by pupils in mathematics can provide excellent opportunities for the teacher to plan with the learner which activity, project, or investigation the latter is to engage in. Certainly, individual needs, interests, and purposes are important to provide for in ongoing lessons and units of study. Mathematics tends to be a rather precise objective academic discipline: thus behavioral stated objectives with its criterion referenced tests (measurement driven instruction) may be used at selected intervals in teaching and learning. A strong argument can also be made for emphasizing a subject centered approach in teaching. Certainly, pupils should attain structural properties of mathematics such as commutative, associative, and distributive properties of addition and multiplication. Thinking of, and reflecting upon, these structural ideas when taught requires abstract learning ultimately. Sequentially concrete, semi-concrete, and abstract materials of instruction be used to think abstractly. Bruner (1960) was a strong advocate of pupils achieving structural ideas inductively and with the use of the following sequential materials: manipulative, iconic, and symbolic. He believed strongly that pupils need to have key or structural ideas so that new content can be analyzed in terms of the subject matter already possessed. Bruner also stressed the importance of a spiral curriculum whereby each structural idea is achieved at a more complex level by the learner as he/she progresses through the sequential years of schooling. The structural ideas then are met up with again and again as pupil achieve on different levels of the public school. Each pupil then is aided in achievement when possessing a structure of the academic discipline of mathematics. Newly acquired content is related to the already possessed structure.

The mathematics teacher should use an appropriate philosophy of teaching at a given time which stresses each pupil learning as much as possible. Pupils differ from each other in many ways such as abilities, interests, purposes, and attitudes. It behoves the mathematics teacher to guide pupils individually to attain optimally be it working by the self or within a committee setting.

The behaviorally stated objectives approach stresses pupils attaining at different rates even though they are following the same mathematics curriculum. Thus with predetermined objectives such as in Measurement Driven Instruction (MDI), each pupil may work at his/her own optimal rate of speed to attain the objectives sequentially. Slow learners may need more assistance as compared to other learners in the classroom. Thus, time becomes the variable; selected pupils need more time as compared to the others to attain the stated objectives.

There are educators who believe that high standards should be set for all pupils to attain regardless of their ability levels. The same objectives should then be achieved by all learners in a class. There should be no tracking or ability grouping of pupils for instruction. Rather the class is taught as a whole. Distinctions are not made among pupils in this definition of democracy. All pupils are to receive the same sophisticated knowledge in the class. The teacher must have high expectations for all pupils in the class. Careful monitoring of each pupil's progress is a must. Evaluation needs to be in evidence to notice if each pupil is learning and achieving.

Gandal (1995) lists and discusses criteria in setting standards for pupil achievement. These are the following:

1. Standards must focus on academics.
2. Standards must be based in the core disciplines.
3. Standards must be specific enough to assure the development of a common core curriculum.
4. Standards must be manageable given the constraints of time.
5. Standards must be rigorous and world-class.
6. Standards must evaluate performance.
7. Standards must include multiple levels of performance.
8. Standards must combine knowledge and skills.
9. Standards must not dictate how the material is to be taught.
10. Standards must be written clearly.

The above standards indicate a strong subject centered curriculum with demanding goals for pupils to attain. Individual differences are provided for in standard seven where Gandal (1995) wrote, "France and Germany have high standards for all their students, but they don't expect all to meet the same standard. It's just not realistic to expect the same from everyone."

Dewey's experimentalist philosophy of education (1938) emphasized that knowledge is subjective as experienced and amenable to change. He stressed that absolutes do not exist in life. One can only know what has been experienced, not what is outside the framework of human experience. Since these conditions exist, knowledge is tentative and as new experiences are encountered subject to modification and change. That is why problems arise and new approaches are necessary in the solving of problems. Since school and society are integrated, not separate entities, Dewey believed that problem solving is important in each arena. In scoiety, people tend to work in groups to solve problems. Thus pupils in the school setting also need to work in committee endeavors. Lifelike, real problems need identification and related solutions are found. Knowledge is used to solve problems and is not an end in and of itself. There should be no barriers as to which pupils are involved in the solving of problems. All should use the methods of problem solving in the school curriculum and the curriculum of life. Dewey was a strong believer in democracy as a way of life. Each pupil could then achieve optimally.

Objectives of Instruction

Tha National Council Teachers of Mathematics (1989) developed high quality standards for mathematics teachers to use in planning for teaching-learning situations. These standards provide objectives of instructions as well as criteria to gauge one's own mathematics curriculum. One's own mathematics curriculum then may be compared with the NCTM standards. Revisions and modifications in the local curriculum might well be an end result. As examples, the NCTM standards that pertain to numbers and numeration for grades K-4 emphasize the following:

1. construct number meanings through real world experience and the use of physical materials;
2. understand our numeration system by relating counting, grouping, and place value concepts;
3. develop number sense;
4. interpret the multiple uses of numbers encountered in the real world.

To achieve standard number one above, pupils need to experience lifelike problems in society in which mathematics is used. Markers and objects should be used to aid pupils in understanding the abstract. For standard number two, pupils need to have good command of counting using the set of counting numbers. Initial counting emphasizes a one-to-one correspondence between the oral number counted in sequence and the related number of objectives in a set. Being able to group markers in terms of five or ten in a set when asked to do so, among others, indicates that meaningful learning is taking place. Sequentially the pupil should understand place value such as the ones, tens, and hundreds column. It is always important for pupils to understand and comprehend what is taught so that meaningful learning is taking place. This would emphasize standard three above. Standard four places much stress upon pupils attaching meaning to the numeration system as it relates to use and application in societal endeavors. The National Council Teachers of Mathematics (1989) emphasizes four standards that are broad in scope that apply to all grade levels. These standards encompass problem solving, communication, reasoning, and mathematical connections. In addition to these four broad standards, nine topical standards are listed for each level of instruction. These are estimation, number sense and numeration, concepts of whole number operation, geometry and spatial sense, measurement, statistics and probability, fractions and decimals, and patterns and relationships. Maturity and capability levels of pupils are emphasized when the standards are stressed in the mathematics curriculum.

To have pupils achieve well, the teacher should use recommended principles of learning from educational psychology. Ediger (1994) recommends that teachers use the following agreed upon criteria when teaching pupils:

1. meaningful lessons in units of study. With meaning, pupils understand and comprehend that which was contained in ongoing learning opportunities.
2. interesting content and skills in the curriculum. With interest, the pupil and the curriculum become one, not separate entities. Pupils attend and achieve from ongoing lessons and units of study.
3. purpose in learning. With purpose for learning, pupils accept reasons for attaining relevant facts, concepts, and generalizations presented.
4. sequence in learning. With quality sequence, pupils relate

newly acquired content with that previously achieved. Previous knowledge attained provides readiness for the new objectives to be achieved. Pupils need guidance to perceive relationship of knowledge in teaching-learning situations.

5. balance among objectives stressed. Thus knowledge, skills, and attitudes–three kinds of obectives need to be achieved by students. These objectives interact and are not in isolation from each other. For example, if pupils possess positive attitudes, they should achieve needed knowledge and skills more readily.

To achieve objectives of instruction, pupils need to experience a multimedia interactive mode of teaching. Hatfield and Bitter (1994) provide the following characteristics of a multimedia approach:

1. Promotes active versus passive learning.
2. Offers models or examples of exemplorary and nonexemplorary instruction.
3. Is illustrative and interactive.
4. Facilitates the development of decision-making and problem solving abilities.
5. Provides user control and multiple pathways for assessing information.
6. Provides motivation and allows for variability of learning styles.
7. Facilitates the development of perceptual and interpretational abilities.
8. Offers efficient management of time for learning and less instructional training time.
9. Allows for numerous data types, e.g. animation, graphics voice, texts and motion video.
10. Offers multilingual presentation. The technology exists whereby programs and units can be presented in different languages.

Learning Opportunities

There are numerous beliefs pertaining to how learning should be encouraged and optimized in mathematics. B.F. Skinner was a strong advocate of reinforcement theory of learning. Thus there must be clearly stated objectives to achieve, written in measurable terms. The teacher teaches so that pupils might attain the precise objectives. If the pupil responds correctly, a reward should follow. The reward could be given on a ratio or time basis. In the ratio approach one reward, for example, for every five correct responses given could be stressed by the teacher. In terms of time, a reward given for five minutes of concentrated attention to the lesson at hand would be a further example of reinforcement theory of learning. Extrinsic motivation is then in evidence.

Bruner (1977) advocated intrinsic motivation as being vital in teaching-learning situations. Learning is its very own reward. Challenging questions through inductive procedures of instruction would assist pupils to value learning for its own sake in problem solving. There has been a long debate in the extrinsic versus intrinsic approaches in helping pupils learn. Good and Teller (1973), in writing about the Lancastrian Monitorial School that was brought to the US in 1805, stressed the rewards that pupils received for doing well. These were badges, offices, and orders of merit. The reward system had been used in England prior to the early 1800's. As an example of intrinsic motivation stressed in the history of education, Cole (1950) emphasized that Pestalozzi in the latter 1700's and early 1800's advocated pupils developing from within, not from without. The teacher then would motivate achievement rather than lecture or force pupils to learn. Instead of stifling a pupul's individuality, the pupil should be encouraged to develop his/her talents. A love for learing by pupils was important in Pestalozzi's thinking. Pestalozzi emphasized progressive methods of teaching pupils in that they should desire to learn from within with no prizes given for learning.

Should a developmental approach be used in teaching and learning situations or should high standards be set for all pupils to attain at the same time? Piaget (1950) whose educational writings based on clinical research have almost become a classic in education. For example, Piaget emphasized the following sequential stages that pupils go through in the school years:

1. preoperational–ages 2 to 7 approximately.
2. concrete operations–ages 7 to 11.
3. formal operations–above age eleven.

Piaget believed that each stage had tremendous implications in terms of what pupils can learn. Within each stage, there would also be important variations as to possible achievement levels of learners. In contrast, Ganal (1995) advocates that high academic standards for pupil attainment should be developed. All need to achieve goals and objectives pertaining to these standards. However in the evaluation process, there might be differences in how pupils of different achievement levels are evaluated.

As a further issue, should mathematics be taught as a separate subjects curriculum or should there be increased correlation, fusíon, and integration with other academic disciplines and with the real world in society? The "get back to the basics" movement is very strong on the part of selected lay people. President Reagan frequently stressed during the 1980's the need to teach the basics. The basics emphasizing the separate subjects curriculum has a rather lengthy history. Among others, William Chandler Bagley (1938) was an essentialist, another name for one who advocates the basics in the curriculum for all pupils. Bagley believed strongly in maintaining a separate subjects curriculum. The academic disciplines were not to be integrated in terms of content to be studied by pupils. He believed a "watered down curriculum" resulted when subject matter areas failed to show their differences. The National Council Teachers of Mathematics, as well as Growth in Education through a Mathematical Mentorship Alliance (GEMMA), advocates that subject matter be related in the curriculum. GEMMA brings together individuals from different walks and professions in life to ascertain what can be done to improve the mathematics curriculum. To emphasize relationships among different curriculum areas, GEMMA (Farrell 1994) stresses the following objectives, among others:

1. helping pupils discover connections between mathematics and science, engineering, and other disciplines used in the workplace.
2. disseminating to teachers materials about current real world applications of mathematics.
3. providing students with examples of mathematical applications that require problem-solving skills in school and in life after school.

4. forming a network between mentors and teachers, mentors and other mentors, and teachers and other teachers.
5. Empowering a group of teachers to become leaders through a unique learning experience and reinforcing their leadership skills with opportunities to interact with other professionals at local, state, and national meetings.
6. Allowing teachers and mentors to examine how present curriculum and instruction follow guidelines set forth in the NCTM's (1989) Curriculum and Evaluation Standards for School Mathematics. Teachers need to notice how these standards can improve student's preparation for careers in science, business, and industry.

Educational psychologists believe, through research results, that knowledge perceived as being related will be remembered longer as compared to that which is compartmentalized.

Evaluation of Pupil Achievement

How should learner progress be evaluated? Numerous workshops, staff development programs, faculty meetings, and professional organizations have emphasized the importance of quality means of appraising learners in mathematics. Sharing ideas pertaining to evaluation guides teachers to develop a larger repertoire of strategies to use in effectively appraising pupil progress. Cain, Kenney, and Schloemer (1994) wrote, "Although there are many possible scenarios for establishing the link between professional development and classroom assessment, perhaps the best one involves 'teachers helping teachers.' As teachers develop the necessary strategies and skills necessary for becoming successful mathematics assessors, it is important that they share their knowledge with their fellow teachers. One single teacher who becomes hooked on using effective methods of alternative assessment in the classroom can serve as an available resource to other teachers in the school."

Collegiality and collaboration in sharing objectives, learning opportunities, and evaluation procedures are needed for teachers to determine the best methods of evaluating pupil achievement in mathematics. These three components of teaching mathematics cannot be separated from each other. Nor should they be. As the teacher teache, he/she evaluates each pupil's progress. The mathematics teachers then raises questions, in terms of self evaluation, pertaining to the following in teaching-learning situations:

1. how are pupils thinking about problems being discussed? It is essential that teachers understand how each learner processes information in mathematics.
2. how can I make mathematics dynamic and useful to learners?
3. how might my observations assist in providing improved sequence in learning for each pupil? Pupils solve problems in specific identifiable ways; the teacher must observe how this is done in order to make quality instructional decisions.
4. how may I guide my pupils to perceive reasons for learning in ongoing lessons and units of study?
5. how can I incorporate adequate manipulative items, pictorial visual materials, and symbolic experience to aid pupil thinking and reflection?
6. how might the concepts of diagnosis and remediation be used more effectively in my teaching?
7. how can I secure my pupils' attention so that time on task will be more in evidence?
8. how can pupils be guided to appreciate and use mathematics in everyday life's situations?
9. how can interests be developed within pupils toward mathematics which will be applicable in the work place?
10. how might pupils be assisted to perceive the relationship of knowledge in mathematics to other curriculum areas and to life in the societal arena?

Self evaluation by the mathematics teacher is vital to improve the curriculum. Each teacher needs to view the self in terms of what is being emphasized in teaching and learning as compared to what should be a normative approach. Quality evaluation is the key to make necessary modifications in mathematics instruction. Ediger (1988) lists and discusses the following techniques to use in appraising pupil's progress in mathematics: teacher written test items including multiple choice, matching, true-false, short answer, and essay; rating scales and checklists with accompanying relevant standards as a basis for evaluating pupil progress; standardized norm referenced tests; criterion referenced tests; anecdotal records and journal entries; discussions and cooperative learning with quality standards used; teacher observation; pupil diary entries and logs; sociometric devices to notice social growth of learners; assessment of peer learning; and portfolios of pupil work. A variety of evaluation procedures should be used to appraise pupil achievement. The results from each approach may be used to compare with other procedures. No one approach is perfect. Thus different procedures need to be used to evaluate learner performance to secure the best appraisal results possible. The National Council Teachers of Mathematics emphasizes a broad based assessment program:

The advantage of using several kinds of assessments, some of which are embedded in instruction, is that students evolving understanding can be continuously monitored. The disadvantage is that such a procedure is perceived cumbersome. Records of student progress should be more than a set of numerical grades or checklists; they can include brief notes or samples of students' work. Such records are evidence of students' continued growth in understanding. Students should also maintain their own records. At all grades, students can keep portfolios of their work; in the higher grades, as they become more verbally fluent and reflective, they should be encouraged to keep a mathematics journal. These journals contain goals, discoveries, thoughts, and observations, as well as descriptions of activities. Journals allow students not only to chart their progress in understanding but also act as a focus for discussion between student and teacher, thereby fostering communication about mathematics itself.

Selected References

Davanport, Linda Ruiz (1993). The Effects of Homogeneous Groupings in Mathematics, ERIC Clearinghouse for Science, Mathematics, and Environmental Education, Columbus, Ohio.

Shepherd, Gene D., and William B. Ragan (1982). *Modern Elementary Curriculum.* New York: Holt, Rinehart and Winston, 59-62.

Ernst, Paul (1991). *Philosophy of Mathematics Education.* Bristol, Pennsylvania:

Falmer Press, 205-210.

National Council Teachers of Mathematics (1991). *Professional Standards for Teaching Mathematics*. Reston, Virginia: NCTM.

Ediger Marlow (1989). Old Order Amish Culture and Stability. *Social Science Perspectives Journal*, 4, 16-25.

Ediger, M. (1994-95). Problem Solving in Mathematics. *SMTS Journal*, 30, 66-67.

Bruner, Jerome (1977). *The Process of Education*. Cambridge, Massachusetts: Harvard University Press.

Gandal, Matthew (1995). Not All Standards are Created Equal. *Educational Leadership*, 52, 16-21.

Dewey, John (1938). *Experience and Education*. New York: Crowell Collier and Macmillan.

National Council Teachers of Mathematics (1989), *Curriculum and Evaluation Standards for School Mathematics*. Reston, Virginia; NCTM, 36.

National Council Teachers of Mathematics (1989), *Curriculum and Evaluation Standards for School Mathematics*. Reston, Virginia; NCTM, 23.

Ediger, Marlow (1994). Early Field Experiences in Teacher Education. *College Student Journal*, 28;302-306.

Hatfield, Mary M., and Gary G. Bitter (1994). A Multimedia Approach to the Professional Development of Teachers: A Virtual Classroom. *Professional Development for Teachers of Mathematics, Reston,* Virginia: Yearbook of the National Council Teachers of Mathematics.

Good, Harry G., and James Teller (1973). *A History of American Education*. New York: Collier-Macmillan Publishers, 129.

Cole, Luella. *A History of Education*. New York: Holt, Rinehart and Winston, 454-489.

Piaget, Jean (1950). *The Psychology of Intelligence*. New York: Harcourt Brace Jovanovich.

Bagley, William Chandler (1938). An Essentialist's Platform for the Advancement of American Education, *Educational Administration and Supervision,* 24: 241-246.

Farrell, Ann M. (1994). Industry Internships and Professional Development. *Professional Development for Teachers of Mathematics*. Reston, Virginia: NCTM Yearbook.

Cain, Ralph W., and others (1994). Teachers as Assessors: A Professional Development Challenge. *Professional Development for Teachers of Mathematics*. Washington, DC: National Council Teachers of Mathematics Yearbook.

Ediger, Marlow (1988). *The Elementary Curriculum*. Kirksville, Missouri; Simpson Publishing Company, 87-93.

National Council Teachers of Mathematics (1989). *Curriculum and Evaluation Standards for School Mathematics*. Reston, Virginia: NCTM, 233.

2

Psychology in Teaching Mathematics

Mathematics teachers need to study diverse psychologies of learning so that individual learners may be guided to attain as optimally as possible. With a thorough knowledge of the psychology of learning, teachers may do a better job of teaching mathematics to pupils of all ability levels. Individual differences among learners must be provided for in order that each pupil may learn as much mathematics as possible. A quality mathematics teacher emphasizes objectives, learning opportunities, and appraisal procedures that assist pupils individually to perceive meaning in the mathematics curriculum.

Meaning Theory in Teaching Mathematics

Mathematics teachers need to be certain that each pupil attaches meaning to facts, concepts, and generalizations, acquired in the curriculum. With meaningful subject matter, pupils may understand that which was taught. Understanding content presented in mathematics assists the pupil to clarify information. Clarity of understanding stresses that pupil comprehend subject matter presented. In deductive teaching, the teacher explains each fact, concept, and generalization so that meaningful learning may accrue. When induction as a method of instruction is used, the mathematics teacher asks numerous questions of pupils to receive feedback if they understand what was taught. We believe that teachers must spend adequate time in guiding pupils to perceive meaning, deductively and inductively, through the use of concrete, semiconcrete, and abstract materials of instruction in terms of content taught.

Directly related to pupils attaching meaning to ongoing content presented, learner must be able to use subject matter acquired. If subject matter acquired is used, the chances are it will be retained better than if it were not used. The teacher should assist pupils to apply facts, concepts, and generalizations acquired. Thus information can be used in solving word problems from the basal textbook used in the classroom. Pupils may also use previously acquired content when solving life-like problems in mathematics. The teacher might write problems and photocopy them for learners to respond to. These problems are directly related to what has been taught in ongoing lessons and units in mathematics. Learners too may write problems and exchange papers with others to solve each problem so that application can be made of what has been learned previously. Discussions led by the teacher can also get pupils wholeheartedly involved in making use of subject matter learned.

The mathematics teacher needs to guide learners to engage in higher levels of cognition when using meaningful materials for learners. Thus pupils need to have opportunities to engage in critical thinking. In separating the relevant from the irrelevant in working to secure answers to a word problem in mathematics involves critical thought. A separation then of what is salient as compared to that which is not important is necessary in critical thinking. That which is significant is then used to obtain an answer to a word problem contained in the basal or written by the teacher or a learner. Life in society demands that pupils become proficient now and in the future as an adult in the area of critical thought. Separating reality from fantasy and the real from that which is imaginary are necessary ingredients in critical thinking.

Novel solutions are needed to solve numerous problems. Creative thinking then needs adequate emphasis in the mathematics curriculum. For example, to solve a word problem, several algorithms may be used to arrive at an answer. Each algorithm might well provide the correct answer. Learners should become familiar with diversity involved here so that the algorithm that works best for the pupil may be used. Unique solutions to word problems should assist pupils to explore different options to each problem in the societal arena. Hopefully, this transfer from the mathematics curriculum to the real world of society will be in evidence. In society, individuals meet up with unique situations in which solutions are needed that are different from any solution used in the past.

Life-like problems actually faced by learners in mathematics need adequate emphasis in the curriculum. These problems involve buying and selling items, how to stay within one's own budget, as well as an increased use of mathematics in society emphasize problem solving involving reality. A creative mind may be necessary presently for the pupil as well as in the future to solve these problems involving mathematics. Creative thinking must be a definite goal in the mathematics curriculum. Critical thought is also necessary for pupils in solving life-like problems in mathematics. Comparing solutions in answer to a problem certainly stresses critical thought. Further situations involving critical thought emphasizes analyzing a problem in mathematics to study component parts. After comparing and analyzing possible solutions in dealing with problems in mathematics in the real world, a synthesis is needed. To synthesize, creative thinking again is in evidence. Synthesizing emphasizes securing wholeness in coming up with a solution to a problem area. Steps inherent in solving life-like problems (or word problems) in mathematics include the following:

1. defining the problem whereby clarity is in evidence.
2. gathering information in arriving at a tentative solution.
3. developing a hypothesis based on the acquired information.
4. testing the hypothesis in step three above.
5. revising the hypothesis, if needed.

In addition to pupils attaching meaning to what has been learned, applying that which has been learned, and engaging in higher levels of cognition, pupils also need to perceive purpose in learning in ongoing lessons and units off study in mathematics. There are selected approaches which can be used by the mathematics teacher to guide pupil to perceive purpose for achieving. A deductive procedure might be used. With deduction, the mathematics teacher explains to learners why the subject matter to be studied is relevant. We believe that the small amount of time needed to explain to learners why the subject matter to be acquired is salient is time well spent in teaching and learning situations. Instead of a deductive approach in guiding pupils to perceive purpose or reasons for learning, there are teachers who prefer an inductive approach. Here, the mathematics teacher asks questions of pupils as to why they believe the content to be studied is relevant to learn. Inductive procedures are more time consuming as compared to deduction since responses must come from learners when determining the relevance in studying vital facts, concepts, and generalizations in mathematics.

A third approach in guiding pupils to perceive purpose in learning is to use extrinsic rewards. Here, the mathematics teacher needs to announce prior to instruction what pupils are to learn as well as the reward that will accrue to learners if they achieve this goal. Rewards to be given might be inexpensive prizes, tokens to be exchanged for prizes, time given for a self selected activity, or extra recess time. The reward must motivate pupils to achieve more optimally in mathematics. It is given to pupils only if they have attained a goal announced by the teacher prior to lesson presentation. The amount of learning that must be acquired before the pupil secures the reward is determined by the teacher. The working for the reward is a motivator for the learner. Receiving the reward for goal attainment is a reinforcer to encourage similar future behaviour.

Interest is a powerful factor in learning. The mathematics teacher needs to obtain the attention of all learners during teaching-learning situations. To demand attention of pupils does not capture learner interest in mathematics. Rather, the teacher needs to use a variety of materials in teaching mathematics to obtain intrinsic interests of learners. These activities include life-like problems which need solution, textbook and workbook assignments, films, slides, video tapes, video disks, illustrations, teaching aids, technology, integrated learning systems, teaching units, as well as resource units of study in mathematics. In using a variety of learning activities, the mathematics teacher has a better chance in securing learner interest as compared to a single type of material. The tone of the teacher's voice must have appropriate voice inflection, pitch, and juncture. A monotonous tone of voice will not tend to obtain learner interest and attention. Quality eye contact with pupils should aid in obtaining pupil attention and promote learning in mathematics. Interest of pupils in ongoing lessons and units of study develops effort for achieving.

Theories of Learning in Mathematics

Selected theories of learning in educational psychology used by the teacher should assist pupils to attain at a more optimal level. Operant conditioning, as developed by B.F. Skinner (1904-1988), has done much as a theory of learning to guide learner progress. Dr. Skinner stressed the use of programmed learning in emphasizing behaviorism as a psychology of learning. Here, a qualified programmer would determine what pupils are to learn in any unit of study in mathematics. The body of knowledge within the unit is broken down into component parts. The steps of attainment are very small when working on a program in mathematics, be it in textbook or software form. The pupil, here, generally reads a sentence or two, depending on the maturity level of the involved learner. He/she then views a related illustration, responds to a test item, and checks the response. If correct, the pupil is rewarded. If incorrect, the pupil now knows the correct answer and is also ready for the next sequential programmed item. The program has been tried out previously in pilot studies with needed modifications made. The content to follow in each program moves from the simple to the increasingly more complex. The same procedure, or a slight modification, may follow in each step of learning such as read a sentence or more, view an illustration, respond to a test item, and check the correctness of the response as provided by the programmer. Answers given by the learner are either correct or incorrect. By being correct approximately 90 per cent of the time in responding, the pupil can make continuous progress with increasingly complex items in programmed learning. A positive self concept could be an end result for pupils if they respond with an approximate 90 per cent correct in terms of accuracy. Tutorial programs using computers tend to stress tenets of programmed instruction. Simulation in computer use may also stress programmed learning, providing it is not too open ended in its subject matter presentation.

B.F. Skinner believed strongly in answers being either right or wrong when learners make responses. Shankaranarayana wrote:

For Skinner (1969), "teaching is an arrangement of contingencies of reinforcement which expedite learning." Skinner believes that promotion of learning is possible by giving attention to the following factors: the behavior that is to be learned, the reinforcers that may be used, and the scheduling of reinforcers.

Skinner recommeds the use of programmed instruction which provides for individual differences by allowing students to achieve at their own rate of speed. In terms of Skinner's operant behaviorism, "a program can be seen as an arrangement of material that will lead students to emit correct responses and will also provide reinforcement for the response...The essential elements of programmed instruction...are (1) an ordered sequence of stimuli, (2) specific student response, (3) immediate knowledge of results, (4) small steps, (5) minimum errors, (6) gradual shaping of terminal behavior and (7) self pacing.

B.F. Skinner has a well known and popular name in education.His experiments in teaching and education have indeed been numerous. Morris and Pai (1976) wrote the following:

As Skinner has pointed out several times, the most important task of the teacher is to arrange conditions under which desired learning can occur. Considering the fact that teachers are to bring about changes in extremely complex behavior, they should be specialists in human behavior. Effective and efficient manipulation of the multitude of variables affecting children's intellectual and social behaviours cannot be accomplished by trial and error alone, nor should such work be based solely on the personal experiences of the teacher, since this covers only a limited range of circumstances..Consequently, a scientific study of human behaviour is vital in the improvement of teaching, because it provides us with accurate and reliable knowledge about learning and leads to the development of new instructional materials, methods, and techniques. Similarly, an empirical analysis of the teaching process is essential, for it clarifies the teacher's responsibility through a series of small and progressive approximations. This approach makes teaching practices more specific, thereby facilitating a more effective evaluation.

James Popham and Behaviorism

James Popham from the University of California is a strong advocate of behaviorism. Dr. Popham (1970, see bibliography entries) developed a series of filmstrips and related cassette tapes proposing behaviorism as a needed central theme of teaching and learning. Behaviorists believe strongly in the use of measurably stated objectives in teaching pupils. These precise objectives are written prior to teaching learners. Ideally, there is no leeway in determining what will be taught when viewing the written statement of objectives. The teacher then is certain as to what will be taught. He/she may announce to pupils that which will be taught before teaching and learning. Pupils then know what is required of them in terms of subject matter to be acquired. Learners need not outguess the teacher to realize what is expected as to precise objectives to be achieved.

According to Popham, the learning opportunities chosen by the teacher must contain only that which is in the stated objective(s), no more and no less. Evaluation of pupil attainment in mathematics needs to be done in terms of the measurably stated objectives. Thus a very close alignment indeed is in the offing among the objectives, the learning opportunities, and the evaluation procedures. Validity, a measurement term, is in evidence if the evaluation techniques harmonize with the stated objectives in mathematics.

James Popham with his stress placed upon behaviorism as a psychology of instruction in teaching mathematics advocates the following:

1. vague hazy objectives need to be eliminated or rewritten so that a sharp focus exists in terms of what will be taught.
2. learning opportunities must be very carefully chosen since each needs to guide pupils to attain that which is in the stated objective.
3. evaluation procedures should ascertain if each pupil has attained the precise objectives.
4. a different teaching strategy needs to be used if a learner did not achieve an objective.
5. sequence of objectives is arranged by the mathematics teacher.

Dr. Popham places extremely strong emphasis upon choosing precise, measurable stated objectives for instruction. He places little stress upon choosing learning opportunities, except that they should match up very precisely with the stated objectives. Evaluation is done strictly in terms of what is mentioned specifically in each objective for pupil attainment.

Robert Gagne and Task Analysis of Objectives

Robert Gagne (1984) is a leading psychologist in education who recommends a behavioristic approach in teaching; however, his thinking is more open-ended as compared to Dr. Skinner and Popham. Gagne's eight sequential steps of hierarchical learning for pupils may be of considerable help to teachers in planning the mathematics curriculum. The eight steps of sequential learning for pupils are the following: signal learning, stimulus-response, chaining, verbal association learning, multiple discrimination, concept learning, rule learning, and problem solving as being the most complex form of achievement. Gagne was a former mathematics instructor and found task analysis as being a very appropriate way of determining sequence for pupils. We will comment on a few of the level we believe to be especially relevant in teaching. Stimulus-response psychology is very relevant for mathematics teachers to consider. For example, once pupils attach meaning through the use of manipulative materials that 7+6 and 6+7=13, this addition fact may be committed to memory. Thus on a flash card or computer program the *stimulus* is 7+6 or 6+7=... If correct, pupils should *respond* with the answer being 13. Drill and practice should not be used prior to meaningful learning by pupils. But, once meaning is there, pupils may need to associate the stimulus and the response in a somewhat rote manner. Gagne's step of chaining might involve pupils using a series of concrete and semiconcrete materials to indicate and show that 7+6 and 6+7=13. Which materials might these be? Sticks, corn and bean seeds, paper squares, and buttons, among other items, may be used by the learner in sequence to show a set of seven and a set of six and by joining the two sets together obtain a set of thirteen markers. The commutative property may also be shown by a learner. Chaining is involved in that the pupil used diverse materials to show the value of two addends. Multiple discrimination, in the Gagne's hierarchy of objectives, stresses pupils noticing differences and likenesses in ongoing lessons and units of study. Analysis is involved here in that pupils separate the relevant from the irrelevant such as in seeking solutions to story or word problems. To do so indicated the need to make separations from what is needed to what is unnecessary. We believe the last three terms used by Gagne are very significant in planning the mathematics curriculum. Thus concept learning is very relevant. It takes a variety of learning opportunities using different materials of instruction for pupil to understand concepts such as addition, subtraction, multiplication, division, inverse operation, radius, radius squared, radius cubed, and exponents. Understanding concepts are needed on the pupil's part in order that sequential achievement is possible in mathematics.

Gagne's principle or rule learning indicates that learners relate concepts so they become usable. A rule of principle such as "to find the area of a circle, square the radius and multiple by the value of pi" is necessary in a specific situation; otherwise pupils could not ascertain the area of a circle. The last idea in Gagne's hierarchy is problem solving. Thus principles or rules are needed to understand how to solve the problem of determining the area of a square, triangle, or parallelogram.

A strong point in Gagne's hierarchy of objectives is that the teacher needs to go back a step or level if a pupil does not understand what is to be done. For example, if a pupil cannot solve a problem, perhaps he/she does not attach meaning to the involved rule or principle. If the rule or principle is a stumbling block to the pupil's progress, he/she may need to go back to learning the meaning of the inherent concept within the rule of principle.

Jerome Bruner and the Structure of Knowledge in Mathematics

Jerome Bruner, professor from Harvard University, advocated a structure of knowledge approach in teaching mathematics. The structural ideas in mathematics would be identified by professional mathematicians in their academic area of speciality. These professional mathematicians then choose key or main ideas for pupil attainment. The structural ideas may be used again and again by learners as they proceed to more complex learnings on sequential grade levels. In mathematics then pupils may attain the following in increased levels of complexity:

1. commutative and associative properties of addition and multiplication.
2. distributive property of multiplication over addition.
3. property of closure.
4. subtraction as the inverse operation of addition.
5. division as the inverse operation of multiplication.

The above examples of structural ideas can be emphasized on sequential grade levels at increasing levels of complexity. For example, first grade pupils may learn that 4+3=7 and 3+4=7; this stresses the commutative property of addition. At a higher grade level, fifth grade pupils may learn meaningfully that 18,996 + 38,649 = 38,469 + 18,996.

Jerome Bruner stressed the use of three kinds of materials in teaching mathematics to pupils. In sequence, these would be enactive, iconic, and symbolic. Enactive materials emphasize the use of concrete materials and other objects for learner manipulation in a hands-on approach in learning. Second, pupils learn through the use of iconic materials which include pictures, illustrations, video tapes, video discs, slides, filmstrips, and other audio visual aids. Third, Bruner stresses the use of symbolic materials, such as printed content in textbooks, library books, and other abstract content. This sequence in pupil learning then emphasizes the teacher using concrete, semiconcrete, and abstract materials in teaching.

Jerome Bruner advocates the use of inductive methods of instruction in which pupils discover structural or major academic ideas of a discipline. To emphasize Bruner's approach in teaching, the teacher should attend to the following:

1. the teacher needs to have an excellent knowledge of the structure of knowledge since these key ideas become objectives for learner attainment.
2. to achieve objectives on the pupils' part, the teacher needs to sequence learning opportunities in that individual

experience the enactive, the iconic, and the symbolic in that order.

3. the teacher must appraise pupils to ascertain how many of structural knowledge objectives are being attained by pupils in a spiral curriculum. With a spiral curriculum, pupils meet up again and again in increasing levels of complexity the structural ideas which serve as objectives of instructions.
4. the teacher needs to become a quality asker of questions involving the ongoing mathematics lesson so that pupils can truly learn in an inductive manner. Inductive teaching then assists pupils to achieve the structural ideas.
5. inductive teaching in mathematics must be used together with the enactive, iconic, and symbolic materials of instruction.

Jean Piaget and Development Psychology in Mathematics

Jean Piaget studied pupils in clinical settings for over forty years in Switzerland. He identified different stages that pupils go through in the maturation process. The first stage called the Sensorimotor Stage occurs from birth to two years in the infant's life. Here, parents need to have objects for the young child to manipulate and experience in a friendly environment. The child then experiences and perceives objects such as toys in the real environment. He/she may touch, smell, and see the objects. Listening to sounds made by these objects is also salient in sensorimotor learning.

The preoperational stage of development of the child roughly occurs from ages two to seven years. Here, the young child preceives one variable largely. Thus the preoperational child when viewing two tumblers of the same brand name and size as having an equal amount of water in each, if this is the case. Now, in front of the child, one of the two tumblers of water is poured into a taller thinner tumbler. The child is asked which has more water inside the tumbler. The preoperational pupil will answer the taller thinner tumbler does. The child perceives one variable in that one tumbler is taller than the other and therefore contains more water. If two spheres of clay are held in front of the preoperational child and both are identical in amount, the child will say neither has more clay in it than the other. But, if the experimenter flattens one sphere in front of the child, he/she will say that the flattened clay has more in it than does the sphere of clay. Again, the preoperational child perceives one variable only and that being the flattened piece of clay is longer than the spherical lump of clay. Teachers of kindergarten and first grade pupils need to be aware that preoperational pupils lack maturation to notice that there is more than one variable to objects being observed. Preoperational pupils are perceptionally oriented. How something looks to the child is the correct perception or view. They tend to center on one variable such as the larger the area that one of two sets of marbles is placed in, even though both sets have an equal number of marbles, the larger the number of members of that set in the enlarged area. Thus if a set of six marbles is placed in a larger area, it will have more marbles than a set of six placed in a smaller region.

From ages seven through eleven, Piaget, in his research, found that these learners still needed concrete objects to learn from. Piaget called this the stage of concrete operations. Here, the learner has matured to emphasize reversibility. Thus the pupil may notice that the order of addends can be changed and yet the sum stays the same. Or, the concrete operations pupil learns that there are number families such as 7+5=12 and 5+7=12, which can be undone through subtraction within that number family such as 12–5=7 and 12–7=5. Reversibility also indicates that one can go back to an earlier stage of working on a project or activity and come back to the original starting point. One may go back (reversibility) to an earlier stage in unit teaching to further analyze what was done. One can also reverse to the original stage prior to emphasizing reversibility. Thus the concrete operations development pupils may perceive several variables when reversibility is in evidence.

Additive composition is also a part of the learner's stage of concrete operations. With additive composition, the pupil in perceiving numerous variables, may define, for example, what the identity elements are for addition and multiplication. There are numerous descriptions which can be given in the definition indicating again the pupil's ability to focus on several items at one time. All the definitions possible add up to a sum pertaining to the identity elements for addition and multiplication.

The principle of associativity is also a part of the concept the stage of concrete operations. With associativity, the pupil can add three or more numbers in any order. Or three or more factors may be multiplied in any order and the product is the same. Many tasks may also be taken up in any order and the results are the same or similar. In all facets of the pupil being in the stage of concrete operations, the teacher still needs to refer to and use concrete materials along with the abstract being emphasized.

At about twelve years of age, pupils enter the stage of formal operations. At the stage of formal operations, learners might be able to think abstractly in mathematics without reference to concrete materials of instruction. Learners in all stages of development need to operate or focus on what is being learned for learning to really take place.

There are numerous implications for teaching mathematics when using Piaget's research in teaching-learning situations. These include the following:

1. The teacher must study the maturational levels of pupils in order to know what and how to teach these learners.
2. There can be much wasting of time in teaching what the maturational level of the involved pupil is not ready for. Then, too, the teacher must teach what the maturational level of the pupil is ready for in mathematics. Otherwise time slips by without the learner attaining as much as possible.
3. Hastening the readiness of a pupil for learning mathematics does not work. The maturational level will indicate what can/cannot be taught.
4. There needs to be an adequate amount of concrete materials available for teaching since through the age of eleven, the stage of concrete operations is still in the offing.
5. Securing attention for learning is salient since learners do not achieve unless they mentally operate upon the content being presented.

According to Piaget and Imhelder (1969), there are definite factors that impinge upon pupils as they progress in intellectual development. These are biological maturation; interaction with experiences in the natural environment; social activities; and homeostasis, a balance between the self and experiences in the physical environment.

Biological maturation stresses pupils going through the stages of sensorimotor, preoperational, concrete operations, and formal thought. However, there are factors that influence these stages of biological maturation. One factor is pupils interacting with the natural environment. The richness of experiences here has much to do with learners developing biologically. Thus a stimulating environment in mathematics definitely affects progression in biological development. Working with others or being in groups that stress collegiality and its influence on both biological and the affects of the natural environment. Certainly, pupils learn much from each other pertaining to the world of mathematics. In supervising student teachers and cooperating teachers, we notice how pupils might affect each other very positively in ongoing lessons and units in mathematics. For example, in one class it was difficult for a pupil to understand and attach meaning to why the divisor is inverted and multiplication is stressed in the division of fractions. When this pupil and three others worked together in cooperative learning, one pupil made it very clear as to why the divisor is inverted and then multiplication occurs in the division of fractions.

Homeostasis emphasizes feelings of satisfaction that a solution has been found to a problem. Thus there is balance between the individual and his/her environment. Equilibration has then occurred. In the previous example, when a learner understood what is involved when fractions are divided with the "invert the divisor and multiply" rule, the pupil also has reached a state of homeostasis at that point. Homeostasis may be followed again by a desire to know a new fact, concept, and/or generalization. A good teacher will guide pupils to reach a state of disequilibrium so that an inward desire to learn is involved to seek new information and subject matter.

Piaget emphasizes that what is learned is grouped together in schemes. These schemes provide key ideas upon which future learning of the pupil is based. Schemes are also called structural ideas. Structural ideas or schemes are patterns of behaviour of the individual. The pupil who has been actively involved in learning that 6+4=10 may now use these learnings to achieve the new to be stressed such as 6+5=.... and 5+6=.... New content might then fit into the older pre-existing structures. In other words, previous content acquired in mathematics now sets the stage to learn more of higher decade addition. The involved process is called assimilation. There had to be accommodation so that the old and the new content might be blended.

Piaget (1971) continually emphasizes active involvement of the learner in the mathematics curriculum when writing the following:

> if we desire...to form individuals capable of inventive thought and of helping the society of tomorrow to achieve progress, then it is clear that an education which is an active discovery of reality is superior to one that consists merely in providing the young with readymade wills to will with and readymade truths to know with.

John Dewey and Problem Solving in Utilitarian Situations

John Dewey (1859-1952) advocated a utilitarian mathematics curriculum in which school and society would be related. Thus what is useful in society should provide the basis for the school curriculum. Thus in mathematics, pupils with teacher assistance identify a problem area. The problem is significant to the learner. He/she feels a definite need to find needed solutions. The problem then must be adequately delimited so that an answer can be found. Data or information is acquired in answer to the identified problem.The answer is tentative and subject to change due to further testing of the results.John Dewey did not consider textbook problems as being life-like and reality based. Predetermined questions raised by the teacher and objectives written prior to instruction for pupils to attain do not stress problem solving. Rather within context in an ongoing unit to study preferably, the learner or a committee of pupils choose a problem in mathematics which is vital to solve. This is a practical problem to solve which emphasizes being useful and stresses application of content/skills acquired.

Problem solving then emphas izes the useful and the

utilitarian in the pupil's life in the school setting. Mathematics is a curriculum area that can truly emphasize that which is functional. Thus situations such as the following may stress a practical mathematics curriculum with problem solving involved:

1. measuring ingredients for a representative food dish of a foreign nation being studied in social studies.
2. planning and preparing a holiday meal in school whereby each pupil brings a certain amount of a food item.
3. averaging scores of the number of words spelled correctly by a pupil from six sequential weeks of spelling test scores.
4. developing a line graph from pupil's individual birth dates in a calendar year.
5. operating a simulated supermarket in the classroom using real or toy money.

The above are merely suggestions for a reality based mathematics curriculum. One needs to remember that John Dewey advocated that problems come from pupils and not from an extrinsic source. The teacher guides learners in selecting and solving problems. John Dewey believed that pupils liked to work on committees rather than individually in solving problems. Learners, too, desired to find out on their own instead of being told how to locate an answer. Pupils were to be active, not passive recipients of knowledge. Creative behaviour is preferred much more so as compared to conformity endeavors.

In summarizing John Dewey's problem solving approach in teaching pupils, the following are salient points:

1. activity centered approaches are emphasized in teaching in that pupils are the focal point to the curriculum.
2. mathematics stresses that pupils with teacher guidance select relevant life-like problems which need solving.
3. a learning by doing, not passivity on the part of pupils, is a must for learning to accrue in mathematics.
4. purpose and interest on the learner's part make for learner effort and perseverance in solving problems.
5. the role of the teacher is to encourage, help, and assist pupils in attaining solutions to problems.

In Summary

There are numerous psychologists who may provide teachers with guidance in teaching mathematics. B.F. Skinner advocated a highly structured curriculum in/which pupils would make few errors when achieving objectives arranged in an ascending order of difficuty. The programmer arranges the frames of learning in mathematics by using a sequence of read, view an illustration, respond, and check order. A psychology of behaviorism is emphasized here. Responses are either correct or incorrect as given by pupils individually.

James Popham believes in using measurement driven instruction with the objectives stated behaviorally. The stated objectives leave no leeway for interpretation. The mathematics teacher then provides learning opportunities which contain only that which is in the stated objective. Appraisal is done in terms of the stated objective to determine if learners individually have been successful achievers.

Robert Gagne emphasizes a hierarchical arrangement of teacher written objectives whereby the learner attains each in ascending order of complexity. Should an objective in mathematics be too difficult to achieve, the teacher needs to assist pupils individually to go back to a previous goal so that background information may have been attained. Then, the pupil should be ready sequentially to achieve the original objective. We will review the last three objectives Gagne stressed in curriculum development. These are in sequence: concept development, attaining generalizations, and solving a problem, by the learner. The mathematics teacher writes the objectives for pupil achievement. Dr. Gagne, a former mathematics teacher, found that the teacher needed to go back to an earlier level of achievement if a pupil could not attain the preset objective being stressed in the curriculum. Thus if a learner did not understand how to solve a mathematics problem, he/she might need to go back to studying the related generalization that is inherent in the problem. Should the learner not understand the generalization, he/she may need to study the related concept(s). Once the concept(s) are understood, the pupil is ready to be taught the related generalization. If the generalization is meaningful; the involved pupil might then be ready to solve the problem. Robert Gagne emphasized going back to an earlier level of achievement if the pupil did not attach meaning to what is presently being taught. Sequence in learing mathematics is very important to Robert Gagne. All good teachers of mathematics prize highly if content, skills, and attitudes are learned sequentially by learners. This may mean reversing to an earlier level of attainment if a pupil does not understand or comprehend that which is being taught presently. The sequence may also pertain to a learner being taught more complex subject matter in mathematics if presently the objectives have been achieved.

Robert Gagne advocated a hierarchy of objectives for pupils to attain in mathematics which meet the following standards:

1. the objectives are arranged so that each pupil may attain an appropriately ordered set of goals which move from the easier to those increasingly more complex.
2. the teacher may place another objective between two others if a pupil makes an error at that point.
3. the problems to be solved tend to be more abstract than those advocated by John Dewey.
4. the objectives are determined prior to instruction.
5. quality sequence in mathematics makes for fewer learner errors when being engaged in a lesson or unit of study. The teacher sequences or orders the objectives for learner attainment.

Jerome Bruner emphasized that pupils on any grade level attain structural ideas in mathematics. Mathematicians at the university level select and agree upon these ideas. The structural ideas are available to teachers who teach pupils. Inductively, pupils are to achieve these structural ideas on an increasingly difficult level as they progress through sequential levels of attainment.

Jean Piaget stressed the importance of pupils going through specific maturational level such as the sensorimotor, preoperational, concrete, and abstract levels. Biological maturation is salient when teachers ascertain what should be taught to pupils. The stage of concrete operations, for example, has associativity as one of its subcategories. The associative properties of addition and multiplication, using concrete materials, should be taught at this stage (ages seven to eleven) of learner development.

John Dewey advocated a problem solving approach in which pupils identify and solve problems. The problems are life-like and practical. The useful and the utilitarian are emphasized. Dewey placed strong emphasis upon democracy as a way of life. Democracy then is more than a political system or a way of governing individuals. Democracy is a way of associating with others and a means of communication. It is a means of involving all who will be affected by a given decision (Dewey, 1916). Democratic means are needed to identify and solve problems. These problems need to be reality based and practical in the social arenas. Pupils then need guidance to select and solve life-like problems in mathematics. To stress democracy in the school and classroom settings, learners should work cooperatively in problem solving endeavors in mathematics.

The teacher of mathematics needs to use a psychology of teaching which will guide the learner to achieve as optimally as possible. There are diverse psychologies available to provide guidance in helping pupils achieve, grow, and learn in mathematics. Pupils need to be able to use what has been acquired. Meaning is then attached to facts, concepts, and generalizations achieved in mathematics. The National Council Teachers of Mathematics in 1989 developed excellent criteria, goals, and objectives for pupils to achieve. These are listed in their book *Curriculum and Evaluation Standards for School Mathematics*. The psychologies discussed above may well be used to guide pupils in goal attainment from those listed in *Curriculum and Evaluation Standards for School Mathematics*.

Selected References

Dewey, John (1916). Democracy and Education. *New York: The Macmillan Company.*

Gagne', Robert (19y. 96-102.84). The Conditions of Learning. New York: Holt, Rinehart and Winston.

Morris, Van Cleve (1979). Philosophy and the American School. *Boston: Houghton Mifflin Company, 340.*

Piaget, Jean (1971). Science of Education and the Psychology of the Child. *New York: Viking Press, 26.*

Popham, James (1970). Alternative Avenues to Educational Accountability;

Appropriate Practice; Educational Objectives; Establishing Performance Levels; Modern Measurement Methods; Opening classroom structures; Selecting appropriate objectives; and Teaching Units and Lessons Plans. *(These are filmstrips and related tapes on behaviorism as it applies to teaching and learning).*

Shankaranarayana, B.L. (1990). Achievement in Mathematics Under Guidance Discovery Learning and Reception Learning Conditions. *Ph D thesis. Mysore, India: University of Mysore, 6,7.*

3

Philosophy of Teaching Mathematics

There are selected philosophies in the teaching of mathematics which can provide guidance to the teacher in developing the curriculum. Each teacher has selected concepts and generalizations which provide a framework for teaching and learning. A study of the philosophy of education may develop a reservoir from which the teacher may secure the background knowledge, attitudes, and skills to do a quality job of teaching learners. Ozman and Craver (1990) wrote:

A study of philosophy of education seems imperative today, for we are in a critical era of transition. There has always been change, but seldom at our present accelerated rate, creating in many individuals what Alvin Toeffler has called the sickness of "future shock." In such an age, it is easy for people either to embrace more and more with little thought to eventual consequences or to resist change with little or no matter what. Educational philosophers, regardless of the particular theory they embrace, suggest that the solutions to our problems can best be achieved through critical and reflective thought. In one sense we can say that philosophy of education is the application of philosophical ideas to educational problems. We can also say with equal force that the practice of education leads to a refinement of philosophical ideas. From this viewpoint, educational philosophy is not only a way of looking at ideas but also learning how to use them in the best way. No intelligent philosophy of education is involved when educators do things simply because they were done in the past. A philosophy of education becomes significant at the point where educators recognize the need to think clearly about what they are doing and to see what they are doing in the larger context of individual and social development.

Idealism in Teaching Mathematics

Idealism is one of the oldest philosophies available which may assist the mathematics teacher to select objectives, learning opportunities, and evaluation procedures for pupils. Plato (427-347 BC) advocated idealism as a philosophy of education in ancient Athens. Above Plato's academy door, it stated that "no one is to enter unless they know mathematics." He believed mind to be superior to the body. Thus a strong academic curriculum in mathematics should be in the offing. Upon death, the mind/soul survives whereas the body decays. The mind must rule the body so that higher levels of choices are in evidence. It is the body that brings an individual to lower or inferior levels of choices and decisions. A study of mathematics assists the learner to attain well mentally. In the Forms (heaven), perfection is there in that a perfect something exists, such as different number systems, and geometrical figures, plain and solid. The here and the now on the changing earth is inferior to what is in the unchanging Forms. Thus a triangle, square, parallelogram, and circle, for example, in the here and now are imperfect models of what is perfect in the Forms. The same is true of all things and life on earth. What exists in stable Forms is much superior to the world of change here on earth.

One only receives ideas about the Forms according to Plato. A person cannot perceive the Forms as they truly are, but receives ideas through thought, mind, meditation, and intellectual endeavors. An idea centered mathematics curriculum pertaining to the abstract assists in achieving thinking individuals who reflect upon subject matter acquired. The well educated and the abstract thinkers have abilities to perceive or receive ideas pertaining to The Forms. Wisdom is a necessary prerequisite to perceive The Forms.

Idealism as a philosophy of education still receives much attention today. A mathematics teacher who is an idealist tends to emphasize mental endeavors as being superior to the physical and its emphasis. The mind is what is truly real about the person. Thus the mathematics teacher needs to stress pupils attaining abstract content in mathematics since this will aid mental development. Higher cognitive level objectives need to be selected and implemented in the mathematics curriculum. These objectives pertain to pupils being able to think critically, synthesize content, and appraise what has been acquired. Mind is real and needs to be developed, according to idealism as a philosophy of teaching mathematics.

Concrete learning opportunities consisting of the use of real objects, and the semiconcrete emphasizing use of illustrations, should be stressed only if they guide learners to understand abstract ideas in mathematics. The focal point of instruction is ideas and mental development. One receives ideas of the natural and social environment only, not a replica of the real world. All information is developed by the mind. Ideas are then secured about the natural and social facets of life. What is in back of this world is mind and the spiritual, not the physical. Scope and sequence in mathematics emphasizes mental and intellectual development of the pupil pertaining to the following topics:

1. base ten system of numeration, estimating, as well as understanding positive and negative integers.
2. addition, subtraction, multiplication, and division on whole numbers, the integers, rational numbers, and irrational numbers.
3. geometry with its space figures, including plane (squares, rectangles, triangles, parallelograms, and circles, among others) and solid (spheres, cylinders, cones, prisms, and Platonic solids).
4. common and decimal fractions, as well as per cents.
5. measurement including linear, square, and cubic.
6. graphs, tables statistics and probability.

For the above named topics, pupils with teacher guidance need to study each in depth with emphasis placed upon learners attaching meaning to content being taught. Mathematics as general education is salient in developing mental maturity to work with numerals and number in the abstract. Critical thinking in the mathematics curriculum stresses mental development. Reason and intelligence are necessary to achieve fully in mathematics. The rational being then becomes increasingly mature mentally to use intelligence in dealing with the world of number and numerals. The teacher stimulates pupils to achieve using a variety of learning opportunities emphasizing inductive and deductive methods of thinking. Idealists stress the concept of purpose for each human being in a purposive world. There is purpose involved in learning mathematics. The purpose involves, among other things, the development of the spiritual facet of the person. Human beings are not a part of the animal world, according to idealists. Rather they transcend that level and are endowed with rational powers that animals do not possess. Mathematics as an academic discipline can assist pupils to reach out from the finite toward the Infinite, in achieving intellectual and rational goals. Mathematical truths are a priori and thus have always existed. For example, any basic number sentence in mathematics such as $12 \times 10 = 120$ has always been true, prior to human experience. Each pupil must be guided by a competent and academically inclined teacher in discovering pre-existent truths in mathematics.

For the idealist, mathematics presents content to pupils to encourage the development of reasoning persons in which the mind achieves in the direction of the Infinite, the unlimited in terms of attaining an ideal. Mind, not matter, represents ultimate reality. The mind and mathematics content stress reaching toward the Ideal or Infinite in achieving a priori content.

Since idealists in mathematics tend to recommend mental development of the learner as a major goal of instruction, a quality series of mathematics textbooks might well provide appropriate scope and sequence in the curriculum. The teacher's role here is to assist pupils to attain optimally in thinking mathematically. Brubacher (1966) wrote :

The most prolific writer on the idealist philosophy of education in the twentieth century was Herman Harrel Horne (1874-1946). At a time when idealism was fast fading as the dominant American theory of education, Horne managed to draw together the various strains of idealism into their more systematic educational exposition. In addition to much that is already familiar, he made two points of this own. One is his emphasis upon volition and effort in learning. The pupil is like the plant, he agreed with Froebel, in that his response is self active. But the child is unlike a plant, Horne continued, in that he can withhold his response. Hence the ultimate responsibility for getting an education rests on the will of the pupil. All education therefore is self education : it is the voluntary effort put forth by a self active mind. If effort is aided and abetted by interest, well and good. If not, then like Kant, Horne urged that the pupil in any case put forth effort in obedience to what he ought to do.

A second and more notable point in Horne's exposition is the fact that he did not make any significant alteration in the developmental theory of education in the light of Darwinian theory of evolution, which was introduced to the world after the deaths of Hegel and Froebel. To be sure, Horne saw that evolution had made the developmental process irreversible and unrepealable, in contrast to the Aristotelian pattern of matter endlessly reproducing the cycle of changes demanded by its form. The Absolute, however, had no difficulty in assimilating this new theory of development, for Horne could still say that the Absolute is; only the finite becomes. Pedagogically speaking, this seems to mean that through education the child still becomes in time what he was meant eternally to be.

Horne was a strong advocate of a subject centered curriculum. An idea centered curriculum in mathematics is then in evidence. The abstract numbers and numerals, the symbols of operation on numbers, as well as the different formulas in determining area and volume, among others, might well provide a significant set of lessons and units in mathematics. Concrete and semiconcrete materials may be used to guide pupils to achieve well in the abstract.

Realism and the Mathematics Curriculum

The mathematics teacher who stresses realism as a philosophy of education believes in using the methods of science in teaching and learning situations. Objective evidence, irrespective of the subjective person, is inherent in mathematics. Thus, subject matter in mathematics is true independent of the observer or person. Precision is a key word to use in teaching mathematics, according to the realist. A realist likes accurate descriptions of what exists. For example, he/she does not care for a person saying that the temperature reading in a room is comfortable. Rather, the exact temperature reading is wanted such as 22 degrees Celsius. If a person states that his/her blood pressure reading is normal, the realist desires to know the precise blood pressure reading using numerals for the systolic and diastolic readings.

A teacher who emphasizes that his/her pupils are attaining well does not satisfy the realist critic. Rather numerical results are wanted to ascertain how well learners are attaining, such as grade equivalents, percentile ranks, quartile deviations, as well as standard deviations from the mean and other derived or standard scores. Testing pupils to notice achievement is quite typical of the philosophy of realism. Thus standardized norm referenced tests may be used to gather data on learner progress. Formative and summative tests are recommended to be given to learners to notice pupil progress in mathematics. The former is given to learners within an ongoing unit of study to monitor achievement along the way, as well as make needed changes in teaching. The summative test is given at the end of a unit of study in mathematics so that changes may be made, if evidence warrants, the next time the same unit is taught.

A mathematics teacher then who is a realist desires objectives of instruction to be stated in measurable terms, prior to instruction. The following are examples:

1. The pupil will add correctly ten number pairs, each containing single digit addends.
2. Given four geometrical figures, the learner will accurately compute the area of each.
3. The learner will change five common fractions to decimals and then to per cents.
4. Given three dimensional values for a rectangular prism, a triangular solid, a cylinder, and a pyramid, the pupil will compute accurately the volume of each geometrical solid.
5. Given data pertaining to the federal budget, the pupil will construct a line graph, a bar graph, and a picture graph.

For each of the above named objectives, pupils will reveal as a result of instruction if they have been successful in goal attainment. These objectives are stated with precision so that the mathematics teacher knows exactly what is to be taught. There is no guesswork in terms of what pupils are to learn. There are realists who advocate that the teacher announce prior to instruction what pupils are to learn as stated in the objective(s). Pupils then do not need to outguess the teacher in terms of what is expected of them as learners. When ascertaining how much pupils have learned as a result of instruction, the teacher receives numerical results such as the per cent of correct responses from a test of each pupil. The results from each pupil could also be computed to secure percentile ranks. Derived scores based on the normal distribution curve would indicate the number of standard deviations above and below the mean for each pupil.

A mathematics teacher who is a realist in terms of philosophy of education desires precise objectives for learner attainment. He/she matches the learning opportunities with the stated specific objectives so that an increased number of objectives will be achieved by pupils. What is in the learning opportunities then harmonizes with what is stated in the objectives, no more and no less. Appraisal procedures harmonize with the objectives of instruction. Validity in appraisal is then in evidence. Results from the appraisal determine the number of objectives achieved satisfactorily by the learner. Results for the appraisal are objective in that independent of any evaluator, the number of correct responses would be the same each time. Subjectivity is then eliminated in the appraisal process.

Pertaining to realism as a philosophy of education, Bowyer (1970) Wrote the following:

> We have noted that there are different forms of naturalism and of idealism. The same is true of realism, which makes it difficult to pinpoint the distinguishing features of realism and to define the realist point of view. One element that the various forms of realism do have in common is a rejection of the idealist theory of knowledge that the various qualities of experience depend upon knower for their existence. Realists believe that the universe is composed of real entities that exist in themselves. These entities can be known, and their existence is not dependent upon a

knower or perceive. Although realists can argue on this point, they do not all agree when they attempt to build a metaphysical system. Here their views range from pluralism to dualism to monism.

The realist's epistemological views include epistemological monism where it is held that objects are presented in consciousness, and epistemological dualism where objects are thought to be represented. The monists define mind as a relation between the organism and an object, while the dualists identify the mind more closely with the organisms. Realists do have a common tendency to view the world as the mechanism described by the physical scientists, and they generally believe in determinism, in orderlines in the universe, and in the objectivity of nature. The unifying theory of realism is that knowledge is thought to have a universal character and comes to man through his sensory capacity. The realists have confidence in their assertions about reality and value which is most discerning to pragmatists.

Since mathematics and its component parts are independent of any person, that is, the content is objective and not subjective, precision and complete accuracy of answers to questions and problems are possible. Mathematics probably possesses the most objective subject matter as compared to other academic disciplines. This makes realism as a philosophy of education very useful in choosing precise objectives for pupils to achieve. The learning activities might well be used to assess learner performance against the stated objectives.

Experimentalism and the Mathematics Curriculum

The world of experience represents ultimate reality for the experimentalist. The realist believes that one can know the real world as it truly is in whole or in part. Also the real world exists independent of any observer or human being. The idealist believes that one can only know ideas about the real world, not as it truly is.

With knowing what is experienced only, the experimentalist realizes that change is all around us. Our perceptions change in time and place. Life in society continually changes. Thus problems arise which need identification. Each problem is life-like and reality based, not fictional. Clarity in problem selection is relevant. Vague, hazy problems do not lend themselves to solution. An hypothesis is developed for the identified problem. The hypothesis is actually an education guess or answer to the chosen problem. The hypothesis is not absolute, but tentative. The hypothesis is then subject to testing in a life-like situation. The consequences of the testing reveal the correctness or the lack thereof pertaining to the stated hypothesis. It is easy to understand how experimentalism with its problem solving situations is very relevant in ongoing lessons and units of study in mathematics. Problem solving is at the heart of the mathematics curriculum.

Problems should come from pupils in the world of society. Utilitarian problems are then identified, not textbook story problems. A practical mathematics curriculum is then in evidence. What is useful in the mathematics curriculum is desired in terms of objectives, learning opportunities, and evaluation procedures. The everyday experiences of people in society pertaining to mathematics provides content then for the experimentalist curriculum. Within a mathematics unit being studied, the learners choose problems to solve. Ediger (1994-1995) wrote the following:

> Problems solving requires deliberation in finding solutions to the unknown. There have been many approaches emphasized as problem solving. One approach has been to use word or story problems from the basal textbook. Higher levels of cognition can be emphasized here depending on the quality of the problem in the textbook. However, the problems therein may not be accepted by learners as having purpose. They may have outdated information in the problem which does not harmonize with what the real world of society has to offer today. Students can then not relate personally to these world or story problems as having merit.

A second approach at stressing problem solving has been for the teacher to devise the problems for students to solve using worksheets. Here again, the problems may emphasize higher levels of cognition, but they fail to arouse student interest and meaning. For problem solving to accrue, students must be involved in working on the life-like which occurs in society. In the societal arena, there are problems in mathematics which need solving. These problems have personal meaning and purpose for the learner. Thus, learners individually or within a committee identify a problem. The identified problem must be specific enough so that it can be solved, but not so specific that rote learning is involved to recall answers. There is perplexity involved in the selected problem in that the student has to think deeply of how to obtain a necessary solution. Next the learner develops a hypothesis or answer to the problem. The hypothesis is tentative, not an absolute. The hypothesis is an educated guess, based upon the best information that the student has. Each hypothesis, being tentative, needs testing. The testing is done situationally and not on a paper-pencil test. If the consequences are positive, the hypothesis stays as is. Should it be warranted, the hypothesis is revised. New problems may be chosen as the tentative answers are chosen or as the hypothesis is developed. Problems might arise as any hypothesis is revised. Problem solving in mathematics is open-ended, not factual nor recall of isolated bits of information. Problem solving does not emphasize memorizing of content. Rather content is acquired to gather data to solve problems.

....which provide experiences for learners in the mathematics curriculum. These are the following, provided as examples:

1. planning how a pupil is to spend his/her weekly money allowance.
2. planning objectives, learning opportunities, and evaluation procedures with pupils for sequential lessons and units in mathematics which stress practical experiences.
3. planning an experimentalist mathematics curriculum which harmonizes with the National Council Teachers of Mathematics (NCTM) *Curriculum and Evaluation Standards for School Mathematics* (published by NCTC. 1906 Association Drive, Reston, Virginia 22091-1593).
4. planning how to divide cookies among a certain number of children who are involved in the lesson presentation. When teaching mathematics, there are numerous situations such as these, whereby pupils need to be actively involved in decision-making.

5. planning a class party related to a holiday in which mathematics is heavily used such as how many cookies, cup cakes, soft drinks to purchase.

Mathematics teachers need to be creative in thinking about developing and implementing an experimentalist curriculum. There are numerous experiences which can be included in mathematics lessons and units of study emphasizing the practical and the utilitarian in life-like problem solving situations. Atkinson and Maleska (1965) wrote the following:

> To a follower of Dewey, education has two sides–psychological and social; neither may be subordinated or neglected. The psychological nature of a child forms the basis for his education–it is the teachers' responsibility to make full use of his natural, spontaneous activities, Describing the original nature as being spontaneously impulsive rather than passive, Dewey divided impulses into four kinds: the societal impulses of communication and conversation; the constructive impulse to make things; the impulse to investigate things; and the impulses of artistic or creative expression.

With these impulses in mind, said Dewey, the school must be changed from a place for sedentary listening to one for active doing or working. The teaching processes must be planned to allow the child to learn wherever possible by his own experiences and, in that way, to acquire the habit of thinking. A proper solution to any problem demands intelligent thinking which becomes the principal factor in the ability to cope with new situations. Thinking as Dewey defined it is the use of the meanings of past experiences in interpretations of new situations.

Dewey felt that when the psychological and the social approaches to learning are separated, there is produced either a forced and external education in which freedom of the individual is subordinated to a preconceived notion of what society should be, or else a barren and formal development of the mental powers in which the learner has little idea of the use to be made of what is being learned. The school is primarily a social institution because its processes are basically no different from those going on continuously in life outside the classroom.

Therefore, Dewey claimed, the manner in which pre-school learning has been taking place should suggest to a teacher the physical and mental growth. The school ideally should be that form of social life into which can be concentrated those factors that most effectively cause a child to share the accumulated knowledge and skills of the race. Education can be considered as proceeding most satisfactorily whenever the individual is actively participating in social relationships with others.

Existentialism and the Mathematics Curriculum

Existentialists stress the individual choosing and making decisions. To be sure, it is very salient that each pupil learn to engage in the making of choices. Life consists of making choices. Experimentalism emphasized also that pupils choose and make decisions, but usually within a committee setting. The belief exists in experimentalism that a pupil is a member of society presently and should be actively involved in the mathematics curriculum, but within a committee setting. Existentialism emphasizes the individual as one who should determine his/her curriculum within a flexible framework. The teacher assists the pupil in achieving the latter's goals. We will mention a few other tenets of existentialism which may or may not apply to the mathematics curriculum. One first exists and then determines his/her essence. Thus the individual pupil should be heavily involved in determining goals, learning opportunities, and evaluation procedures in mathematics. We truly believe this to be a difficult method of teaching, but it certainly has its values and benefits. In all of teaching, it is the learner that is the focal point of instruction. Jean Jacques Rousseau (1712-1776) in him book *Emile* (see Brubacher, 1966) emphasized a one-on-one relationship between teacher and pupil. Thus a pupil would be taught by a mentor or teacher. Here, the teacher could truly provide for individual differences (one pupil and one teacher). The learner asks questions that would be of personal interest. The out of doors or nature provides the necessary curriculum for the pupil, according to Rousseau. The teacher then assists the pupil to find the needed information. Induction as a method of teaching is used here. The pupil does not need to depend upon other pupils for help in learning, but is to be an independent being, removed from the ills of society. Nor is the learner hindered in optimal achievement since no other pupil is there to hold the former back. The pupil does not need to gauge his (a boy in this case) learning against that of others in making comparisons. Uncomfortable comparisons between learners in achievement then cannot be made in the one-on-one teaching situation. Rousseau's philosophy of instruction had definite tenets of existentialism. Which are selected mathematics experiences for pupils that Rousseau recommenced?

1. estimating the height of a cherry tree so that an appropriate ladder may be found or made to reach and pick cherries.
2. measuring the size of boards to make necessary items and objects.
3. becoming independent as a carpenter so that one does not need to be a servant of others. (Rousseau was very critical of norms in society). In being a carpenter, arithmetic and geometry are salient to learn within the framework of life-like situations.

Rugged individualism can be a term used to describe existentialism. Soren Kierkegarrd (1813-1855), a theistic existentialist, advocated that the person is first born and then finds his/her essence, meaning the individual must find his/her own purposes in life. These purposes or goals are not given to anyone, but must be found. The individual makes the self in an open-ended universe, very limited in restrictions. Prior to this time, most philosophers stressed that the essences or purposes of persons were given to all first, and then the individual would be more certain as to what his/her role in life would be. Idealism was a prominent philosophy during the centuries and emphasized that the Infinite was ultimate reality and had purposes established for all. Kierkegarrd was a theistic existentialist who also believed that the Absolute was ultimate reality; however, a long struggle was necessary in reaching this goal involving personal choices made. Jean Paul Sartre (1905-1980) emphasized atheistic existentialism as a philosophy of life. He also emphasized, as did Kierkegarrd, that an individual is born and then must find his/her own essence or purposes. With no Absolute, Sartre stressed that there is no one to manipulate the individual from above to determine purpose in life. Sartre's famous words that "Man is condemned to be free" certainly would make for a world of free choices for the individual. There are no absolutes.

Sartre (1971) in his essay "Man is Freedom," wrote the following :

> It is strange that philosophers have been able to argue endlessly about determinism and free will, to cite examples in favor of one or the other thesis without ever attempting first to make explicit the structure contained in the very idea of action. The concept of an act contains, in fact, numerous subordinate notions which we shall have to organize and arrange in a hierarchy; it is to produce an organized instrumental complex such that by a series of concatenations and connections the modification effected on one end of the links causes modifications throughout the whole series and finally produces an anticipated result but this is not what is important for us here. We should observe first that an action is on principle intentional. The careless smoker who has through negligence caused the explosion of a powder magazine has not acted. On the other hand the worker who is charged with dynamiting a quarry and who obeys the given orders has acted when he has produced the expected explosion; he knew what he was doing or, if you prefer, he intentionally realized a conscious product.
>
> This does not mean, of course, that one must foresee all the consequences of his act. The emperor Constantine, when he established himself at Byzantium, did not foresee that he would create a center of Greek culture and language, the appearance of which would contribute to the weakening of the Roman Empire. Yet he performed an act just in so far as he realized his project of creating a new residence for emperors in the Orient. Equating the result with the intention is here sufficient for us to be able to speak of action. But if this is the case, we establish that the action necessarily implies as its condition the recognition of a "desideratum," that is, of an objective lack or again a negatite...

Stumpf (1971) wrote:

> Whether they were theists or atheists, the existentialists all agreed that traditional philosophy was too academic and too remote from life to have any meaning for them. They rejected systematic and schematic thought in favor of more spontaneous mode of expression in order to capture the authentic concerns of concrete existing individuals. Although there is no "system" of existentialist philosophy, its basic themes can, nevertheless, be discovered in some representative existentialist thinkers.

Existentialists believe strongly in conscious choices made by individuals as being desirable. Moral judgments made in an atmosphere of freedom is a key concept stressed by existentialists. An existentialist mathematics teacher needs to give learners as many options as possible in learning. The pupil chooses that option in a very open-ended mathematics curriculum. Most teachers of mathematics would tend to feel that existentialist philosophy is too free of borders and boundaries. Mathematics has its own scope and sequence. The scope and sequence has much agreement in and among mathematics educators. We would like to describe a mathematics unit which a few of our students and regular teachers have used. The approach we will describe emphasizes the use of learning stations. The mathematics teacher here needs to decide upon the number of stations needed. Perhaps for twenty five pupils, there should be at least eight stations. Each station must possess concrete, semiconcrete, and abstract materials of instruction. Also at each station, there is a task card which lists possibilities for pupils individually to choose from in terms of learning activities. The pupils may select which station and which tasks to work on sequentially. There should be an adequate number of tasks so that a pupil may omit that which does not possess perceived purpose. Sequence resides within the learner, not textbooks nor the teacher, in that the pupil orders his/her own experiences. If the pupil cannot find a station or task which meets personal purposes, he/she may plan with the teacher which learning opportunities to complete in mathematics. The learner is the chooser in deciding upon these tasks. The teacher encourages, assists, and guides the pupil in finding tasks and materials to complete that which has perceived purpose. Tasks at the different stations should have individual endeavors as well as those which stress committee work. The pupil then can work individually or with others, depending upon perceived purpose. In all cases, pupils individually sequence their very own learning opportunities.

There are mathematics teachers who stress additional tenets of existentialism in their teaching. The following are examples:

1. having pupils choose extra work to do in mathematics, beyond that which is required.
2. completing a contract with individual learners to indicate what he/she is to complete. The contract lists specifically what a pupil wishes to complete with a due date listed. What is in the mathematics contract represents that which the learner desires to complete with teacher assistance, not teacher direction.
3. using teacher-pupil planning in the mathematics curriculum in which the latter determines what will be learned in sequence with instructor guidance. Thus the objectives, learning opportunities, and evaluation techniques are chosen by pupils with teacher guidance in mathematics.

Each of the above three enumerated items contains mathematics learning opportunities which can be incorporated into any classroom. To stress tenets of existentialism, the teacher must lean upon pupils in determining what they wish to learn. From within or intrinsically, the learner is the decision maker in terms of selecting objectives, learning opportunities, and evaluation procedures in the mathematics curriculum.

Pertaining to existentialism as a philosophy of education and humanism as a psychology, Ediger (1994-1995) wrote:

> Humanism, as a school of thought in psychology, emphasized input from students into the mathematics curriculum. Input for students may stress problem solving or it may stress other kinds of experiences. A learning center approach may be used. The teacher develops the different centres with approximately five tasks per center. Teacher-pupil planning may be in evidence to plan the centers and the tasks. There needs to be more tasks at the

> different centers than what any student can complete so that decision-making is possible in choosing what to learn and what to omit. Time of task is important!

The student decides what to learn sequentially. A psychological mathematics is then in evidence when the learner chooses what to learn and what to omit. Sequence resides within the student, not the teacher nor in textbooks... Tasks which choose, from among others, need to possess challenge, interest, and purpose. The mundane and routine should not be a part of the learning activities offered. If tasks do not meet personal needs of learners, student-teacher planning can be implemented so that the former might work on activities that do motivate. The individual then chooses which tasks to pursue and which to omit, be they problem solving or other kinds of experiences. There is no core or body of knowledge which all should pursue and complete.

In Closing

Four philosophies of teaching mathematics were discussed. Idealism stressed that pupils live in an idea centered mathematical world, but not an objective real world. Mental development of the pupil is a number one goal of instruction. The mathematics curriculum is viewed here as a part of the general education curriculum. Abstract content is prized higher than that which is concrete and semiconcrete. Ideas only can be known by an idealist. One only receives ideas of the real world of the realist. Ideas alone are also received of the experiences that experimentalists say can be known only. Realism emphasized that a person can know the real world in whole or in part as it really is. With pupils attaining precise measurable stated objectives in mathematics, they become more and more knowledgeable of the real world as it truly is. Each objective attained assists the learner in knowing more and more about the real world as it truly is, not merely ideas of this world. Bertrand Russell (Quoted in Wahlquist 1942) wrote:

> The first characteristic of the new philosophy is that it abandons the claim to a special philosophic method or a particular brand of knowledge to be obtained by its means.

> It regards philosophy as essentially one science, different from the special sciences merely by the generality of its problems, and by the fact that it is concerned with the formation of hypothesis where empirical evidence is still lacking. It conceives that all knowledge is scientific knowledge, to be ascertained and proved by the methods of science. It does not aim, as previous philosophy has usually done, at statements about the universe as a whole, nor at the construction of a comprehensive system. It aims only at clarifying the fundamental ideas of the sciences, and synthesizing the different sciences into a single comprehensive view of that fragment of the world that science has succeeded in exploring.

Bertrand Russll was a mathematician and a philosopher. He believed strongly in two possible sources of information, mathematics and science. Why? These two academic areas alone provided empirical knowledge. The other subject matter areas, to Russell, were subjective and lacked reliability. Mathematics is precise and exact with its many patterns and formulas, according to Russell.

Experimentalism emphasizes pupils learning that which is useful and utilitarian. Within a given problem area, mathematics is used to solve selected problems. Committee work is emphasized in that in society, people work in groups to solve areas.

Existentialism stresses individual choices made by a pupil in selecting sequential tasks and experiences in mathematics. The pupil is the chooser. The tasks may involve problem solving as well as other kinds of tasks. The teacher needs to select that philosophy to implement which assists a pupil to attain optimally. Pupils differ from each other in numerous ways such as native abilities, past experiences, interests, motivation, and purposes. It behoves the mathematics teacher to prepare well and guide learners individually to attain optimally. Use of diverse philosophies of education to provide for individual differences should assist each pupil to learn as such mathematics as possible.

Pertaining to attitude and the affective development of pupils in mathematics, Ediger (1934) wrote:

> In providing for individual differences and to guide

optimal affective achievement, the mathematics teacher needs to guide students to achieve an adequate self concept. Adequate self concept development comes about when teachers assist students to:

- achieve meaningful knowledge so that understating of acquired subject matter is in evidence.
- develop readiness for learning in order to have pupils' experience sequence in ongoing activities.
- increase interest in the mathematics curriculum to attain attention to achieve worthwhile objectives.
- perceive purpose in achievement to understand reasons for attaining in ongoing lessons.
- enjoy mathematics and thus develop quality attitudes in the affective dimension.

Selected References

Atkinson, Carroll, and Eugene T. Maleska. The Story of Education, *New York: Chilton Books, 1965, pp. 87 and 88.*

Bowyer, Carlton H. Philosophical Perspectives for Education. *Glenview, Illinois : Scott, Freshman and Company, 1970, p. 17.*

Brubacher, John S. A History of the Problems of Education, *New York : McGraw hill Book Company, 1966, pp. 128-129; 204-205.*

Ediger, Marlow (1994). "Mathematics and the Affective Domain," Tennessee Association of Middle Schools Journal. 21 : 44.

Ediger, Marlow (1994-1995). "Problem Solving in Mathematics." Saskatchewan Mathematics Teachers' Society Journal, 30-31: 66-67

Ozman, Howard, and Samuel Craver. Philosophical Foundations of Education. Columbus, Ohio : Charles Merrill Publishing Company, 1990. p xii.

Sartre, Jean Paul. "Man Is Free," as quoted in Introductory to Philosophy *by Tillman, Franklin A., et. al. New York : Harper and Row, 1971, pp. 220, 221.*

Stumpf, Samuel Enoch. Philosophy. History and Problems. *New York : McGraw hill Book Company, 1971, p. 455.*

Wahlquist, John T. Philosophy of American Education. *New York: The Ronald Press Company, 1942, pp.60-61*

4

Grouping Pupils in the Classroom

A major task involved in teaching pupils is to group wisely for instruction. Means of grouping pupils should reveal respect and acceptance of each learner. Learners need to be placed within a group in which optimal achievement is possible. Flexible grouping should be in the offing whereby pupils can get to know and appreciate learners from diverse backgrounds. Rigid, formal approaches which are outdated in grouping pupils for instruction would be avoided. Teachers and principal need to study and appraise diverse means of grouping pupils for learning. Ultimately, the best grouping procedures should be used in which pupils achieve as well as possible in knowledge, skills, and attitudes.

The Self-Contained Classroom

Most elementary schools group learners in terms of being in a self contained classroom. Thus the teacher teaches a single set of pupils in a classroom for most of the school day, except perhaps for music, art, and physical education. The teacher has numerous opportunities to get to know pupils well in self-contained classroom. Thus the teacher should be able to provide for diversities among learners so that each may achieve as much as possible. Teachers here should also be able to provide for different learning styles of pupils. We believe that teachers in the self-contained classroom can plan objectives, learning opportunities, and evaluation procedures well due to observing the same set of pupils frequently in the classroom setting. There are ample opportunities then to understand each pupil so that he/she might learn as much as possible. Pupils, too, can get to develop selected expectancies of teachers due to seeing them teach each sequential day of teaching. We feel that pupils develop feelings of security when they know what to expect of teachers. Should there be a conflict which hinders a pupil to benefit from a teacher's instruction, he/she could be transferred to another classroom and teacher. Further advantages of the self-contained classroom include the following :

1. the teacher can relate subject matter from different curriculum areas effectively.
2. the teacher may use knowledge acquired from each pupil to more adequately provide for individual differences among learners.
3. the teacher might communicate with parents more effectively by knowing more about each parent and child due to the self-contained classroom.

Shepherd and Ragan (1982) list the following advantages and disadvantages of the self-contained classroom:

1. The self-contained classroom calls for placing a group of pupils with a teacher for the major portion of a school day. This enables the teacher to learn a great deal about individual pupils through long association and observation of them in a wide variety of learning activities.
2. The teacher in the self-contained classroom is in a good position to help pupils understand the interrelatedness of subject matter fields.
3. Pupils in a self-contained classroom have more opportunities for learning to participate effectively in group enterprises; they stay with the same group under the same teacher for a major portion of the school day.
4. The self-contained classroom permits a more flexible use of time; significant learning experiences are not brought to an abrupt end because pupils must go to another class. It is easier to schedule field trips and other experiences that involve more than one period in the daily schedule.
5. Although subject matter knowledge is important for elementary teachers, other competencies, such as understanding child growth and development and ability

to organize learning experiences, are also important. The scope and depth of subjects taught in elementary schools are not so great that they cannot be acquired by the regular classroom teachers.

6. The self-contained classroom can be modified to permit teachers who are weak in certain fields to exchange with other teachers.

Limitations Claimed for the Self-contained Classroom

1. The need for increased achievement in a basic subject calls for greater depth of preparation on the part of the teacher than teachers in the self-contained classroom generally have.
2. Critics of the self-contained classroom maintain that pupils need experiences with many teachers.
3. Teachers who are not well prepared in all areas may neglect the areas in which they lack competence; this leads to an imbalance in the school program.
4. Teachers in self-contained classrooms tend to become isolated from other teachers, rather than working as members of a team.

It almost appears that for every action, there is an opposite and equal reaction when analyzing the pros and cons of the self-contained classroom.

Departmentalization and the Pupil

One may departmentalize all curriculum areas on each grade in the elementary school. This would seem rather extreme, especially on the primary grade levels where the self-contained classroom holds strong sway. For selected educators, to departmentalize completely on the intermediate grade levels would be equally severe. However, Intermediate grade children are older as compared to primary grade pupils and can adjust more so to complete or modified departmentalization. Generally, modified departmentalization is emphasized on the intermediate grade levels. Thus a teacher may teach science only in departmenta-lization. Or, mathematics might be taught by a single teacher to several classes of pupils. With departmentalization, the teacher may specialize in teaching one academic area only. Here, the teacher might truly develop proficiency in knowledge and skills of teaching one academic area only. We have observed numerous teachers teach two curriculum areas only, such as mathematics and science which is then a modified approach in a departmentalized elementary school. These teachers appear to feel more proficient in teaching when they can concentrate on teaching two curriculum areas only, as compared to the entire gamut of courses that a self contained classroom may emphasize.

There are disadvantages in a departmentalized plan of instruction in that a teacher may not be able to assist pupils to perceive relationship of subject matter taught as compared to the self-contained classroom. However, one of the anothers has talked to departmentalized teachers who plan together with other teachers of additional academic areas in relating content. These teachers appear to feel that departmentalization in grouping of pupils does not necessarily make for a separate subjects curriculum. Thus a teacher can work with other teachers to emphasize relationship of subject matter taught. These teachers do feel that a little inconvenience is involved in planning with other teachers, but the consensus is that classroom teachers should always have opportunities to work together in planning the objective, learning opportunities, and evaluation procedures.

In some ways, we believe that departmentalization harmonizes more with a separate subjects curriculum as compared to the self-contained classroom approach in grouping pupils for instruction. If teachers and administrators do want more of integration of content in the curriculum, teachers in a departmentalized plan of instruction must work cooperatively with others to make this come about. Perhaps a modified plan can help such as one teacher teaching both mathematics and science and a second teacher teaching both language arts and the social studies to different classes of intermediate grade pupils. The modified plan would assist pupils to become oriented to a departmentalized procedure when entering the senior high school years. The sequence could be quite abrupt when a pupil has experienced a self-contained classroom only and then the next school year experiences a strict departmentalized plan of grouping for instruction. A more gradual sequence could be recommendable.

Homogeneous versus Heterogeneous Grouping Controversy

There is continuous controversy over homogeneous versus heterogeneous grouping of pupils for instruction. Homogeneous grouping emphasizes a uniform group of achievers being taught in a single classroom. Here, the principal and teachers determine how best to arrange pupils in a given grade so that similar attainment levels of pupils are taught in one room. A wide range of achievement is not wanted in homogeneous grouping. The belief emphasized in homogeneous grouping is that pupils of similar achievement can best learn from each other. Learners might then challenge each other more so if the attainment levels are more equivalent in a classroom.

With heterogeneous grouping, learners are of mixed achievement levels in a classroom. The fast, average, and slow are placed in the same room. There are numerous reasons for doing so according to its advocates. Democracy is more in evidence here as compared to homogeneous grouping. Learners need to work together with each other regardless of ability levels. We believe there should be both homogeneous and heterogeneous grouping. When grouping learners for reading instruction, we definitely believe that pupils should be grouped homogeneously. Why? For example, when teaching directed reading and pupils are reading orally to reveal word identification strengths and weaknesses, pupils should be somewhat uniform in reading attainment. If not, the fast learners will become restless in listening to slow learners read and slow learners might become embarrassed when fast readers listen to the many problems revealed in oral reading. The problems become even more pronounced in silent reading when the teacher in a mixed achievement level group has pupils read for a definite purpose. The fast readers finish quickly whereas the slow readers take much more time to complete the same reading activity. The teacher here may become ill at ease if the fast readers need to wait for what seems like a long time to have the slow learners complete the same reading selection. Pertaining to reading instruction, Ediger (1936) wrote:

> Many teachers group students homogeneously to

> minimize a wide range of reading achievement. Thus, a more uniform set of learners in demonstrating skills in reading is in evidence. It is easier to provide for individual levels in reading achievement if the range of achievement is somewhat uniform. Within a classroom, the teacher might then place the top, middle, and slower achievers into three reading groups. A single series of basal readers may be utilized in teaching and learning. Or, a multiple series might also be used on ongoing lessons and units. A major goal of reading instruction is to guide each student, whether in the fast, average, or slower group, to learn as much as possible.

There are numerous plans of instruction which may be used which does not place pupils into high, average, and slower groups. As one example, Veatch (1959) wrote the following pertaining to individualized reading :

> One of the advantages of individualized reading over other methods is the elimination of pressure and tension from the student...to meet the standards of the group...Why should he be compared with anyone else? He is not like anyone else. When group competition is removed and the child is allowed to compete against himself, his own ability becomes the standard by which he is judged and tensions and pressures will give way to a more relaxed type of study. The removal of this pressure should eliminate the development of possible emotional blockages and undesirable attitudes toward reading.

Maximum efficiency of the child's time is another advantage of individualized reading. The student does not drill with a group on words which only certain members of a group do not know. Instead, he spends time on his own list of words he does not know. The amount of time which the student spends in silent reading is also increased because he does not need to wait while others are reading orally. Instead, he spends his time in doing his own silent reading or in activities related to this reading.

Even though individualized approaches in teaching may focus upon a person, not persons, there still is adequate time in a school day for committee work in cooperative learning. Rational balance needs to exist between individual and group endeavors. Cooperative learning might well stress homogeneous or heterogeneous grouping of pupils for instruction. The same is true for individualized reading. It does not matter how pupils are grouped in individualized reading. We recommend here that pupils be grouped heterogeneously. Presently for pupils and at the work place later, each person works with others of diverse ability and achievement levels.

At various times during the school day, we recommend strictly heterogeneous grouping such as when pupils view an audio-visual activity in an ongoing unit of study. After the presentation, all pupils in a mixed achievement level classroom can benefit from discussing its contents. We believe that one should not become dogmatic on emphasizing one approach only, such as selected educators are doing today in favoring heterogeneous grouping only. These educators quote research stating that pupils achieve at a higher rate in heterogeneous grouping as compared to homogeneous grouping. Generally, slow learners learn better in heterogeneous grouping settings. Why? There are motivated learners here who set the pace in learning and others then also need to achieve at as an optimal rate as possible.

Frequently, advocates of heterogeneous grouping look only at slow learners and their achievement in heterogeneous grouping. They have one role for the fast learner only and that is to assist the slow learner. There are times when this should be a goal. However, the fast learner needs to have a challenging curriculum of his/her own with proper scope and sequence. We believe the dilemma can be resolved between heterogeneous versus homogeneous grouping with looking at what assists a child to achieve optimally. Which plan of grouping pupils for instruction then assists pupils to learn as much as possible on an individual basis?

The heterogeneous versus homogeneous controversy then might be summarized in terms of advantages for each plan of grouping pupils for instruction. Thus the former emphasizes

1. mixed achievement levels of pupils in one classroom.
2. pupils of diverse abilities learning from each other.
3. learners working more like the social environment

emphasizes in that people of different attainment levels interact with each other.

4. usually, cooperative learning goes along with heterogeneous grouping advocates in that pupils of diverse ability levels work together on a project.
5. the composition of heterogeneous groups should change, making for flexibility.

Homogeneous grouping advocates believe the following:

1. pupils who possess more of homogeneous characteristics can do a better job of challenging each other.
2. the teacher can do a better job of providing for individual differences in a homogeneous grouping setting due to a smaller range of pupil achievement in a classroom.
3. each pupil can do more of his/her fair share of the work when committee endeavors are emphasized.
4. less looking down upon slow learners should be in evidence when pupils are quite similar in achievement within a classroom.
5. there can be numerous opportunities to stress heterogeneous grouping when pupils are in physical education, art, and music classes.

Again, there are approaches in teaching whereby it does not matter much if pupils are grouped homogeneously or heterogeneously. A language experience approach in learning can be used on any grade level no matter how pupils are grouped for instruction. Pertaining to the language experience approach in teaching reading, Bush and Huebner (1979) wrote the following:

In the initial stages when children dictate their own stories, the teacher as recorder points out letters that stand for sounds, good words the children have used to express their ideas, and sentence structure. He or she helps the child notice similarities in beginning and ending sounds of some words and helps the children build a basic stock of sight vocabulary useful in their reading and writing.

Meaningful experiences with clay, paint, and other materials provide opportunities for further self-expression. As children spontaneously talk about their activities, they are encouraged to write their stories. They write again in content areas as they record information on topics of interest, contributing to classroom newspapers or class books. The teacher encourages self-expression and helps children as they ask for spelling, punctuation marks, and other aids to writing. Reading practice is obtained as the children read their own writing, each other's and, finally, the adult writing in published material.

The language experience approach may be used on any grade and age levels. As long as one's own experiences are written down by others or by the self, the language experience approach is in evidence. Pupils may be grouped homogeneously or heterogeneously in the language experience approach in learning to read and write. The content here may come from any academic area.

Learning Centers

An open-ended approach to grouping pupils for instruction is to use learning centers. The teacher can develop each center and tasks therefor or teacher-pupil planning might be emphasized to develop the tasks for each center. The latter approach may take considerable time to implement but is well worth the time to do so. Being able to plan is so vital for each pupil to do and do well. There needs to be ample input from learners when teacher-pupil is used to develop the curriculum. The former approach in which the teacher develops all the tasks for the diverse centers can be quite open ended if there are more tasks available for learners to select sequentially than what can be completed. Thus learners individually may work on sequential tasks of their very own choosing and omit those not possessing perceived purpose. If tasks do not meet personal needs of individual pupils, the latter can talk to the teacher and negotiate more worthwhile activities from the pupils' point of view.

Humanism is inherent as a psychology when learners individually select their own preferred tasks to complete. Humanists are strong believers in guiding the pupil to make choices and decisions in the curriculum. Sequence here resides with the pupil and not within textbooks nor the teacher. The pupil is the focal point of instruction.

Thus the pupil needs to be heavily involved in choosing the

objectives of instruction, learning opportunities to attain the objectives, and evaluation procedures whereby the learner appraised the self. A humane curriculum should thus be an end result.

Pupils may select tasks that harmonize with their very own individual levels of attainment. They may choose activities that are worked on individually or activities may be chosen which emphasize committee endeavors. The choice is for the pupil to make. The problems of homogeneous versus heterogeneous grouping have been greatly minimized when using a learning centers philosophy in teaching learners. When pupils choose sequential tasks, they may work on an activity individually. Thus it does not matter if the learners are somewhat uniform in achievement or mixed achievement levels are in evidence in the classroom. When a pupil chooses committee work as a task, then homogeneous or heterogeneous grouping may be in evidence. Perhaps, the teacher can guide pupils here to work with learners from both categories. The teacher encourages, stimulates, and motivates learners to achieve optimally in a learning center approach in teaching pupils.

The Dual Progress Plan

The dual progress plan in grouping pupils for instruction is generally implemented on the intermediate grade level. The curriculum areas of mathematics and science are taught as being ungraded, there are no grade levels here. Pupils individually, however, achieve as much as possible. There are separate teachers for mathematics and for science, resulting in departmentalization. Those who wish to teach a separate academic discipline in the elementary school in mathematics and in science may do so. Teachers might also teach English and the social studies as an integrated classroom. There are homeroom responsibilities here for the teacher in teaching English and social studies. Guidance and counselling of pupils may be stressed during homeroom time.

Teachers who teach both social studies and English emphasize the graded concept here. Thus there are definite grade level standards for pupils to attain in social studies and English. The social studies English teacher is in a modified self-contained classroom with two curriculum areas only, that need to be taught by one person. Team teaching could be emphasized here in the dual progress plan. It could also stressed in homogenous and heterogeneous grouping.

Team Teaching and Grouping Pupils for Instruction

The team approach in teaching learners emphasizes that two or more teachers plan together the objectives, learning activities to achieve these ends, and the evaluation procedures to ascertain how much pupils have learned. Notice the teachers must plan instructional strategy cooperatively, not individually. With cooperative planning participants may think critically about ideas presented from team members. The best possible procedures presented should be used in teaching pupils. More than one mind is better than a single mind in preparing for teaching.

There are three levels of teaching using a team approach. Large group instruction is one level. After planning for teaching, one team member may teach pupils in large group instruction. How many pupils are there in large group instruction? If two elementary school classrooms are joined together, there might be fifty pupils from the two rooms. If three classroom are joined together for large group instruction there might be seventy-five learners from the three rooms. Could a team approach be used in large group instruction? The answer is in the affirmative. What is salient in large group instruction is that the teacher/teachers do a good job of motivating pupils. Thus audio-visual aids that engage pupils in learning should be used in large group instruction. Teachers not involved in direct teaching in large group instruction may assist in monitoring learners' progress.

The second level of team teaching is to assist pupils in small group endeavors. Within the small group, teachers guide pupils to clarify and discuss what was presented in large group instruction. Teachers here should use a variety of materials such as audio-visual and printed content such as in textbooks and trade books to assist each pupil to attain as optimally as possible. In small group endeavors, pupils will ask questions and identify problem areas. The teacher needs to guide pupils to locate relevant information.

A third level of team teaching is to emphasize individual study. Each pupil will have a topic to pursue or an area of interest to develop within the framework of individualized study. The leaner identifies a problem or wishes to pursue a task of personal interest. These kinds of learning activities can be planned by the pupil and teacher. There must be a purpose in doing the project. Planning needs to accrue to achieve the purpose or goal. Next, the pupil needs to follow through with the work involved to attain the purpose. Ultimately, criteria should be developed to appraise the completed project. There needs to be heavy involvement by the pupil in working on the project method. Individual study goals must grow out of the large group session as well as from the small group work stressed. There is a definite relationship among large and small group instruction as well as of the individual endeavors emphasized.

There can be an interdisciplinary team as well as team members emphasizing a separate academic area domain. The former would be more typical of elementary school teachers in which the concept of the self-contained classroom has been stressed in teacher education training at a college or university. Thus most elementary school teachers have not majored in a single academic area such as history or biology, but they have experienced a general education curriculum plus professional course work and student teaching in becoming a licensed teacher. If an elementary teacher was educated at a college/university school of education with a double major such as history and elementary education then a team of teachers with similar training may teach social studies in a departmentalized classroom. An interdisciplinary team also could comprise team members having majors in the social sciences/elementary education; English/ elementary education; and biology/elementary education. These teachers would then plan the objectives, learning activities, and evaluation procedures for teaching a given set of learners in large and small groups as well as in individual work. Relationship of diverse academic disciplines might then be in evidence.

In team teaching, a leader of the team may be appointed and receive additional salary for being the designated leader. Team teaching has also to be emphasized in which there is no designated leader, but leadership emerges within each planning session.

To implement team teaching, participants should have a voice in which team they wish to participate in. No teacher should be forced to serve on a team. Perhaps, with stimulating workshops on team teaching, teachers may feel motivated in desiring to be a member. Thus teachers must be knowledgeable, skillful, and possess appropriate attitudes prior to being members of teaching team. We have known teachers who feared being a member of a teaching team and yet with inservice education felt motivated in becoming a team member. Ediger. (1996) wrote:

> ...The term "team" implies that teachers work together cooperatively in determining objectives, learning opportunities, and evaluation procedures when teaching a specific set of learners. Team teaching needs to be differentiated from "turn" teaching. In turn teaching, each teacher does his/her own planning for teaching and then takes a turn teaching pupils either in a large group or small group session. Other teachers also take their turn teaching these learners. However, there is little or no interaction among teachers when planning the objectives, learning activities, and evaluation procedures.

Democratic planning is very important when team members work together. Team teaching emphasizes that members learn from each other in planning sessions. Thus inservice education is an inherent part of team teaching as a plan in grouping pupils for instruction. If a leader or a member of a teaching team would be very domineering or autocratic, the chances are that individuals, of course, would not learn from each other. There needs to be mutual respect of personalities and ideas presented when team members select the best objectives, the best learning activities, and the best evaluation techniques to be utilized in teaching a given set of learners.

The talents of each teacher should be utilized when providing learning activities for pupils. For example, when large group instruction is utilized in teaching ninety pupils, each team member's strengths should be analyzed to determine who should do the teaching in the large group session. If pupils are studying a unit on "New England–Past and Present," a team member may have travelled extensively in this area as well as studie its past history thoroughly. This team members may have excellent slides, pictures, filmstrips, and booklets pertaining to the new England area. Thus, large group instruction, no doubt, would heavily involve using the talents of this member of the team. At other times, different members of the team will be utilizing their talents involving large group instruction in team teaching.

After the large group session has been completed, all teachers on the team should guide learners in small group sessions. Here, learners can ask questions pertaining to the content presented in large group instruction. Additional learning activities, carefully selected, can be provided in small group sessions. The teacher needs to select activities which are meaningful, interesting, and purposeful to learners. Pupils need to be actively involved in ongoing learning activities. A variety of learning activities should be provided for learners in small group sessions. It should be pointed out that in large group instruction, the teaching team must consider and select those activities which capture pupils' curiosity and are relevant for learners. If activities are not carefully selected, it will be difficult to hold the attention of pupils and valuable time in learning will be lost.

Ample opportunity also needs to be given to pupils to work on individual projects and activities. With the guidance of the teaching team, pupils should work on purposeful projects and activities on an individual basis which relate the large and small group sessions.

On the second level of instruction, team teaching places much stress upon pupils working in committees. Presently, many educators emphasize learners working in groups, known as cooperative learning. For group work to be successful, there is much that a teacher can do to assist in its success. In reviewing research pertaining to group work, Burk (1996) wrote:

> ...Acquaintance pairs in which one partner possessed a higher popularity status than the other tended to benefit least from the experience. The friendship/popularity effect was even more pronounced with pairs of children who began the task with the same understanding of the balance. Acquaintances with a similar understanding of the task

> were more likely to learn if their partner's popularity status was different from their own. Why would popularity status have an influence on learning? Just as friendships evolve within the larger social world, children develop views of their classmates, whether or not they are friends with them. Popularity status is influenced by the number of friends a person has, but not by the intensity of those friendships. It may also be influenced by such things as stability, physical attractiveness and reputation... Popularity status may also affect the equal footing within the relationship that allows for greater cooperation. Because children may be friends with others whose popularity status is similar or different from their own, the two constructs must both be considered.

We as teachers need to facilitate the development of a psychologically safe environment that promotes positive social interaction. As children interact openly with their peers, they learn more about others as individuals, and they begin building a history of interactions. Some interactions will be very positive and develop into lasting friendships. Others will not, but an atmosphere of acceptance and respect in the classroom will help them to see each other as equal members of their social world.

The influence of friendship and popularity on learning is still not well understood...If we focus our attention on cognitive development without consideration for the social realm, we may inhibit development of both realms. The common practice of not allowing friends to work together on projects is, therefore, open to question. Children need experience working with their friends as well as with acquaintances, who are potential friends. By recognizing and appreciating children's relationships, teachers show additional respect for children as members of the social world.

The above quote indicates the many factors that need consideration when grouping pupils for instructional purposes. Cooperative learning is salient since pupils presently need to work harmoniously well with others as well as at the work place later. It is an uncomfortable situation if an individual cannot work well with others and feels uncomfortable in doing so. The teacher then has important responsibilities in knowing how to group pupils to maximize learning for all.

Interage or Multiage Grouping

There are advocates of having pupils of different age levels being taught in a single classroom. For example, pupils in grades one and two could be taught in a single classroom. This could be a team teaching situation or it might emphasize a single teacher teaching a given set of pupils in interage grouping. The children taught here in one classroom could be quite heterogeneous. It could be also that learners in the two grades were grouped homogeneously by placing a somewhat uniform level of attainment of first and second graders combined in a single classroom. What is the focal point of placing pupils into interage groups? People interact with each other in society who are of different age levels. Second, it means little when speaking of a pupil being in grade one or two. Thus selected first grades read better than some second grade pupils. Third, learners need to get along well with others regardless of age levels. Social development is very important. Fourth, dividing pupils in classrooms by age levels is not too relevant. Pupils mature at different levels even though they are of the same age or similar age levels. Interage grouping of pupils for teaching has a different motive today as compared to when small rural one or two teacher schools were in evidence. Today, the emphasis is upon interage grouping to assist learners to work effectively with others so that social development may be more optimal...Hopefully, academic achievement will also be at as high a level as possible for all pupils.

The Joplin plan for teaching reading emphasizes interage grouping. Here, pupils from grades four through six are regrouped in toto. Thus, fourth, fifth, and sixth grade pupils may be together in a separate room of twenty five pupils to make for homogeneous grouping in reading instruction. These fourth, fifth, and sixth grade pupils then emerge in interage grouping whereby there are fast, average, and slow readers grouped homogeneously from the intermediate grade levels. Joplin plan advocates have made salient research claims from their research results on interage grouping in reading.

Mainstreaming of Pupils

Mainstreaming of pupils has made for an increased amount of heterogeneous grouping of pupils in the United States. Handicapped pupils are then to be educated in the least restricted environment and receive an appropriate education, according to the Education for all Handicapped Children Act of 1975. Before that time most children were continually taught within the framework of the handicap possessed, in separate classrooms from that of normal pupils. Thus an orthopaedically handicapped child was in a special room from that of learners in a regular classroom. Selected aggressive educators felt that pupils were being segregated based on the handicap possessed. Thus mainstreaming came into being whereby a handicapped learner was to be placed in the least restricted environment. This has usually meant the regular classroom.

Each child who is handicapped is to have a planned individual educational plan (IEP) to follow as far as the curriculum is concerned. An IEP consists of behaviorally stated objectives agreed upon by the involved parents, the teacher(s), the principal, as well as specialists in the field such as speech correctionists, physical therapists, hearing and sight resource personnel, as well as counselling services. No child is to be refused an appropriate education. If a child has not been placed appropriately, the parents can ask for a reevaluation. Parents may also sue the school if misplacement or diagnosis has been in error. If the judge or court rules in favor of the parents of the handicapped pupil, the school must incur all costs of the lawsuit. Judges tend to be generous in ruling in favor of the parents of the handicapped. With mainstreaming as a federal law, classrooms have become increasingly heterogeneous in grouping. Questions that can be raised of mainstreaming are the following :

1. Do these pupils achieve more in a regular classroom as compared to where the numbers are smaller such as being taught by an appropriate teacher of the handicapped?
2. Are regular teachers trained and educated properly to teach the handicapped in the classroom?
3. Would handicapped pupils attain more in a special class

in which the pupil-teacher ratio is very low and where the teacher is properly trained and educated?

4. Do regular teachers receive aid service to assist with teaching the handicapped in the classroom?
5. How do normal children achieve in a mainstreamed classroom in which handicapped pupil demands or needs much assistance?

In their research study on "Teacher Perceptions of Mainstreaming/Inclusion, 1958-1995 : A Research Synthesis," Scruggs and Mastropieri concluded the following:

The primary implications for practice form this research synthesis derive from this consistent finding that teachers need support in teaching classes that include students with disabilities. These needs relate time, training, personnel, materials, class size, and consideration of severity of disability as follows :

- Time–Teachers report a need for 1 hour or more per day to plan for students with learning disabilities.
- Training–Teachers need systematic intensive training either as part of their certification programs as intensive and self-planned inservice, or as an ongoing process with consultants.
- Personnel resources–Teachers report a need for additional personnel assistance to carry out mainstreaming objectives. This could include a half-time aide and daily contact with special education teachers.
- Materials resources–Teachers need adequate curriculum materials and other classroom equipment appropriate to the needs of students with disabilities.
- Class size–Teachers agree that their class size should be reduced to no fewer than twenty students, if students with disabilities are included.
- Consideration of severity of disability–Teachers are more willing to include students with mild disabilities than students with more severe disabilities, apparently because of teachers' perceived ability to carry on their teaching mission for the entire classroom. By implication, the more severe the disabilities in the inclusive setting, the more

the previously mentioned sources of support would be needed.

In Closing

Teachers and principals have a salient responsibility in determining the best approach in grouping pupils for instruction whereby each learner achieves optimally. There are numerous recommended procedures in grouping pupils for instruction which are recommended. Each has its pros and cons. Educators and parents need to study and analyze each method of grouping pupils for instruction. A well informed constituency in terms of how learners may be placed into groups for teaching and learning is necessary. A plan must be implemented which provides for each pupil to learn as much as possible. The plan or plans of grouping chosen need to be based on a sound philosophy of education as well as a recommended foundation of the psychology of instruction. Rigid approaches must be avoided since flexibility is a key term when thinking of how learners should be grouped for instruction. Thus teachers and principals need to have an open mind in terms of how learners should be grouped so that each pupil can attain as much as possible in the school curriculum.

We make the following recommendations when emphasizing how learners should be grouped in the school curriculum:

1. the plan of grouping stressed must benefit the individual child in ongoing lessons and units of instruction.
2. an integrated curriculum whereby each subject matter area is related within the total curriculum should be implemented in grouping for instruction. The child should perceive knowledge and skills as being related.
3. parents need to be involved and informed about proposals for grouping learners for teaching and learning.
4. inservice education for teachers may well be necessary when implementing a new plan in grouping pupils for instruction.
5. the school curriculum and the approach to grouping learners for instruction need to be congruent and not separate in philosophical and psychological beliefs.

Selected References

Burk, Deborah I. (1996). *"Understanding Friendship and Social Interaction,"* Childhood Education, *285.*

Bush, Clifford L. and Margaret Huebner (1979). Strategies for Reading in the Elementary School. Second edition. New York: McMillan Publishing Company. 256-257.

Ediger, Marlow (1996). *Curriculum Improvement* (A Collection of Essays). Kirksville, Missouri: Simpson Publishing Company. 59-60.

Ediger, Marlow (1996). Elementary Education (A Collection of Essays). Kirksville, Missouri: Simpson Publishing, 82.

Scruggs, Thomas E., and Margo A. Mastropieri (1956). "Teacher Perceptions of Mainstreaming/Inclusion. 1958-1995: A Research Synthesis," *Exceptional Children.* 72.

Shepherd, Gene D. and William B. Ragan (1982). *Modern Elementary Curriculum,* Sixth Edition. New York : Holt, Rinehart and Winston, 50.

Veatch, Jeanette (1959). *Individualizing Your Reading Program.* New York: G.P. Putnam's Sons. 105.

5

Problem Solving in Mathematics

Much is written and spoken about the merits of pupils solving problems in mathematics. There are numerous questions that need to be answered pertaining to problem solving in mathematics. We have spoken at numerous teacher education conferences on problem solving in mathematics. There are numerous questions from participants at the end of the presentation which have helped to clarify thinking in this area of teaching and learning.

What is Problem Solving?

This is a broad question and needs to be delimited. First of all, let us discuss who owns the problem. Better yet, who faces the problem in mathematics. Piaget's research (1950) indicates that pupils go through different stages of development. The sensorimotor stage, birth to two years of age, need not concern us directly as public school teachers. The preoperational stage, two to seven years of age, is of concern to kindergarten and first grade teachers. Here the pupil can perceive one variable only or largely. The inverse operation of addition may involve too many variables for the preoperational learner to understand and use. This, however, is not an absolute, but needs to be tested as a hypothesis. We have had graduate students in class who state that their children can go beyond the one variable perception even though these youngsters are in the preoperational stage of development.

To the five and six-year-old, a valid problem of personal concern might be how much money the child has if he/she had two cents and was given or found three cents. The learner here had not committed the 2+3 = 5 to memory at this stage of development and the child truly wishes to know the answer. Thus a problem is involved. Information needs to be gathered, through thinking, as to what the solution is. If the learner finally determines that five or six is the correct answer, he/she needs to test the answer in terms of correctness or lack thereof. To the concrete operations and formal thought stage of development pupil, according to Piaget, 2+3=5 is no longer a problem. Maturation has taken place within the pupil and he/she is now at a different stage of development. Thus, 2+3=5, using markers, may be a problem to solve for the young learner in the preoperational stage of development.

Supposing the teacher in context asks a pupil what 2+3 is, can that be considered a problem to solve? We think not. The teacher here raises a question pertaining to the value of a number pair. No doubt, pupils have had experiences with the number pair 2+3=–, and pupils are being drilled on what the answer is. A stimulus response learning is involved whereby pupils are to respond with "five" as being the answer to the stimulus of what 2+3 is. The question raised by the teacher requires an abstract answer; nothing is presented in the concrete in terms of materials of instruction.

Should problems always be identified by the pupil, not by the teacher. We would say "yes." It is the learner who must identify and solve problems in school and in society. Each person faces problems in life which will require solutions. However, we have noticed many times how pupils do accept mathematics problems chosen by the teacher and others as their very own. The learner appears to develop ownership of these problems.

Selected problems in mathematics take longer to solve as compared to others. For the young child referred to previously in wanting to know how much money he/she has with two cents and three cents, a considerable amount of time might be required to determine the amount. If someone else says how much money is then in evidence, this would not be problem solving. It is the pupil himself or herself who needs to find ways of securing the answer and testing the correctness of the answer. John Dewey (1915), who is still the most frequently referred to educator in educational literature, emphasized that learners needed to select a problem, gather data or information to solve the problem, develop a hypothesis or tentative answer to the problem, and then test the answer in a life-like situation.

Textbooks and Problem Solving

Do word or textbook problems provide opportunities for pupils to engage in problem solving? These kinds of problems are written by writers of the adopted text. First of all, are these truly to be considered as problems for learners to solve. Generally, I would say "no." Why? The problems do not represent life in all of its manifestations. I have observed pupils in class who have disagreed with the price of items stated in a textbook word problem or the amount of pay per hour that a worker secures. To be sure, some of the money items definitely are not realist. A second problem pertains to the pupil, accepting as his/her own, those written by writers of textbooks or problems written by the teacher. Most do not personally perceive these word problems as being realistic and life-like. The problems become an exercise to work to complete requirements and to receive grades, hopefully a top grade.

There are times when the teacher can make these problems realistic and life-like. We have seen teachers who update prices and wages received for work performed. This helps to breathe life into the mathematics curriculum. The problem, however, still does not belong to the pupil unless the learner accepts the problems as his/her very own and this has happened, according to my observations. We would encourage teachers to assist pupils to select and solve personal problems related to the world of mathematics. Thus if a pupil wishes to buy a baseball glove for #17.98 and he/she has #9.29, how much more money is needed? This represents a problem to solve. The pupil does not know the answer nor is he/she able to come up with immediate processes in obtaining solutions. Deliberation and thought are necessary on the part of the learner. We have noticed many, many pupils who have problems to solve that are realistic, not text or worksheet oriented. We as teachers must provide ample opportunities for pupils to select and solve mathematics problems experienced.

Do pupils ask questions in which the procedure is too difficult to use in solving problems. The answer is definitely "yes." Should these problems then become a part of the school's mathematics curriculum? Definitely. We would suggest cooperative learning as one approach. Thus in a committee setting, pupils may work toward solutions of these problems. Pupils should be encouraged to bring personal problems in mathematics to the school setting. The curriculum of life presents some of the best opportunities to learn mathematics and achieve worthwhile objectives.

The Basics in Mathematics

Mathematics has its very own scope and sequence. It is precise and orderly. There is no academic discipline that contains the patterns and exactness as is true of mathematics. Few would disagree about the exactness and orderliness of mathematics. Single digit addends are taught prior to addition of two digit and two digit addends. Carrying in addition would follow the single digit addends in sequence or the two digits number pair in each addend provided no carrying is involved. We could go on and on with an appropriate scope and sequence in the mathematics curriculum. Should pupils learn these basics within the framework of problem solving or outside the problems solving sequence? Our answer is that problem solving should be stressed as much as possible. However, there still may be a need to use the basal text and selected worksheets. Textbooks, workbooks, and worksheets are neither good nor evil in and of themselves, but they are neutral in nature. The uses made of textbooks, worksheets, and workbooks made these teaching devices good or bad. If pupils achieve new goals in mathematics and satisfaction results therefrom, the chances are these traditional materials of instruction have had quality implementation. If learners are forced to use textbooks, worksheets, and workbooks and feelings of dislike result, the chances are that these materials were not used in a way that assists pupils to feel success and interest. Teachers need to observe that pupils benefit adequately from any material of instruction used, including a multimedia approach. Merely using multimedia does not guarantee success in learning. If teachers force pupils to memorize subject matter from the diverse media, the chances are that learners will tend to dislike learning. Learning and achievement seems to be such an individual matter that even having memorized much poetry, as an example, selected pupils have enjoyed it presently or later as adults. A colleague of ours memorized much poetry as requirements in elementary and secondary levels of learning. He still can recite in an enjoyable manner many poems from the public school years of forty years ago. One problem is to ascertain if learning is to be enjoyable, interesting, and goal attainment presently, or if a teacher in the future looks back to what benefited learners ten, twenty, thirty, or more years ago. The latter is impossible to engage in presently as a classroom teacher. How pupils react presently to ongoing learning opportunities, of course, is much easier to determine. It could be good if the teacher could ascertain what actually benefited individuals after they have left the public school. Test results, be they norm referenced or criterion referenced, do a rather poor job of determining learner progress, interest, and meaning. All tests are written by human beings and have their many flaws. Tests have a problem with validity in that what is covered therein might not harmonize with truly stressing achievement or what is needed to be successful in the real world of mathematics. Reliability or consistency of measurement results can be ascertained much more accurately be it test-retest, alternate forms, or split half. Something, however, needs to be used to ascertain learner progress. Teachers, properly educated and trained, can do as good a job, using observational methods based on quality criteria, as any other evaluation technique in determining pupil achievement. One problem here is that numerical results are lacking in reporting learner progress to parents and other interested persons. Too frequently, numerical results are looked upon as being holy and objective. There is little objectivity here and results are not scientific. There is as much subjectivity in norm and criterions test results as there is in teacher observation. Perhaps, the problems can be resolved somewhat by using a variety of evaluation procedures including portfolios.

We believe there are some very valuable guidelines that should be used in teaching and learning situations. Thus the teacher should (Ediger 1994)

1. emphasize meaningful lessons and units of study. With meaning, pupils understand and comprehend that which was contained in ongoing learning opportunities.
2. stress interesting content and skills in the curriculum. With interest, the pupils and the curriculum become one, not separate entities. Pupils attend and achieve from ongoing lessons and units study.
3. indicate purpose in learning. With purpose for learning, pupils accept reasons for attaining relevant facts, concepts, and generalizations presented. Purpose development by the teacher may take little time indeed. With deduction, the teacher explains clearly and concisely why pupils should achieve the objectives to be stressed. With inductive approaches, the teacher raises a few questions about the new lesson whereby the pupil responds and perceives reasons for achieving. Extrinsic rewards can be emphasized. Here the teacher announces prizes and awards that pupils may secure if they attain the objectives of the lesson. Pupils need to know precisely what is to be learned to receive the rewards.
4. obtain sequence in learning. With quality sequence, pupils relate newly acquired content with that previously achieved. Pupils need guidance to perceive relationship of knowledge in teaching learning situations.
5. implement balance among objectives stressed. Thus knowledge, skills, and attitudes–three kinds of objectives need to be achieved by pupils. These objectives interact and are not in isolation from each other. For example, if pupils possess positive attitudes, they should achieve needed knowledge and skills more readily.

With good teaching then, pupils may master the basics and use this information in the solving of problems. The teacher must be a good thinker of problem areas for pupils to solve directly related to the basics. The teacher also needs to encourage pupils to raise questions and identify problems so that the level of application may enter in as well as mathematics and problem solving becoming one, not separate entities.

Role of the Textbook

What should be the role of the basal mathematics textbook in a problem solving curriculum? Writers of these texts have developed their very own scope (what is taught) as well as sequence (when subject matter is taught) in the mathematics curriculum. Mathematics texts may soon become outdated, especially with prices listed for what goods and services cost; pupils are to use these prices in computing the total cost of items purchased. Newer series of texts, carefully chosen in terms of desired criteria, may stress more of critical and creative thinking as well as problem solving.

When modern school mathematics came out in 1960 and was incorporated in numerous texts, the emphasis was quite different as compared to today's mathematical curriculum. Many study groups were federally funded and hired leading professors of mathematics to revise the curriculum. Little or nothing is heard of modern mathematics, if anything, today. But in the 1960's, it was a wrong not to incorporate the many findings of federally funded study groups into the new mathematics curriculum. We believe modern school mathematics as indicated by their findings and reports in the early 1960's was very strong on the following structural ideas in mathematics.

1. the commutative property of addition and multiplication.
2. the associative property of addition and multiplication.
3. the distributive property of multiplication over addition.
4. the inverse properties of subtraction and division.
5. the property of closure for counting numbers in addition and multiplication.

Jerome Bruner (1977) was a strong advocate of the structure of knowledge theory in teaching pupils. His well-known hypothesis was "any subject matter in some intellectually honest from can be learned by any child at any stage of development." Bruner emphasized that academicians on the higher education level should identify major generalizations or key ideas from their academic area of speciality. These key ideas would then be available for teachers to use in teaching pupils. The above enumerated structural ideas as identified by mathematicians at the college/university levels provided pupils with background content that held consistently true in pursuing mathematics subject matter. The structural ideas can certainly be valuable in problem solving. Too frequently, what a pupil has learned is separated from its use and that use being problem solving. That which has been learned should be integrated into higher cognitive level objectives.

Textbooks are used in the mathematics curriculum in most schools and can definitely be adapted to knowledge acquired by pupils to be used in problem solving.

Our recommendations in textbook usage include the following:

1. be certain the pupil can read the content meaningfully, particularly when reading word problems. Meaningful learning can only accrue with learners understanding content read.
2. provide background experiences for pupils so that new content in sequence may be meaningful.
3. guide pupils to perceive application in society of what has been learned.
4. use other sources or materials of instruction in addition to the text. The additional materials should assist pupils to become numeracy literate and attain critical and creative thinking skills within the framework of problem solving.
5. help learners to develop positive attitudes toward mathematics within and outside the framework of textbook use.

National Council Teachers of Mathematics Standards

The National Council Teachers of Mathematics (NCTM) strongly emphasizes problem solving in the curriculum. The following are listed for kindergarten through grade four, standard one:

Mathematics as problem solving. In grades k-4, the study of mathematics should emphasize problem solving so that students can.

1. use problem solving approaches to investigate and understand mathematical content;

2. formulate problems from everyday an mathematical situations;
3. develop and apply strategies to solve a wide variety of problems;
4. verify and interpret results with respect to the original problem;
5. acquire confidence in using mathematics meaningfully (NCTM 1989, p75).

Grades five though eight

Standard one : Mathematics as problem solving

In grades 5-8, the mathematics curriculum should include numerous and varied experiences with problem solving as a method of inquiry and application so that students can

1. use problem solving approaches to investigate and understand mathematical content;
2. formulate problems from situations within and outside mathematics;
3. develop and apply a variety of strategies to solve problems which emphasize multistep and non-routine problems;
4. verify and interpret results with respect to the original problem situation;
5. acquire confidence in using mathematics meaningfully (NCTM 1989, p98).

There is overlapping between the two sets of NCTM standards k-4 as compared to grades 5-8. However, these NCTM standards do show the emphasis placed upon problem solving in mathematics.

Kennedy and Tipps (1994) suggest the following strategies, among others, that learners may use in the solving of problems;

1. look for patterns, e.g. 1,3,5,7, and...Mathematics is orderly and contains many consistent patterns.
2. use model. e.g seeds, sticks, geometrical figures, and beads, among others.
3. draw a picture or diagram. The picture or diagram represents using semiconcrete materials and can replace or represent numerals in order that the problem is clarified and meaningful. Use of Venn diagrams, for example,

assists learners to understand a process or procedure.

4. act it out. Many pupils have developed accurate concepts and generalizations through buying in a "make believe" classroom store.
5. Construction tables and graphs of mathematics phenomena being studied.
6. guess and check. Reasonable or educated guesses are acceptable and should be welcomed in mathematics. Estimations are necessary in numerous situations involving the real world of number and numerals.

When pupils ask or answer a "why" question, the chances are that meaning and understanding is desired in mathematics. Higher levels of cognition are necessary in these situations. The mathematics teacher needs to motivate pupils to think critically, creatively, and engage in problem solving activities and experiences.

Philosophy of Education in Teaching Mathematics

Ediger (1992) wrote the following:

Diverse schools of thought in the philosophy of education have much to offer in terms of objectives, learning activities, and appraisal techniques for pupils in ongoing units of study in the curriculum areas of mathematics. Teachers and supervisors need to study, analyze, and implement selected strands from the diverse philosophical schools of thought.

As one philosophy, experimentalism emphasizes that pupils solve real problems, generally identified by pupils with teacher guidance. Subject matter is used to solve problems and is not an end to be learned in and of itself. Solutions to problems are tentative and subject to change. Problem solving then should be at the heart of the mathematics curriculum, according to experimentalists. Committee work or cooperative learning is salient since people in society work together to solve problems.

A second philosophy, namely, existentialism, advocates much pupil input into the curriculum. Individual decisions and choices, generally, should be at the heart of the mathematics curriculum. Pupil/teacher planning of the mathematics curriculum needs much stress, a learning centers approach could be excellent here in that pupils may choose which task to complete and which to omit. There are an adequate number of tasks so that choosing by the pupil may truly be in evidence. Tasks at the different centers may or may not stress problem solving, according to existentialists; but the opportunities are there for the authentic self to select and solve problems. A learner becomes responsible for choices and decisions made. We would recommend here that the major focus on objectives should stress problem solving tasks at the diverse centers in the mathematics curriculum. Ozman and Craver (1990) wrote the following:

> Because the individual human is so important as the creator of ideas, existentialists maintain that education should focus upon individual human reality. It should deal with the individual as a unique being in the world, not only a creator of ideas, but as a living, feeling being. Most philosophies...existentialists charge, tend to focus on the individual as a cognitive being. The individual is this, but also a feeling, aware person, and existentialists think that this side deserves attention.

A third philosophy to emphasize in mathematics is realism. Teachers stressing realism believe that objectives be selected prior to implementation. The objectives are highly precise and stated in measurable terms. After instruction, it can be measured if the pupil has/has not attained an objective. If an objective has not been achieved by a pupil, a new teaching strategy needs to be implemented in teaching. The teacher sequences the objectives, chooses the learning opportunities, and appraises achievement of learners against the stated objectives. The precise objectives are the measuring stick to gauge learner achievement and progress. Prior to a lesson presentation, the mathematics teacher may announce to pupils what they are to learn so as to be successful in goal attainment.

Realists tend to look at products of pupil learning as compared to processes. Answers to basic number pairs or to problems provide specificity in terms of what pupils have learned, according to realists. Processes such as critical and creative thinking as well as problem solving are very difficult to state in measurable terms. However, accuracy in terms of pupil responses to questions and problems is salient.

Equally important are the processes that pupils engage in and yet are highly complex to measure and state results in numerical terms. Our concern with realism as a philosophy of education pertains to the emphasis placed upon precision and accuracy largely perhaps to the exclusion of thought processes which cannot be measured with precision. When stressing realism as a philosophical school of thought in teaching, my recommendations would be to stress the processes of learning equally so.

A fourth philosophy of education to incorporate advocates idealism. Idealists emphasize mental development of pupils thoroughly as a major goal of instruction. The abstract is preferable to the concrete and semiconcrete in learning. Academic subject matter taught needs to stress learning opportunities that reflect the abstract. Concrete and semiconcrete experiences are appropriate to the degree that pupils achieve concepts and generalizations that truly emphasize academic learning. Subject centered approaches are to be preferred above that of the practical and the utilitarian. The teacher's goal is to stress/impart knowledge such as pupils attaining relevant subject matter ideas as well as to have learners analyze, synthesize, and appraise content acquired. Mathematics is a part of general education and needs to have an academic emphasis, according to idealists.

We believe strongly that pupils need to attain vital concepts and generalizations in a subject centered environment, but I also believe that learners need to be able to apply that which has been learned. Application brings into the curriculum problem solving in mathematics. The idealist stresses that individuals cannot know the real world as it truly is and exists, but ideas pertaining to reality represents what is ultimately true.

Evaluation of Achievement

Traditionally test results have been used to gauge pupil progress in mathematics. These include teacher written, norm referenced standardized tests, criterion referenced tests, as well as test results from those tests developed by the writer/publisher of textbook content. Parents and the lay public, in many cases, desire numerical results to show where and at what level pupils are achieving. Numerical results include the per cent of problems worked correctly by a learner for specific lesson, percentile rank, standard deviation from the mean, and stanine scores. Test results have as much subjectivity attached to the scores as do other evaluative techniques. Why? Human beings write test items and are then subject to bias or to write poorly written test items.

Today's mathematics educator believes in a broader scope of evaluation techniques to appraise learner performance as compared to the use of test items only or largely. Columba and Dolgos (1995) emphasize using a broad range of assessment procedures in portfolio development for each pupil in the school and class setting. The scope of assessment procedures might well include the following :

1. self evaluation by the pupil using a Likert-like scale.
2. student attitude scale in which learners reveal affect pertaining to feelings possessed toward mathematics.
3. problem solving strategies whereby pupils file in the portfolio different strategies used. Perhaps, this section would be the heart of the portfolio since problem solving is a major goal of mathematics instruction.
4. student journal entries pertaining to concepts and generalizations acquired in mathematics lessons and units of study.
5. project/investigation reports which contain summaries of individual and cooperative learning conclusions.
6. quizzes, tests, and homework data and information.
7. Classroom observations which record information about a pupil's progress. The items are dated to notice learner progress as sequential lessons and units are taught.
8. Student interview record. Dated statements of pupil responses to interview questions raised by the teacher.
9. conference recorded in which data is recorded by the teacher of discussions conducted with the pupil on mathematics achievement and progress.
10. checklist for mastery. Here the teacher checks pupil progress against statements contained in a checklist.
11. miscellaneous items such as photos of committee work, video presentations, tapes of oral reports, and computer

generated work.

The contents of a comprehensive portfolio provides opportunities for teachers, administrators, parents, and other responsible person to notice the sequential achievement levels of a pupil.

In Conclusion

Pupils need the best mathematics curriculum possible in terms of objectives, learning opportunities, and appraisal procedures. Teachers and principals should develop a systematic approach in staff development whereby both benefit from inservice education. A professional library in school pertaining to the teaching of mathematics with the latest journal and other teacher education materials should be available to improve the curriculum. A love of knowledge, teaching skill, positive attitudes, and a desire to guide each pupil to attain optimally should be the lot of all professionals entrusted with the care of learners in the school setting.

Selected References

Piaget, Jean (1950). *The Psychology of Intelligence.* New York: Harcourt Brace Jovanovich, Inc.

Dewey, John (1915). *Democracy and Education.* New York: The Macmillan Company.

Ediger, Marlow (1994). Early Field Experiences in Teacher Education, *College Student Journal,* 28: 302-306.

National Council Teachers of Mathematics (1989). *Curriculum and Evaluation Standards for School Mathematics.* Reston, Virginia : NCTM, page 75.

NCTM (1989), page 98.

Kennedy, Leonard, and Steve Tipps (1994). *Guiding Children's Learning of Mathematics.* Belmont, California : Wadsworth Publishing Company, Seventh edition, pages 123-161.

Ediger, Marlow (1992). Philosophy of Education and the Mathematics Curriculum. *Journal of Instructional Psychology,* 19:236-240.

Ozman, Howard, and Craver, Samuel, (1990). Philosophical Foundations of Education. Columbus, Ohio: Charles Merrill Publishing Company, fourth edition, page 249.

Columba, Lynn and Dologs, Kathleen (1995). Portfolio Assessment in Mathematics. *Reading Improvement,* 32: 174-176.

Bruner, Jerome (1977). *The Process of Education.* Cambridge, Massachusetts, Harvard University Press, page 33.

6

Challenge and Learning Opportunities in Mathematics

To achieve objectives, pupils need to experience learning opportunities. The mathematics teacher needs to choose those activities which will assist pupils to achieve relevant objectives. Thus the chosen learning opportunities should provide for pupils of different abilities and achievement levels. Pupils do differ from each other in terms of the complexity of mathematics problems they can benefit from. They also differ from each other in terms of interests possessed, motivation, and purpose in studying ongoing lessons and units of study in mathematics. It behooves the mathematics teacher to plan well and thoroughly to guide each pupil to learn as much as possible in mathematics.

Using Single or Multiple Series of Textbooks

Textbooks in mathematics are still popular to use in assisting pupils to achieve relevant objectives. These texts should be chosen carefully so that the best possible learning opportunities are available for pupils. The textbooks need to be clearly written so that learners might understand their contents. Illustrations contained in the textbook should be of value to pupil in clarifying ideas and stimulating interest for learning. Quality sequence needs to be in the offing in that the activities move gradually from the easier to the increasingly complex subject matter. Pupils should experience the sequence that assists continuous achievement. If subject matter in mathematics is too complex, pupils may not learn as much as otherwise would be the case. If it is too easy, boredom and a lack of challenge may set in.

A good accompanying manual provides mathematics teachers with suggestions for objectives, learning opportunities, and evaluation techniques. Pre-tests for pupils and their results may assist the teacher in determining if a pupil needs to complete work in that unit of instruction or be placed at a different level of achievement. However, the teacher's judgement is a better indicator of where a pupil is specifically in an ongoing lesson and unit of study as compared to a pre-test or post-test contained in the basal textbook. No doubt, a variety of information sources should provide the mathematics teacher data on where the pupil is presently in achievement. From that starting point, the pupil, through learning opportunities, should be assisted in achieving continuous progress.

There are simulated problem areas which do stimulate pupils to learn from a quality mathematics textbook. The text needs to be on the reading level of the involved learner. The pupil can then understand and attach meaning to what is being read. Failure to possess an adequate reading vocabulary will hinder a pupil from doing quality work from using a mathematics textbook. The mathematics teacher needs to assist pupils who have difficulty in reading abstract words contained in the basal textbook.

There is no reason why pupils cannot engage in higher levels of cognition when working story problems from the textbook. Each problem then has a question which is perplexing for the learner to answer. The question requires thought, deliberation, and critical analysis. Hasty answers do not make for problem solving situations. It takes time and effort to solve problems. Pupils need guidance to think through what is wanted in an answer. Learners then gather information to secure the answer. The tentative answer is evaluated to determine its accuracy and feasibility. Reading materials and discussions must be on the understanding level of the individual pupil. Ediger (1988) lists the following criteria of content to be included in a quality basal textbook in mathematics.

1. Proper order or sequence in learning for pupils is in evidence.

2. Adequate illustrations and diagrams are inherent to help pupils understand mathematical concepts, facts, and generalizations.
3. The textbook captures pupil appeal and interest.
4. Key structural ideas are in evidence such as the commutative property of addition and multiplication, the associative property of addition and multiplication, identify elements for addition and multiplication and the distributive property of multiplication over addition.
5. The teacher's manual section presents ample suggestions for teaching-learning situations such as objectives or goals, learning activities, and appraisal procedures.
6. The authors are reputable from the point of identifying relevant learnings for pupils to achieve in mathematics.
7. Adequate attention is given to guide pupils to develop proficiency in problem solving and using various algorithms in computation.
8. Opportunities are given for pupils to utilize what has been learned previously.

A carefully selected textbook can be an excellent material of instruction to assist pupils to achieve as well as possible. It is, however, up to the teacher to use the basal textbook in a manner which encourages pupil interest and purpose in learning mathematics. To clarify meanings from textbook instruction, the teacher needs to use concrete, semiconcrete, and abstract materials. Markers of different kinds might then help make clear to pupils what otherwise would be vague.

Using Markers

We believe each primary grade pupil should have a kit of markers to make subject matter understandable. We have noticed when supervising student teachers and regular teachers how many kinds of markers are used in teaching. One teacher had pupils show a set of five and a set of four using corn seeds from their kit. It is relatively easy for a teacher to see which pupils can or cannot do what is asked for. Those who fail to put out the correct number of seeds may need assistance in using one-to-one correspondence in counting the correct number of seeds for each set. The teacher's role here, for example, is to guide pupils to attach meaning to the abstract sentence 5+4=9. The commutative property of addition was also stressed by the teacher in having a learner put out four seeds and then five seeds for two different sets. The sets were then joined together to show a value of nine.

It is important for the teacher to change off using different kinds of markers in addition and other operations on number. We have noticed teachers who have pupils use bean seeds, wheat, oats, paper strips, blocks, paper clips, pencils, and crayons, among other markers. Pupils, for example, needed to learn that 4+5 and 5+4=9 regardless of the kinds of markers used in teaching. Children themselves should be involved to show that 4+5 and 5+4=9.

The mathematics teacher should use different markers or materials of instruction effectively so that each pupil may achieve optimally. One time, one of the authors frowned at a teacher using sticks to teach addition in which each pupil kept clicking the stick loudly. Pupils were playing rather than learning. Disruptions occurred here. The teacher, in this case, is recommended to demonstrate what is to be learned by pupils using the large sticks which all could clearly see in the demonstration. Otherwise, we believe strongly in a hands-on approach in pupil learning.

Teacher-Made Materials

We have seen in many classrooms outstanding teacher aids made by classroom teachers which truly assist pupils to achieve objectives. These aids are attractive, well made, and are excellent materials to use as learning opportunities. Flannel boards may be made by teachers and used on any grade level to teach pupils. With the flannel boards, there should be felt cutouts to guide pupil achievement of objectives. We would suggest having cutouts of different colors to attract learner attention in teaching and learning situations. What kind of cutouts might teachers make? These can be felt circles, squares, rectangles, and parallelograms. These cutouts may be used to have primary grade pupils learn geometrical figures. Pupils may also count how many members there are in a set of cutouts. Addition, subtraction, multiplication, and division may be taught using the flannel boards and cutouts.

Cardboard, three feet by four feet, covered attractively with flannel can make for an excellent teaching device on which the felt cutouts may by placed. One teacher had the headings from right to left– ones, tens, hundreds, and thousands on the flannel board. Intermediate grade pupils might then place cutouts to show a value such as 4,567 with four circle cutouts under the thousand's column, five under the hundred's column, six under the ten's column, and seven under the one's column. Borrowing and renaming can easily be stressed using the place value chart. For example, subtracting 1,328 from 4,567 in the set of counting numbers, one cannot take away 8 from 7, so one ten from the six tens needs to be taken. Thus one 10 and 7 ones equal 17. Now 8 can be taken from 17 leaving 9. Further more, two tens may be taken from the five tens leaving three tens. Three hundreds may be taken from the five hundreds and one thousand may be taken from four thousand leaving 3,239 as the answer.

Most teachers make place value charts from paper by stapling pockets labelled for the thousands, hundreds, tens, and ones columns. Congruent strips of paper are then cut out and placed into each pocket. The strips protrude from each pocket so pupils can readily see how many are under each heading. For example, in the number 3,245, there would be three congruent slips of paper in the thousands column, two in the hundreds column, four in the tens column, and five in the ones column. If 2,134 are to be subtracted from 3,245, the pupils can remove four slips from the ones column, three strips from the tens column, one from the hundreds column, and two from the thousands column (of 3,245), leaving a value of 1,111.

For multiplication, pupils may use the place value chart to show meaning. Thus if pupils are attaching meaning to $3 \times 23 = 69$, three congruent slips or paper may be placed in the ones pocket and two sets of ten each in the tens pocket. Next three sets of three each may be placed into the one's pocket and three sets of two tens may be put into the tens pocket. Thus, pupils understand that $3 \times 3 = 9$; this numeral would represent how many would be in the ones column. Also, three sets, two tens in each set, would make for six tens in the tens column. The final product of $3 \times 23 = 69$.

Place value charts may well be used to help pupils understand division. If pupils are developing understandings pertaining to the division problem 42 divided by 2, the dividend of 42 may be represented by two congruent slips of paper being placed in the one's column and four sets, with ten members in each set rubber banded, being placed in the tens pocket. To divide, the learner may place one member in each of two sets to represent the one's column. Next, the four sets of ten each, rubber banded, may be separated into two equal sets. Thus the answer to the division problem 42 divided by 2 = 21.

Using Transparencies and the Overhead Projector

Overhead projectors may be wisely used in the classroom setting due to the following factors:

1. The teacher faces pupils when using transparencies in a class discussion.
2. Specific content that pupils are to learn only, are placed on the transparency, no more and no less. Irrelevant content then is not a part of ongoing learning activities.
3. Transparencies can be developed which are interesting and appealing to learners.
4. The order of discussing several transparencies may be arranged sequentially from the point of view of the child's own unique perception.
5. Content may be added to a transparency as needed. Content may also be omitted from a transparency.

Transparencies and the overhead projector may be used in the following ways:

1. Pupils count how many members there are in a set as given in a specific transparency.
2. Learners tell how many members make a new set if two previously given sets are combined or joined together.
3. Pupils tell how many members are left if, for example, there were nine circles and two are taken away.
4. Pupils begin initial learnings in multiplication, e.g. three sets of circles with four members in each set, 3 x 4 = 12.
5. The inverse operation of multiplication (division) may be shown and discovered from the previous example,

e.g. twelve circles are to be divided equally into three different sets. Thus four members are in each of these three sets.

Using Filmstrips

Filmstrips are excellent devices to use in teaching inductively as well as deductively. The use of filmstrips involves an older device in teaching as compared to modern day videotapes. However, they are excellent to use provided the content is clear and related directly to the objectives of instruction. We have heard teachers and administrators say that filmstrips are outdated to use. We do not believe so. Our feelings are that it depends upon the quality of content and how the teacher uses this approach in teaching mathematics. One thing is certain, the frame of the filmstrip remains constant as long as the mathematics teacher wishes to focus on it for meaningful teaching. The teacher can point out items to pupils in a frame and stay on that frame as long as necessary. Content in filmstrips should follow the following guidelines :

1. The content should capture the interests of pupils.
2. Ordered frames must follow a desired sequence so that each pupil may learn as much as possible.
3. Learners should have ample opportunities to learn inductively as well as deductively from sequential frames in a filmstrip. The mathematics teacher may develop questions for a frame which assists and challenges a pupil to respond in a manner stressing learning by discovery.
4. There are good opportunities for the teacher to emphasize a problem from which pupils need to seek answers for a tentative solution involving filmstrip content.
5. A manual should accompany a filmstrip so that teachers may follow the teaching suggestions, if desired.

The following are examples of how filmstrips may be used:

1. to introduce a new unit in mathematics. If pupils are to study addition of unit fractions with unlike denominators, a carefully chosen filmstrip may give learners an overview of the new unit. Pupils can then see how knowledge of unit fractions with unlike denominators is useful in

problem solving in class and in life outside the classroom. The unlike denominators need to have a relatively easy greatest common factor so that numerators may be added and placed over the common denominator.

2. To develop learnings in greater depth, the content of filmstrips guides learners in attaching meaning to fractions such as one-fourth one-sixth =...or one-third plus one-sixth=...Social situations stressed in the filmstrip presentation guide learners in perceiving practical application of abstract learnings. In the filmstrip presentation, numerous experiences would be provided pupils in understanding what is involved if unit fractions with unlike denominators are added.
3. To end or culminate a unit of study. In the filmstrip presentation, pupils should have ample opportunities to review what has been learned previously. If pupils can use that which has been learned previously within the framework of purposeful learning experiences, it will be possible to retain these learnings in terms of understandings, skills, and attitudes for a longer period of time than would otherwise be the case.

Content in the filmstrip should provide opportunities for pupils to:

1. respond to questions and problems.
2. make practical application of what has been learned previously,
3. arrive at relevant concepts and generalizations at their own unique rate of speed,
4. assess their own achievement in learning,
5. branch out in the direction of new related learnings,
6. experience success and satisfaction in learning,
7. achieve understanding of selected major structural ideas in mathematics such as the commutative and associative properties of addition and multiplication,
8. perceive diverse operations in mathematics as being related such as division undoes multiplication.

The above-named eight guidelines may also be stressed in any learning opportunity involving the use of a variety of materials of instruction.

Slides are similar to filmstrips in their use in teaching mathematics. Instead of a frame on a filmstrip, there is a slide to convey information to pupils. Many of our student teachers and cooperating teachers whom we supervise have made slides to use in teaching mathematics. These teachers have placed on each slide what they wish to have pupils learn to achieve objectives. As much time as is needed may be spent discussing and elaborating on mathematics concepts contained in a slide.

Using Graphs in Teaching Mathematics

Pupils need to experience making and using graphs. Graphs developed by pupils with teacher guidance should

1. emphasize content within the experiences of pupils. No pupil should be left out in left field or fall through the cracks in ongoing lessons and units of study.
2. present generalizations in an understandable manner.
3. contain a heading to orientate viewers to inherent content in the graph.
4. provide interesting, meaningful, and purposeful learning activities.

Kinds of graphs to be made by elementary school pupils in mathematics include

1. picture graphs. Picture graphs may be the easiest to develop and read by pupils. As an example the birthdays of pupils in a classroom may be placed on a picture graph. Thus pupils whose birthdays are in January should have their pictures placed horizontally next to the name of that month. The same should be done for the rest of the months of the year with pupils' pictures coming horizontally next to the respective months.
2. line graphs. We have seen excellent line graphs made by pupils with teacher guidance on temperature readings for the five days of a school week. Learners may then quickly notice how the line goes up or down to show temperature reading covering a given interval of time.

   The line may also stay horizontal from one day to the next when reading the thermometer at the same time each day of the week

3. bar graphs. Information contained in a picture or line graph may also be shown using a bar graph. We have seen several high quality bar graphs in classrooms showing the gross national product in the United States covering the decades from 1940 to the present. The bars became longer as each of these decades passed. The graphs were neatly made and had attractive titles or captions.
4. circle or pie graphs. One very good pie graph we observed showed what part of the circle in a family budget was spent on food. Clothing, shelter, insurance, car expense, and miscellaneous. The figures contained in this graph were actual from a specific family. There are a variety of data sources which can be used to develop pie graphs.

We viewed a pie graph which contained the land areas of different countries in Europe such as the per cent of land of Germany, England, France, Spain, among others.

It is very relevant that pupils learn to make and read information from graphs. Why? The contents in a graph can be quite misleading if made incorrectly. We recently read information from a line graph contained in a reputable newspaper. The cost of living was shown as rising very, very rapidly, when actually this was not the case. How was this done? Rectangles rather than squares were used to show the rising cost of living. The rectangles were placed so that the width of these were placed horizontally. The length of each rectangle then was placed vertically, making the cost of living shown in an upward spiralling situation. In a line graph, there should be equal sized intervals, horizontally as well as vertically. This is a fundamental rule in statistics. A person merely looking at a line graph might truly be deceived when looking at unequal sized intervals.

Using Songs

There are numerous songs that pupils may learn which are enjoyable and yet stress counting using the set of whole numbers. Young children, in particular, benefit from songs involving counting. In learning to sing the song Ten Little Indians, pupils are learning the correct order or sequence of the set of counting numbers. Later on, pupils need to attach meaning to the set of counting numbers when engaging in rational counting. Here, pupils count objects in one-to-one correspondence. The learner then touches an object and says one, counts a second object by pointing to it and saying two. This sequence in rational counting is continued until achievable goals have been accomplished. Learners need to be ready before stressing rational counting as continuous progress needs to be made.

Using Money

Real coins and play money should be used in teaching-learning situations to guide learners to understand currency values. Real and play money should be used in the following ways:

1. pupils counting members given in a specific set, such as five coins pertaining to the cardinal number of five. Pupils may also develop learnings here pertaining to cardinal numbers, such as coin is fourth in a specific set. The concepts of first, second, third, fourth, fifth and so on indicate ordinal value within a set. Thus the ordinal value answers the question of "which one?"
2. pupils joining two sets together to make a third set. Thus if a pupil spends 25 cents for a candy bar and 20 cents for a package of chewing gum, how much is spent for both items? A set of 25 cents is joined together with a set of 20 cents to make a new set of 45 cents.
3. pupils subtracting where regrouping is involved such as a pupil having 50 cents and spending 22 cents for a candy bar. Here, the teacher needs to help pupils understand that the five tens on 50 cents need to be regrouped in terms of four tens and 10 ones (ten ones come from one ten formerly in the five tens column). Now two ones can be taken from the ten ones leaving eight. Two tens may also be taken from the four tens.
4. multiplying a factor times a factor such as a pupil had 25 cents and needed six times that amount to buy a used baseball glove, thus there are 25 cents in a set; six of these sets are needed to buy the used baseball glove. The factor 25 needs to be multiplied by the factor of 6, making

for $1.50.

5. dividing such as where there are 12 doughnuts and these need to be divided so that each of six boys gets an equal number. Learners then need to use division to determine that 12 divided by 6=2.

Pupils need to use real money to realize that

1. money is used to buy needed goods and services in society. Puplis may list which goods and services they or their parents have purchased recently. Money use should strongly stress the practical and the utilitarian.
2. application should be made using real money. Too frequently, learners fail to perceive ways of applying that which has been learned and yet, being able to use what has been learned becomes a major goal of mathematics instruction.
3. meaning in learning is of utmost importance. Pupils should attach understanding to the use of money. Much time is wasted in teaching unless pupils show they understand subject matter taught. Through discussions and questions, pupils reveal what is understood and is meaningful.

Using Geoboards

To assist pupils to understand geometrical forms, the teacher may wish to have pupils use a geoboard. We believe geometry is so vital to a pupil's experiences that the mathematics teachers should devote adequate time in making geometrical instructional aids. Geoboards may be made of plywood. A twenty by twenty square inch piece of plywood should be adequate. Shingle nails, a square inch apart, may be driven in lightly into the square piece of plywood. However, the nails should be stable and sturdy in the plywood.

Rubber bands may be used by pupils, stretched around selected nails, to show diverse geometrical forms such as squares, triangles, rectangles, trapezoids, and other figures.

It may be wise to have pupils develop a mathematics glossary that relates directly to geometrical concepts read about as well as shown on the geoboard. Pertaining to reading for meaning and a mathematics glossary, Ediger (1996) wrote:

Pupils with teacher guidance should have ample opportunities to become independent in attaching meaning to words read. With the use of context clues, the learner may ascertain the identification and meaning of a word by noticing surrounding words within the sentence. If a pupil, for example, does not know the meaning of the underlined word, the rest of the words in that sentence may take care of the unknown.

We would suggest that teachers assist pupils to develop a mathematics glossary individually or within a committee. This activity indicates that pupils can be authors and be empowered with their very own writing. Arranging words alphabetically is involved here as well as the correct spelling of words. Relevant terms need to appear in the glossary. Definitions of each word must be clear. Examples may clarify meanings of mathematics terms sooner than definitions. It would be good to use each term in sentence within a contextual situation.

Using Drill and Practice

Pupils need to have opportunities to be drilled on essential basics in mathematics. Generally, addition, subtraction, multiplication, and division facts can cause problems to few pupils in retaining content. The mathematics teacher always needs to remember that pupils should first understand what a basic addition fact, for example, means. Thus 4+5=9 is symbolic and stands for something concrete and semiconcrete. A pupil should then be able to show a set of four marbles and a set of five marbles. The learner should also be able to join the two sets together to show a set of nine members. Pupils should be able to explain what is involved in any basic addition, subtraction, multiplication, and division fact. We recommend strongly that each pupil be able to show comprehension by indicating with concrete and semiconcrete materials the meaning of any operation performed on number pairs such as $4 \times 7 =$ ......

A variety of materials need to be used to vary the kinds of learning activities that are involved in drill and practice. Flashcards may be used to have pupils respond to what, for example, $7 \times 8=$... There are excellent computer software packages whereby learners may experience rich experiences in drill and practice. The mathematics teacher needs to capture the interests of pupils in these kinds of experiences. We have seen student teachers and cooperating teachers make excellent teaching aids which stress pupils playing games. These games emphasize drill and practice. Thus these teachers have made a spinner together with a game board, consisting of squares sequentially marked two inches by two inches. If a child hits the value of "five" after using the spinner, he/she may move forward five spaces if a correct response is given to a basic number pair such as 9 – 5=... This number pair is printed on a card, face down-learners with others playing the game take sequential turns drawing cards. Each players moves forward the number of spaces on the game board as indicated by the point of the spinner. The first pupil that reaches the end of the game board is the winner. Instead of individual pupils playing against each other, a committee may challenge another committee in playing this game.

We have also observed teachers making fish cutouts from different colors of construction paper. On each fish, a number pair is printed. A paper clip is placed into the mouth of each paper fish. A fishing pole or stick with an attached string and a magnet at the end is used to catch fish. If a pupil catches a fish, he/she may keep it provided that a correct response is made as to what is printed on the paper fish such as 3 × 7=... The fish for fishing should be placed in a paper box or other container whereby the pupil cannot see which numbers pair is printed on the fish.

Worksheets developed by the teacher, transparencies and the overhead projector, software and the personal computer, as well as pages from workbooks may contain quality drill and practice activities for pupils. Each activity should be goal centered in that pupils remember an answer to a basic number pair better than formerly. We believe that mathematics teachers should always point out to pupils why drill and practice activities are important. These activities are not engaged in for the sake of doing so, but rather that pupils can use and apply what has been learned. It is always important to remember that pupils should comprehend and attach meaning to whatever is being stressed in the drill and practice activities

Using Video Tapes

We have observed several video tapes that provide excellent learning opportunities for pupils. These videos bring movement and motion into learning opportunities in mathematics. Teachers need to be certain that a video presentation is properly introduced to provide readiness and background experiences for involved learners. Readiness experiences might involve discussing new vocabulary terms with learners as well as presenting needed information that will assist pupils to understand the video presentation in an optimal manner.

The video definitely should be on the understanding levels of pupils, not the frustration nor boredom levels of pupils. The pace of the presentation should harmonize with the sequential comprehension of content of learners. What pupils do not understand, they should receive clarification of these ideas, concepts, and generalizations from the teacher. Monitoring of pupils before, during, and after the video is important. Time on task needs to be emphasized by the teacher. Learners should be guided to become responsible individuals and assume self direction roles in mathematics achievement. Most videos tend to secure pupils' interest. The teacher also needs to be certain that there is pupil-perceived purpose in observing the contents in the video. Thus the mathematics teacher may give a few reasons as to why the contents in the video are important to comprehend.

Video presentations may pertain to :

1. one or more problems in mathematics that pupils individually or in committees need to solve. Assistance needs to be provided to pupils in securing the necessary information for the identified problems areas.
2. practice and drill that pupils need in order to work more proficiently in addition, subtraction, multiplication, and division. Drill and practice activities may truly stimulate learner achievement when using videos.
3. games that pupils may play individually or collaboratively, have observed much interest in pupils being actively involved in videos that stress the playing of games. Positive attitudes toward mathematics may well be an end result here.

4. history of mathematics. A video that instills much interest in pupil learning pertains to information on the history of measurement such as how the foot, yard, and inch was initially determined. We have observed much pupil excitement in these kinds of learning opportunities involving videos.
5. geometry in the mathematics curriculum. Here, learners are assisted in determining areas, as well as perimeters of squares, rectangles, circles, and trapezoids Recently one of the authors observed a film that presented outstanding content stressing finding areas and perimeters of selected figures, There are educators who will say that films are outdated in the mathematics curriculum. That would depend more upon the content presented rather than is it a film that is used as a teaching material.

Using Technology

Advocates of using modern technology believe schools should move in the direction rapidly of being very updated in the use of technology. Why? Society uses computers, modems, internet, worldwide webs, and modern search engines to locate needed information. Unless schools use the state of the art technology, they and their pupils will be left further and further behind in developing skills needed in the twenty first century. Learners need to be productive individuals now as well as in the future in the use of technology. The technology skills developed will update a pupil for his/her future roles as a productive member in society. Pupils need to use knowledge and skills which assist in being contributors to an improved society. Today's pupils should not lose out on the modern and the futuristic in the school setting. Losing out now will hinder pupils in developed harmoniously well with what is and exists in society and what will be in the future.

There are others who believe that too much money can be spent in having a school possess state of the art technology. Repair and maintenance costs are heavy in keeping modern technology moving forward. Technology, it is stated by selected educators, cannot meet the needs of pupils as can good teachers who creatively devise materials or instruction which guide optimal progress for individual pupils.

Kinds of software. Mathematics teachers need to select software carefully for computer use. Computers should not be used for the sake of doing so, but rather to assist learners to attain more optimally in mathematics. Computer use should stress what other kinds of materials cannot accomplish when used in teaching and learning. Thus, computer programs should assist pupil to learn that which, for example, a textbook or a workbook cannot provide.

Computer programs should guide pupils to attain relevant objectives in mathematics. Programs used should assist pupils to make continuous progress and to attain optimal achievement. We will review different kinds of software programs available to guide pupils to achieve as much as possible in mathematics. A first kind of software program emphasizes relevant subject matter such as sequential facts, concepts, and generalizations that pupils need to learn. These learnings are presented in a sequence which moves in ascending order of complexity. Vital knowledge in mathematics needs to be in the offing here. For example, if pupils are to learn to divide using a two place divisor with a remainder in the quotient, the inherent facts, concepts, and generalizations need to be presented in program form. The software program moves forward to increasing levels of complexity. Thus a pupil looks at content expressed in one or two sentences containing numerals and or operation signs in most cases. He/she then responds to a test item covering what was read and studied in one or two sentences. If the learner responded correctly, he/she is rewarded and may go on to the next pair of sentences to be read. A pupil that responded incorrectly may try again in making a response that is correct. If it is incorrect again, the correct answer is given and the learner may go on to the next sequential content to read and respond to. Being correct in responding the first time is the reward, operant conditioning is in evident here. Operant conditioning stresses rewarding the correct response made so that the learner is conditioned to respond correctly each time the situation requires the same answer. Facts, concepts, and generalizations in mathematics require specific content to be learned. The content is exacting and specific. Facts pertain to such items as answers to the basic addition, subtraction, multiplication, and division number pairs i.e.6+5=... 4+3=....2+3=..., among others. Concepts emphasize single words or phrases such as addition, subtraction, multiplication, division, square root, cube root, dividend, quotient, divisor, factor, and diameter, among others. Generalizations are usually stated orally or in writing within complete sentences using subjects and predicates in each. The following are examples of generalizations :

1. The associative property of addition states that we can add numerals in any order and the sum is the same.
2. To find the circumference of a circle, we need to know the diameter and multiple it times pi (3.14 approximately).
3. To determine the area of a right triangle, we need to multiply the base times the height and then divide by two.

Each generalization needs to be clear and meaningful. Thus in number two above, pupils should attach meaning to the concepts of circumference, diameter, and pi, prior to working on securing the circumference of circle. Seeing circles in circular windows, drawings and models, as well as in illustrations should aid learners to attach meaning to the concept of "circle." Teacher explanation of the concept of diameter using actual circles in the semiconcrete or in the concrete assists learners to attach meaning and understanding to the term "diameter." Emphasizing meaning theory in teaching mathematics is vital and salient.

A second type of software material available in teaching mathematics stresses pupils reviewing that which has been learned previously so that forgetting is minimized. We would suggest here that the software program emphasize interest in learning on the part of learners. Too frequently, reviewing what has been learned previously is boring. Must it be that way? The answer is "definitely no." We have noticed software and teacher made materials in mathematics which are highly interesting to pupils. Using flash cards containing basic number pairs for review and drill is only one method of assisting pupils to rehearse that which has been learned previously. These number pairs such as 5+3=....might then be shown on a card clearly visible to the learner receiving the review opportunities. Smudge marks and other visible marks should be erased or new cards made so that learners identify what the answer to the basic number pair is, 5+3=...in this case, and not by the smudge marks that are on a card. We have observed pupils who state that they recognize the answer to a basic number pair by the smudge marks rather than by the numerals provided on a three by five inch card. Pupils may also work in dyads with the two involved learners drilling each other on what has been learned.

An amusing incident occurred when a pupil in using an electrically wired answer board stated he did not know many of the basic multiplication number pairs presented but he could find out quickly by looking on the back of the board to see how it is wired. Thus in responding to 9×8=.... the pupil did not know the answer but could determine the answer by looking on the back to see what the answer would be by noticing the connections of the electrical wiring used. In this electric board, a light would go on if the pupil took the two wires to match up 9×8=72. The 9×8=... was in one column and the 72 in the second column, in random order with the answers to basic multiplication number pairs previously studied in class. The mathematics teacher then needs to be sure that pupils respond to the numerals in the multiplication facts rather than how the electric board is wired. One great advantage in using software and the computer to stress drill and practice is that pupils cannot identify answers through smudge marks on the monitor or see how the computer is assembled to determine which answer is correct.

A third type of software program emphasizes using problem solving. Here, pupils may simulate real life situations in a virtual reality situation. Each problem stresses higher levels of cognition involving critical and creative thinking within the framework of problem solving. Each problem should be challenging to pupils. Thus there is a perplexing situation in which the learner needs to ascertain what the problem is which needs solving. Critical thinking is involved when the learner analyzes that which is needed to solve the problem. Thus the relevant needs to be separated from the irrelevant. A problem may have many steps involved in working toward a solution. Creativity is inherent when the pupil determines which algorithm to use as well as which sequence to stress in problem solving. In short, the pupil needs to perceive the problem clearly with meaning involved. He/she needs to develop an hypothesis in answer to the problem. The hypothesis is tentative and needs testing or trying out to see if it truly works. Thus an hypothesis is always tentative, not an absolute. If testing the hypothesis reveals that it did not solve the problem, then a revision of the hypothesis needs to be forthcoming.

Simulated software stresses pupils engaging in problem solving activities. Reality is emphasized as much as possible in simulation. The content herein is different as compared to computer emphasis upon learners acquiring new content outside problem solving. Simulation also differs from drill and practice activities in that the latter advocates pupils practicing what has been learned previously so that it will not be forgotten.

A third approach in computer software use is to stress a game approach. We have observed on several occasions how fascinated and interested mathematics can become in a gaming approach. Pupils may work individually or in a committee when computerized games are used in teaching and learning situations. Games can be a regular inherent part of the mathematics curriculum or be stressed during free time or during recess time.

A pupil when competing against the self can observe how well he/she can do in a recreational approach in learning mathematics. If a learner competes against another pupil, he/she must learn to respect others and not stress a dog-eat-dog approach in mathematics. If committees compete against each other in a game, wholesome attitudes need to be developed. The goals are to acquire new subject matter as well as achieve wholesome attitudes toward mathematics and toward others. The use of games can be an excellent way for pupils to learn vital mathematics content. If the home setting has a personal computer, the mathematics teacher should assist parents in securing software games which will challenge and nurture the learner. The home and school should work together for the good of the pupil. Too frequently, the goals of the home and school are so opposite to each other that learner optimal achievement is not possible.

Learning Activities in Mathematics in the Home Setting

Through parent/teacher conferences, the goals of the home and of the school might be harmonized. The mathematics teacher needs to have positive suggestions to parents as to how they can help the learner do well in mathematics. We would suggest the following as guidelines for a parent/teacher conference:

1. Respect the thinking of parents in the face-to-face situation.
2. Find out how the child feels toward mathematics.
3. Diagnose what the child needs in mathematics; the home setting might be able to assist the child to overcome these deficiencies.
4. Guide parents to encourage the pupil to learn and to achieve.
5. Suggest to parents learning activities which will guide the pupil to achieve in mathematics in the home setting.
6. Listen carefully to the concerns of parents.
7. Have parents consider the physiological as well as the social dimensions of the pupil's development, if there are indications that this needs to be done. A tired and hungry child cannot do well in school. The school also should do as much as possible to meet nutrition, clothing, emotional, social, and other needs of the learner. If these needs are met of pupils, learners should then attain more optimally in mathematics.
8. Guide parents in being able to reward the learner for doing well in mathematics.
9. Assist parents in discussing what the offspring has learned in mathematics for a given school day. Parents should show much interest in the child's welfare.
10. Have the child involved in discussing everyday problems in mathematics, such as how much a given set of items purchased in a supermarket cost.

Kennedy and Tipps (1991) wrote:

Teachers have another resource for helping children. Teachers can involve parents to help children learn mathematics. Teachers have a variety of ways in which to include parents or guardians in the program. Some write weekly or monthly newsletters that communicate the topics being studied and make suggestions for home activities. Some textbooks now include model newsletters in their teaching manuals. Other teachers ask parents to volunteer in the classroom. Parent volunteers need tasks organized for them such as reading books or working with a mathematics game. Some teachers have created take home versions of mathematics materials. Students check out the games, manipulatives, or investigations to use with parents at home. Homework can also be designed to include home projects. A geometry scavenger hunt and a survey of favorite foods are good ways to involve parents and siblings.

In Closing

A variety of learning activities need to be in the offing for pupils so that each may achieve as much as possible. The learning activities need to assist pupils to achieve stated, relevant objectives. Each activity should provide for individual differences. Thus a learner is guided to attain more optimally. Each pupil should learn as much as possible in mathematics. To vary learning activities makes it possible for each pupil to achieve more optimally in mathematics. Learners need to achieve knowledge objectives with its vital facts, concepts, and generalizations. They also should attain relevant skills objectives which include creative and critical thinking as well as problem solving. These skills are vital for pupils to achieve and cannot be left to chance. Rather the mathematics teacher plans relevant skills within lessons and units of study so that each pupil might attain these higher cognitive level objectives. The teacher then has definite learning opportunities that focus upon pupils achieving problem solving skills as well as becoming proficient in creative and critical thinking. Pertaining to problem solving, Ediger (1996) wrote the following:

Learners need to have ample opportunities to engage in solving realistic problems. Situations in life demand that human beings become proficient in problem solving Thus, pupils should have ample opportunities to engage in the solving of real problems. Pupils with adequate background information could solve problems such as the following :

1. A miniature supermarket could be housed in the class

setting. Learners may bring empty cereal boxes, fruit and vegetable containers, candy bar wrappers, flour sacks, and sugar bags. These items should be placed on a counter, properly labelled and priced. Pupils may "buy" needed items using toy money. Thus, needed addition, subtraction, multiplication, and division facts may be learned in this manner.

2. A "cafeteria" could also be set up in the class setting. Cutouts of appropriate food items may be pasted on paper plates. Each food item would need to be priced meaningfully. Learners again may use toy money to purchase selected food items in the "cafeteria".
3. The mathematics laboratory concept of teaching and learning can well become an important facet of the mathematics curriculum. Thus, pupils may measure areas, distances, and determine volumes of specific containers in actual problem solving situations utilizing the English as well as the metric systems of measurement.
4. Realistic problems may also be solved by pupils within the framework of the use of reputable textbooks, films, filmstrips, slides, video-tapes, and life-like situations in society.

A third type of objective for pupils to achieve are attitudinal goals. If pupils attain important attitudinal objectives, they should do better in realizing knowledge and skills objectives. Attitudinal objectives include pupils appreciating, valuing, being interested in, and perceiving purpose in studying mathematics. To achieve any vital objective, the mathematics teacher needs to select and adapt specific learning opportunities to the present achievement level of the individual learner. Pupils should also learn to work together well with others in ongoing lessons and units of study. Being able to work effectively with other learners is significant. Later, in adult life at the work place, it becomes exceedingly important that the pupil be able to work well with others. At the present time in school, pupils need to tolerate, understand, and value each other.

To assist pupils to achieve optimally in mathematics, the teacher needs to be able to work harmoniously with parents of children in the classroom. Parent/teacher conferences are important to harmonize the efforts of the teacher and school with these of the involved parent. There are many ways in which parents can help in having their offspring achieve as much as possible in mathematics. Parent/teacher conferences should stress good human relations as well as look at what a child needs in mathematics to do as well as possible. Cooperatively, the parent and the teacher can work out a plan for the pupil to achieve well in mathematics. There are advocates of having pupils being involved in the parent/teacher conference. This has much to offer if arrangements can be made for this to occur. The pupil might then evaluate the self in terms of what is needed to be more successful in mathematics. The pupil may tell about his/her work in mathematics in terms of products completed. Within this endeavor, the learner may reveal personal talents, interests, and attitudes toward mathematics. Journal writing can be very personal in which the learner records on a daily basis what has been learned and what is left to achieve. The pupil in a parent/teacher conference may wish to share his/her written journal entries to indicate achievement and diagnosis. Good human relations and working together for the good of the child in mathematics are ultimate objectives in parent/teacher conferences.

Selected References

Ediger, Marlow (1988). *The Elementary Curriculum.* Second Edition. Kirksville, Missouri : Simpson Publishing Company, page 131.

Ediger, Marlow (1996). "Principles of Learning and the Mathematics Curriculum," *Experiments in Education,* published by the SITU Council of Educational Research (in India), pages 156-157.

Ediger, Marlow (1996). "Problems in Reading in Mathematics, *School Science,* Vol. 34, No. 4. Page 9.

Kennedy, Leonard M., and Steve Tipps (1991). *Guiding Children's Learning of Mathematics.* Belmont, California: Wadsworth Publishing, pages 64-65.

7

Multiple Intelligences and Their Implementation in the Mathematics Curriculum

There have traditionally been many ways to label and determine multiple intelligences. Classroom teachers, for example, have taught different subject matter areas such as the following with each having a separate identity:

1. reading and the language arts, including listening, speaking, reading, literature, and writing.
2. mathematics, including arithmetic, geometry, algebra, statistics, and trigonometry.
3. science, including biology, botany, zoology, chemistry, geology, astronomy, and physics.
4. social studies, including history, geography, political science, anthropology, sociology and economics.
5. art, including Discipline Based Art Education (DBAE).
6. music, including vocal and instrumental.
7. physical education with its numerous activities such as competitive athletics, exercise, hiking, jogging, intermural sports, golf. tennis, and dance, among others.

The above-named curriculum areas are separated into component areas. It appears that multiple intelligences are/were involved in making these divisions due to each academic or curriculum area being separated from the others. There are a few pupils who would do well in all curriculum areas listed. Some achieve well in one or two areas. Then too, it is common knowledge that there are a few pupils who do poorly in all curriculum areas. One reason being that there has been a lack of stimulation and motivation developed for achieving interest and purpose for learning. It is not always the school's fault, by any means, when this interest and purpose are lacking. There are pupils who grow up in exceedingly poor environments making it difficult to achieve at an appropriate level. The teacher, however, must attempt to the best possible to stimulate interest and meaning in each curriculum area. This is a professional responsibility, regardless of the complexity involved.

Each of the above-named curriculum areas has been taught in different ways. Thus in the area of reading, pupils have experienced a strong program of phonics instruction on the primary grade levels together with a basal reader approach in teaching and learning. Or, whole language procedures have been used whereby holism in subject matter read becomes important rather than pupils experiencing an analytical reading program of heavy emphasis being placed upon phonics.

Reading has also been emphasized as "reading across the curriculum". Here, a philosophy of instruction stresses the importance of reading in all academic disciplines mentioned above as well as in the literature curriculum. Thus there have been several ways of organizing the curriculum:

1. The separate subjects curriculum whereby arithmetic is taught as a single academic discipline in ongoing lessons and units of study.
2. The correlated curriculum whereby botany and zoology are taught as being related and not as separate entities.
3. The fused or broadfields curriculum whereby history, geography, political science, anthropology, sociology, and economics are planned and taught as being interrelated in lesson/unit planning as well as in implementing.
4. The integrated curriculum whereby diverse academic disciplines lose their boundaries and borders such as in problem solving approaches in the curriculum. With a problem solving philosophy of instruction, a problem is identified in context, the problem is developed, data from a variety of reference sources is gathered to evaluate the

hypothesis, and the hypothesis is revised as necessary.

Which of the above ways of organizing the curriculum should be emphasized by teachers and supervisors? During the 1960s and early 1970s, Dr. Jerome Bruner (1963) from Harvard University came out with a very popular hypothesis in which pupils should learn the structure of knowledge as advocated by college/university academicians in their academic areas of speciality. Each academic discipline then has its structure separate from other subject matter areas. Arithmetic then has the commutative, associative, distributive, and identity elements properties. These are key ideas in arithmetic that provide a structure of knowledge just as buildings have a structure. Dr. Bruner (1963) recommended that pupils learn that structure just as the college/university mathematician recommends. He was very instrumental in stressing the following belief: Any subject matter can be learned in some intellectually honest form by any child at any stage of development. This statement was very optimistic in terms of what a pupil can learn. We believe if/we look at the phrase "in some intellectually honest form," there is much that the teacher can emphasize. Thus the commutative property of addition can be stressed on any grade level in the public schools such as early primary grade pupils learning that 2+3=3+2. Or, sixth grade pupils may learn that 3,467+6,893=6,893+3,467. A variety of methods and materials should be used here to guide meaningful and purposeful experiences.

Dr. Bruner also advocated that pupils should acquire information just as the academician does; a pupil achieves objectives by using the same methods as does a mathematician. Each academic area then has its processes and procedures to follow in securing content and subject matter. The approach stressed here would tend to emphasize a separate subjects curriculum. A pupil would then be given opportunities to understand and attach meaning to the content and methods of a single academic discipline as a professional academic would perceive his/her area of speciality. Ediger (1988) wrote the following:

Various educators have emphasized that pupils should achieve key structural ideas as identified by academicians. Social scientists from colleges and universities include historians, geographers, political scientists, anthropologists, sociologists, and economists. The methods that each of these social scientists uses should also be used by elementary school children, according to social science educators. Advantages given for using this approach in teaching in the elementary school would be the following:

1. Pupils would be achieving relevant concepts and generalizations.
2. Learners would be using appropriate methods for gathering data, such as using primary and secondary sources of information as historians do or using and making maps and globes to gather and summarize information as geographers do.
3. Teachers have more security in teaching selected vocabulary terms, main ideas, generalizations, and structural ideas pertaining to each academic discipline. Statements of structural ideas would be available to public school teachers to implement in teaching-learning situations.

Disadvantages inherent in using the structure of knowledge concept in teaching would be the following:

1. Pupils may not be interested nor perceive purpose in gaining these structural ideas.
2. Methods that academicians use in gathering information may not harmonize with the needs and abilities of elementary school pupils.
3. Within each discipline, academicians may not be able to agree upon relevant structural ideas.
4. An adult centered curriculum may be in evidence if pupils are to achieve structural ideas as identified by academicians in their academic area of speciality.

The Theory of Multiple Intelligences, developed by Howard Gardner (1993), has certainly had its impact on American education as well as abroad. Here, Dr. Gardner recognizes seven areas of intelligence; these are verbal/linguistic, logical/mathematical, visual/spatial, musical, bodily/kinesthetic, interpersonal, and intrapersonal.

Dr. Gardner further divides intelligence into three component parts. These are :

1. Intelligence referring to one's psychological and biological makeup.
2. Domain referring to one's talents, or craft being used in society.
3. Field referring to what the societal arena believes to be important in terms of processes and products.

Dr. Gardner (1993) states that Western culture too frequently stresses the importance of verbal/linguistic and logical/mathematical intelligences when the other five also have much value. Opportunities need to be provided to pupils so that all seven intelligences may be cultivated and used. Individuals have strength in using one intelligence more so than the others, but people learn from/through each of the seven intelligences, according to Multiple Intelligences Theory. Learning styles of pupils are based on ways of acquiring and achieving which cut across subject matter lines. Learning styles research came from test score results of learners whereas Multiple Intelligences emphasis is based on scientific research and are directly related to separate subject area fields.

Dr. Gardner believes in nurturing and recognizing the importance of the pupil in teaching and learning in order to provide for individual differences in the educational setting. There is a major way that people have of expressing themselves and that way comes from one of the seven multiple intelligences. In early childhood, pupils should have opportunities to express themselves and experience all seven modes in intelligence. Skills should be developed in all seven categories; otherwise learner chances to grow will be hindered. Pupil achievement, development, and growth are necessary in the different areas of Multiple Intelligences. General education is needed in early childhood.

On the elementary school level. Dr. Gardner (1993) advocates using an evaluation specialist, a curriculum developer, and a school community worker to coordinate and harmonize learning activities in the classroom.

The evaluation specialist notices and measures pupil talents. Learning activities based on pupil intelligence need to be appropriate for the individual and the surrounding culture. Teacher observation is necessary here to use information in developing an appropriate curriculum for the individual learner. Tests should not be used to determine individual differences since these are strong on linguistic and/or logical/mathematical. From observations made pertaining to each individual child, the curriculum specialist may recommend subject matter content as well as techniques of teaching that would assist the individual pupil to achieve more optimally. The school/community specialist would study and find activities in the community for pupils. Community organizations may include Scout work, 4H clubs, religious, organizational endeavors, as well as civic and business efforts in providing for pupils in the curriculum. Multiple Intelligence development on the elementary school levels will provide readiness for the secondary school years. Weaknesses in previous development of Multiple Intelligences should be noticed and provided for on the secondary level of instruction. Pupils should have confidence in Multiple Intelligences possessed and use these in school and in society.

Pupils need to understand personal profiles on Multiple Intelligence and use these to learn content in a particular curriculum area. Awareness of their skills in Multiple Intelligences, individual pupils may then relate approaches in learning that are preferred to acquire new skills in including verbal/linguistic, among each of the others. Dr. Gardner (1993) has as a definition for intelligence "the ability to solve problems, or to fashion products that are valued in one or more cultural or community settings." Heredity as well as cultural influences are important in Multiple Intelligences. Tests should not be used in determining Multiple Intelligences, but rather contextual situations should be emphasized. Thus with observations made of pupils in context, the observers may determine which Intelligence is inherent. Teachers need to observe pupils in school in a variety of situations to determine what intelligence the learner emphasizes. Individual pupils have different strengths and interests. The traditional intelligences such as verbal/linguistics as well as logical/ mathematics need to be in evidence; however, other ways of revealing knowledge and skills also need to be stressed, such as music and art.

An unusual feature of Multiple Intelligences as identified by Dr. Gardner is that science and social studies as content areas have been omitted. We live in a world of science with its technology and innovations. If we view the field of medicine and medical practices, the changes have been tremendous and have greatly improved human life endeavors. For example, the use of lasers has made surgery obsolete in numerous cases. No doubt, continuous progress will be made in eliminating many kinds of surgery. Surgery made recovery a lengthy process, as compared to the use of laser beams. There are people who say we need to return to an earlier time with its quality values and honesty. We believe this Golden Age never existed. We do not believe there was a time when people were more honest than now. There is a song that says, "Grandpa, tell me about the good old days when people were honest and right was right and wrong was wrong." We do not believe that there was such a time of nostalgia.

There are many pupils who love science intrinsically and have a philosophy of realism to view the world objectively. A very old school of thought and still modern in philosophy is realism. Realists believe the world can be known in whole or in part as it truly is. Realism can be contrasted with the following philosophical schools of thought:

1. Experimentalism whereby one can only know experiences and not know the world as it truly is.
2. Idealism whereby one can know ideas about the real world but not know it as it truly is.
3. Existentialism whereby truth resides with the observer; all of knowledge is subjective and the individual makes his/her own moral truth.

Realism as a philosophy of education emphasizes the methods of science. Objectivity is stressed in that all can come up with the same results in knowledge of the real world. In using the methods of science to acquire information, facts, concepts, and generalizations, objective results are obtained regardless of who the observer is. Ediger (1995) wrote the following:

> Realism emphasizes a world, in existence, independent of observers. The objective world, natural and social phenomena exist and is. The real world is not dependent

> upon any observer being present. The independent world can be known in whole or in part as it truly is Thus, any observer may receive a replica of the natural and social environment, rather than ideas only, from these phenomena.

Accuracy in describing the real world is a must. Numerically, this can be done. The independent universe might then be described with the use of numbers. Accurate description is possible with assigned numbers. The amount of each element and compound present can be described numerically. Mind being like a blank sheet at birth receives subject matter directly from reality. Philosophy in realism becomes scientific. The methods of science are important to the realist. Objectivity is a key concept of realism in securing subject matter knowledge. Subjective ideas have no place in the scheme of things, according to realists. Emotions and feelings are left out. A true statement is one that corresponds with objects, items, and matter being described. Factual information, not opinions, are desired. Reality is not created, but may need to be changed as new discoveries are made.

Bertrand Russell (1992) was a leading realist in philosophy and in being quoted by Wahlquist wrote the following:

> The first characteristic of the new philosophy is that it abandons the claim to a special philosophic method or a particular brand of knowledge to be obtained by its means. It regards philosophy as essentially one with science, differing from the special sciences merely by the generality of its problems, and by the fact that it is concerned with the formation of hypothesis where empirical evidence is still lacking. It conceives that all knowledge is scientific knowledge, to be ascertained and proved by the methods of science. It does not aim, as previous philosophy has usuallly done, at statements about the universe as a whole, nor at the construction of a comprehensive system. It aims only at clarifying the fundamental ideas of the sciences, and synthesizing the different sciences into a single comprehensive view of that fragmemt of the world that science has succeeded in

exploring.

Certainly, Multiple Intelligences should include the world of science and its methods in obtaining and appraising content or subject matter.

A second traditional curriculum area which Dr. Howard Gardner omitted is the social sciences, also called the social studies for public school pupils. The academic areas of history, geography, political science, anthropology, sociology, and economics have had a long sequence of being taught in the public schools. History is usually considered to be the most important social science/humanities area taught. It is doubtful, if it is more valuable for pupils than the other previously listed social science areas. Why? History and its contents are so often written from a nationalistic and traditionally patriotic point of view. The writer of history tends not to perceive the weaknesses in his/her own nation when dealing in world affairs and also in domestic situations. We would like to see more of history written from an objective point of view, as advocated by realists. Atkinson and Maleska (1995) wrote the following:

> The rising spirit of nationalism set forces into motion that began by replacing Latin with vernacular languages. Folk tales and literature received new emphasis. The American Revolution brought with it a realization that if people were to rule themselves, they had first to learn how to exercise their newly found liberties. For this they required an education to free from blind dependence upon their leaders. The fact that declaratoin gained an important place in the common schools during our early national period indicated the eagerness of the people to use their schools to prepare themselves for active participation in democratic processes.

But a more significant result of the spirit of nationalism was the inclusion of history and civics in the curriculum of the elementary schools. Later, along with geography, the whole area came to be known as social studies. Finally, educators borrowed a page from the Athenians and added such subjects as music and calisthenics to promote cultural interest and physical fitness.

However, these nationalistic and political ideals were slow

in creating a truly effective education system–there was much more talk than action. Even in the twentieth century the average elementary school was in session fewer than six months each year, and three/fourths if the instructional time was being spent in formal subjects that were usually taught in a very mechanical manner. Little that was done in school bore any true relationship to the needs of the society in which the pupil was living.

The teaching of history and geography in the school curriculum has a long history in the United States. These two areas of curriculum were already taught in colonial times, from 1750 on. Certainly, one of the multiple intelligences would need to be the social studies, perhaps history and geograpy in particular. However, any individual is a product of his/her culture (anthropology and sociology); we also are economic beings in that we buy goods and services for daily sustenance, as well as live in and under a specific form of government (political science).

We believe that the Seven Cardinal Principles of Education developed by the Commitee on the Reorganization of the National Education Association in 1918 listed a fairly well balanced set of objective for pupils to achieve; these included the lollowing;

1. heath
2. commamd of fumdamental processes (basic subject matter knowledge)
3. worthy home membership
4. vocation
5. civic education
6. worthy use of leisure time
7. ethical character (Drake 1995).

The above-named objectives for pupil achievement represent that which has relevancy and indicates what is important for pupils to attain. There is balance among the categories here in emphasizing goals in health instruction, subject matter knowledge, membership in the home setting, vocational education citizenship, education for leisure time use and ethical behavior. Could it be that objectives such as these also represent diverse intelligences?

What Does It Take to be Intelligent?

There are people who when in the public school years were labelled as being slow in learning and not having much to offer later in society. Perhaps, these pupils eventually behaved as if they cannot be successful and cannot achieve adequately. In the video *The Bells of St. Marys,* Bing Crosby plays the role of a nonchalant headmaster of a parochial school. His ideas on education are quite different from those of teachers in the school, especially those of a teacher played by Ingrid Bergman. The latter is interested in tradition and upholding standards for achievement. We should all be interested in upholding high standards of achievement. But, sometimes, these standards get in the way of assisting pupils to do well in school. The headmaster, played by Bing Crosby, favored flexible standards and the bending of rules in certain situations. At the end of the school year, one pupil did not quite measure up to the exact per cent of achievement in test scores to warrant promotion. The needed per cent to pass was traditional and had been upheld for sometime in the parochial school. The headmaster wanted to pass the pupil to the next grade level where the teacher, played by Ingrid Bergman, believed strongly that standards are standards and should not be lowered. The headmaster told of Elmer Hathaway who as a pupil was a dreamer who came late to school many times and did not have his mind on school work. Later, Elmer Hathaway became a very wealthy, successful man and offered a job to any unemployed person who had been in his graduation class.

To the viewer of the *Bells of Marys* it appears that the successful person as an adult had not experienced a curriculum that met personal needs and interests. Elmer Hathaway might not have had ways to reveal his achievement in school. This is true of many pupils today.

There is a very strong emphasis upon all pupils achieving at a high level in the academics. We gather the academics refers to courses such as history, geography, literature and language, science and mathematics. We do not believe art, music, and physical education are included in the academics for most writers. And vocational education is not worthy of any attention, according to advocates of a strong academic approach in determining the curriculum. The question arises, "Will a curriculum of the academics be valuable to and for many pupils?" We believe not. Why? There are so many fields of endeavor in the world of work that the academics may not be too important for many at the work place. We believe educators minimize practical and utilitarian learning opportunities making the non-academic person appear to be inferior to other lines of endeavor and work.

Vocational education should not be abandoned in our schools. Individuals who work after high school graduation do provide us with what is needed to live well. There are different learning styles and diverse interests in finding what our life's work should be. We believe vocational education and the practical, utilitarian facets of society to be of utmost importance. The entertainers and television personalities with their huge salaries do not contribute to society as much as carpenters, educatores, plumbers, automobile mechanics, farmers, and those who provide food, clothing, and shelter. By emphasizing application of what had been learned by pupils, perhaps, a more useful curriculum is an end-result.

Pertaining to futurism in vocational educations, Ediger (1994) wrote the following:

A curriculum of futurism in vocational education must be given adequate consideration. A clear vision of the future is necessary. What might be in a vocational education curriculum stressing the concepts of futurism? The writers suggest the following:

1. much emphasis being placed upon research results.
2. new theories of instruction.
3. theory providing a basis for decision-making.
4. objectives in school harmonizing with goals of a quality workplace.
5. balance among understandings, skills, and attitudinal objectives within teaching-learning situations.
6. varied learning opportunities to provide for individual differences.
7. effective diagnostic and remediation procedures.

8. improved evaluation procedures to evaluate learner progress.
9. higher levels of training and education required of instructors in vocational education.
10. quality programs of inservice education for instructors.

Present-day inservice education programs for vocational education instructors should be varied and diverse. These include:

1. attendance at professional meetings and conventions.
2. attempts at improving the curriculum through personal methods and approaches.
3. completion of research projects.
4. enrolment in independent studies offered at a college or university.
5. video-tape models for inservice education.
6. planned series of meeting with other instructors to improve the curriculum.
7. opportunities to interact and discuss problems with other vocational education instructors.
8. inservice education through team teaching.
9. paid sabbaticals to further study vocational education on college/university campuses.
10. utilization of materials at a local professional library emphasizing vocational education.

Futurism in vocational education will stress a quality curriculum to assist each student to attain optimally.

The above enumerated items pertaining to vocational education are guidelines that pertain to emphasizing any curriculums area, including the academic arenas.

Encouraging Diversity in Objectives and Outcomes

There cetainly are multiple outcomes that can be expected of learners. Pupils differ from each other in many ways. How can teachers provide for the diversity present in any classroom? Sternberg (1997) is another leading advocate of encouraging and fostering diversity among pupils. Sternberg indicates what can be done to encourage memory, analysis, creativity, and practicality–four areas of revealing what has been learned:

Languags Arts

Memory Remember what a gerund is or what the name of Tom Sawyer's aunt was.

Analysis Compare the functions of a gerund to that of a participle, or compare the personality of Tom Sawyer to that of Huckleberry Finn.

Creativity Invent a sentence that effectively uses a gerund, or write a very short story with Tom Sawyer as a character.

Practicality Find gerunds in newspapers or magazine articles and describe how they are used, or say what general lesson about persuasion can be learned from Tom Sawyer's way of persuading his friends to whitewash Aunt Polly's fence.

Mathematics

Memory Remember the mathematical formula (Distance = Rate × Time).

Analysis Solve a mathematical word problem (Using the D = RT formula).

Creativity Create your own mathematical word problem using the D = RT formula.

Practicality Show how to use the D = RT formula to estimate driving time from one city to another near you.

Social Studies

Memory Remember a list of factors that led to the US Civil War.

Analysis Compare, contrast, and evaluate the arguments to those who supported slavery versus those who opposed it.

Creativity Write a page of a journal from the viewpoint of a soldier fighting for one or the other side during the Civil War.

Practicality Discuss the applicability of lessons from the Civil War to countries today that have strong internal divisions, such as the former Yugoslavia.

Science

Memory	Name the main types of bacteria
Analysis	Analyze the means the immume system uses to fight bacterial infections.
Creativity	Suggest ways of coping with the increasing immunity bacteria are showing to antibiotic drugs.
Practicality	Suggest three steps that individuals might take to reduce the likelihood of bacterial infection.

Sternberg (1997) states that "When we expand the range of abilities we test for, we also expand the range of students we identify as smart."

Educators have been writing and speaking about individual differences among learners for a long period of time. The differences among pupils are great so that each pupil needs a specially designed curriculum and yet at the same time it is necessary for learners to be able to work together with others harmoniously. Those educators who advocate teaching the academics largely or only are leaving out a large segment of the human population. There will be those who will be doing very important kinds of work in the work place that are definitely not academic in nature, such as in the vocational arenas.

The vocational should not be separated form the academic in terms of worth in the school curriculum. Pupils should be able to show what has been learned in vocational courses which truly indicates what has been achieved. It might not be possible for pupils to reveal achievement if it has to be shown in academic learnings only. The vocations are so necessary in society as revealed by the goods and services all of us need to live a quality life or even to survive at a minimal level. We also believe the practical curriculum can be integrated with the academic arena so that pupils receive a balanced perspective of the world scene.

McCarthy (1987 and 1996) emphasizes the 4MAT learning styles in providing for learners in the classroom. She identifies four types of pupils, basically, in a classroom:

1. the highly creative pupil with a feeling and reflecting style of learning. These pupils ask many questions in ongoing lessons and like brainstorming method of instruction.

2. the analytic pupil who is well organized classifying and analyzing details. These learners engage reflectively in step by step learning in a highly sequential way. They tend to have difficulties with open-ended tasks.
3. problem solvers in thinking who are doers and like concrete situations, basically not reading activities to obtain information.
4. learners who like to work cooperatively as well as independently on open-ended tasks in which inductive learning is stressed using kinesthetic/.auditory/visual materials. Firsthand experiences are important to these pupils in teaching and learning. Learners in this category do not like formal, rigid schedules.

In the above four named types of pupils, a natural cycle sequentially of feeling, reflecting, thinking, and acting or doing occurs.

In Closing

There are unanswered questions pertaining to multiple intelligences of pupils. In the traditional divison of content areas in the curriculum, the following are listed: reading and the language arts, mathematics, science, social studies, art, music, and physical education. These divisions have been used for a long time and appear on most report cards when pupil progress is being reported to parents.

The above-named traditional curriculum areas have, in time, been organized in terms of separate subjects, correlated, fused or broadfields, and integrated/interdisciplinary approaches.

Dr. Jerome Bruner in the 1960s and early 1970s received much attention for his work on the structure of academic disciplines. Each academic discipline has a structure or framework which identifies it separately from other academic disciplines. Pupils were to learn the structure of these disciplines as academicians in their academic areas of speciality do. Learners were also to use the methods of acquiring information as each academician does in his/her area of speciality. Dr. Bruner emphasized a strong academic curriculum with inductive learning for pupils.

In many ways, diverse philosophies of education suggest different ways of teaching pupils in the curriculum:

1. Realism advocates the methods of science and mathematics be used with its objectivity and measurability of pupil learning.
2. Idealists believe in an idea centered curriculum in which history and the social sciences as well as literature provide exemplars. Ideas acquired by pupils tend to be broad such as concepts, generalizations, universals, and main ideas. Rational thinking is salient to idealism as a philosophy of education.
3. Experimentalists believe that one can know experiences only in a rapidly changing world. With change, problems arise which need identification and needed solutions. Problem solving becomes the number one objective in the curriculum.
4. Existentialists advocate a world of individualism in which the feelings of the pupil are paramount. There are feelings of anxiety through the making of vital choices and being accountable for choices made. Each person makes his/her own world in a completely subjective world.

The seven cardinal priniciples of education have stood the test of time in terms of providing objectives stressting areas of living. These seven areas of living are not styles of learning, but they do emphasize what is salient in life to learn. We think there will be a continual debate in time and place as to what is important for pupils to learn. Life in society does change continually and rather rapidly.

We have frequently brought in the values of vocational education for pupils. We do not believe that the continual emphasis upon the academics for all pupils is a valid argument. Pupils differ from each other in many ways and the learning styles approach is attempting to determine under which conditions and situations pupils can learn best. Vocational education tends to deal with the concrete and the practical. We have observed many pupils that are orientated toward desiring to learn from the concrete and the real rather than the abstract and the classical.

Dr. Howard Gardner advocates pupils showing in diverse ways what has been learned, not through abstract methods of testing only or largely. Pupils have unique intelligences and need to have opportunities to reveal learning acquired in numerous and diverse ways.

Sternberg has provided us with a classification system of learning styles which makes it possible for pupils to learn from diverse sources and approaches and reveal what has been learned in numerous ways. Teachers here need to think of Sternberg's categories of memory, analysis, creativity, and the practical when providing instruction to pupils. These categories are different one from the other and do provide guidance in teaching regardless of the subject matter area taught.

McCarthy's 4MAT approach also has a sequence attached in teaching pupils which cuts across different subject matter areas. Regardless of subject matter area or academic disciplined being considered, this sequence is feeling, reflecting, thinking, and acting or doing. Teachers need to observe if in their teaching they stress the previously named sequence. Whichever model is followed in whole or in part needs to be evaluated continuously with a view to changing to something better in guiding more optimal pupil achievement. Ediger (1997) wrote:

Careful selection of objectives is needed so that pupils achieve that which is vital and relevant. Objectives should reflect knowledge, skills, and attitudes. They can be stated as general or behaviorally stated objectives. There are pros and cons for either kind of objectives. The important point is to state worthwhile objectives that stress higher levels of cognition such as critical and creative thinking as well as problem solving. Objectives for each learner should be challenging and yet achievable.

Educators disagree on what is truly important in the school curriculum. To indicate what is vitally important in the curriculum, Mlel (1996) wrote:

> First, I would emphasize experiences that would develop group membership skills. As learners are given opportunities to plan such matters as the best use of time together, how to take care of their classroom, what will

be appropriate in some new situation, and what studies in service projects they wish to undertake, they will be learning discussion skills. They will find out how to play both leadership and followership roles in turn. They will find not to settle for a simple majority but listen first to minority and majority opinion, gather the best ideas, and weave them into a useful consensus. Second, we must help learners extend their life-space by bringing new persons into it. Face to face or, if necessary, vicarious contacts can help students become aware of persons different from themseleves in race, religion, socioeconomic status, language and nationality. The intent here is to help learners develop good feelings toward an interesting member of their group or others with whom they may have contact and–if possinle–foster respect and caring relations with them.

Third, people in a democracy are often called upon to be problem solvers. They should gain experience in locating problems that require attention, taking steps to find solutions to a problem for group attack, and promising solutions to action.

These brief suggestions regarding the necessary content of a curriculum for democratic social learning make evident the importance of the group setting that educational institutions provide. The many kinds of human relationships that teachers encourage in such settings will make all the difference in developing student's social learning based on creative uses of information, emphasizing democratic behaviors, and leading in active and warm-hearted citizenship.

What is being emphasized presently in teaching and learning should come under intense scrutiny and assessment so that objectives, learning opportunities, learning styles, and appraisal procedures guide pupils to learn as much as possible on an individual and cooperative endeavor basis.

Selected References

Atkinson, Carrol, and Eugene T. Maleska (1965). *The Story of Education.* New York: Chilton Books, pages 113-114.

Bruner, Jerome (1963). *The Process of Education.* Cambridge, Massachusetts. Harvard University Press, page 33.

Drake, William E. (1955). *The American School in Transition.* Englewood Cliffs, New Jersey: Prentice-Hall, Inc., page 460.

Ediger, Marlow (1988). *The Elementary Curriculum. a Handbook.* Second Edition. Kirksville, Missouri: Simpson Publishing Company, pages 61 and 62

Ediger, Marlow (1995). *Philosophy in Curriculum Development.* Kirksville, Missouri: Simpson Publishing Company, pages 2 and 3 .

Ediger, Marlow (1997). *The Modern Elementary School.* Kirksville, Missouri: Simpson Publishing Company, page 23.

Ediger, Marlow (1993). "Futurism in Vocational Education," *Journal of Educational Psychology.* page 207

Gardner, Howard (1993). *Multiple Intelligences: The Theory in Practice.* New York: The Basic Books.

Marsh, David (1996)."Making School Reform Work," *Thrust for Educational Leadership,* pages 10-14.

McCarthy, Bernice (1996). *About Learning.* Barrington, Illinois: Excel, Inc.

McCarthy, Bernice (1987). *The 4MAT System: Teaching to Learning Styles with Right/ Left Mode Techniques.* Barrington, Illinois: Excel, Inc.

Sternberg, Robert J. (1997), "What Does It Mean to be Smart?"

Educational Leadership Vol. 54, No. 6, pages 20-24.

Wahlquist, John T. (1942). *The Philosophy of American Education.* New York: The Ronald Press Company, pages 60 and 61.

8

Reading in Mathematics

There are problems in reading, unique to the academic area of mathematics. If a learner does not attain well, the problem may lie in the area of reading of subject matter. Sometimes, teachers may confuse ability with experience. Thus if a pupil is not attaining as adequately as the teacher would wish, the mathematics teacher may speak of the pupil as lacking in ability. Rather than lacking in ability, the pupil may lack background experiences which hinder in mathematics achievement. A rich background of experiences can certainly aid the pupil in attaining more optimally. We recommend very strongly that teachers provide a variety of rich experiences so that the learner may acquire knowledge and skills, as well as quality attitudes. All pupils need to experience success in the mathematics curriculum so that a better self concept evolves. Adequate background experiences should accrue so that improved reading in mathematics is an end-result. Ripley and Blair (1983) wrote the following:

Reading has been defined as comprehending and learning from written materials. Facilitative reading factors facilitate the ability to read but by themselves are not reading. Functional reading factors are actual reading abilities and their level of development depends on the facilitative factors that a child brings to the reading situation and the instruction offered by the teacher. Teachers must analyze facilitative factors and determine if these factors are in the domain of their influence and responsibility. The areas over which the teacher has an influence should be strengthened through instructional practices. The purposes that reading serve in a school setting include instructional purposes. Recreational purposes, and learning-tool purposes. Instructional purposes are found in a reading instructional setting. As children progress in reading ability, subsequent instruction builds on this reading growth. Children who have reading problems cannot be expected to improve in reading ability if reading instruction does not build on their strengths. Such children need corrective or remedial instruction to improve their reading skills so that future instruction can build on their ability to read.

The use of reading as a tool focuses on reading in the content areas. Skills used in developmental reading often differ from those used in content reading. If the students' ability to read is not sufficient for the content area learning tasks, then the tasks should be modified and reading instruction should be provided to improve students' ability to use reading as a tool....

Improvement in Reading

Pupils do differ from each other in quality of reading exhibited in mathematics. Ideally, a learner should be able to read approximately 95-98 per cent of the running words encountered without any previous practice. As the learner pronounces fewer than 95 per cent of the running words correctly, comprehension will tend to go downhill. If more than 98 per cent of the running words are read correctly, recreational reading is in evidence. This kind of reading is good for leisure time reading, but not adequate for continued growth to occur in reading. Thus with an approximate 95 to 98 per cent of running words pronounced correctly without previous practice, there is room for growth in learning to identify additional new words. Those whose reading level without previous practice is below the 95 per cent of words pronounced correctly from the content contained in the reading selection may well need additional assistance. The assistance might come in the form of help given in pronouncing words correctly in mathematics. The teacher, another pupil, or a high school student who is a member of the Future Teachers Association (FTA) may provide this assistance. This assistance can give the help needed for the pupil to do well in mathematics. We would recommend here that a pupil be given a chance to pronounce an apparently unknown word correctly. We recommended that a learner be given about five seconds to determine the unknown word before the teacher or an aid pronounces that word. Pupils do need time to ascertain what an apparent unknown word is in terms of pronunciation. The teacher must want to develop independent readers of mathematics content.

For all pupils, the mathematics teacher should identify unknown words and print these on the chalkboard clearly for learners to see. Undivided learner attention to these new words should assist pupils to recognize them when reading from the basal. The teacher needs to be certain here that pupils are on task and receive necessary definitions for understanding the meaning of these new words. Thus success in contextual reading may be possible for most learners. With this learning opportunity, pupils develop their reading vocabularies in mathematics to take care of the unknown words in the 95-98 running words category of words pronounced correctly without previous practice.

Should phonics be emphasized in the mathematics reading curriculum? We would answer with generally "no" it should not be. However, the teachable moment is there in which assisting a learner with a word in which an unknown consonant or vowel is in evidence may take seconds of a teacher's time to do a little bit of teaching in phonics to guide learners to read more proficiently in mathematics. As a whole, phonics instruction belongs in the language arts areas. But, increased relationship among different curriculum areas is being emphasized in teaching-learning situations, such as reading across the different academic areas. Phonetic analysis is a part of the act of reading.

Carlo (1996) wrote the following pertaining to the use of recorded books for pupils:

> For many young children and poor readers, there's a substantial time lag between when they see and say a word. That lag produces slow, laborious reading that makes comprehension all but impossible. It's terribly difficult for students to recall what a passage is about when they have to spend so much effort figuring out each word.

A recorded book can, in effect, do what the child is not yet able to do naturally. It verbalizes the printed words with the correct pace, phrasing, and expression. As a result students make fewer reading errors, and the possibility of forming incorrect reading patterns is diminished.

Best of all, it's not necessary to record dull, simple reading materials to develop a student's sight vocabulary...

Many pupils might be assisted in reading word problems if the recorded voice is there to provide direction to pupils as the reading act progresses in solving word problems. Too frequently, pupils are unable to identify unknown words, even with the use of phonics and other word attack skills. The recorded voice, clear and concise, might well provide pupils with the assistance needed to read through and complete a problem solving experience.

Reading Abstract Symbols in Mathematics

Early primary grade pupils may benefit much from developing and reading from experience charts. These young learners need to have concrete and semiconcrete experiences involving concrete and semiconcrete learning activities. Ediger (1988) wrote:

> Following this experience. pupils with teacher guidance would present related content for the latter to record on the chalkboard or on a chart in neat manuscript letters. After the ideas have been recorded, pupils read the abstract words with the teacher pointing to the content as it is being read.

The concrete materials could consist of markers such as corn, beans, wheat, and oats seeds. These materials might also consist of real objects and children themselves in the environment. Semiconcrete materials may consist of pictures of automobiles, trucks, people, chairs, tables, among other items. The teacher here needs to be a good leader in stimulating pupils to talk about numerical values which can be recorded in an experience chart. The psychology of teaching here is excellent since pupils presented the content. They should find it easy to read after being recorded by the mathematics teacher. The subject matter pertains to their very own experiences, not something external. The teacher writes in neat manuscript letters content presented by learners. Readiness for reading is there since pupils presented the ideas for the experience chart. The teacher then points to the words and phrases as the pupils read orally together with the mathematics teacher that which was printed. A word processor might be used to type the content rather than printing it. Either way, learners may see their ideas in print as they are given. Together with the teacher, pupils read the printed content. Generally, pupils desire to read the content again until the words are mastered. Here might be a good way for selected pupils in learning to read content in mathematics. The related ideas deal with content in mathematics that learners developed•covering concrete and semiconcrete mathematical materials.

Starting with the kindergarten level and progressing sequentially through the ensuing school years, pupils need to read meaningfully those numerals used in the basic four operations, the number names in word form, the abstract symbols for greater than and less than, parenthesis and brackets used in mathematics, radius, diameter, and radius squared, among other abstractions. Reading of these abstract symbols presents a unique kind of experience peculiar to mathematics alone. Thus reading the set of counting numbers–1, 2, 3, 4, 5, 6, 7–represents skill in being able to read mathematics content and ideas. Or the operation of multiplication and addition that has the following expression: $3\times7+5\times4=$ .... indicates that reading is not always done in a left to right progression. Several of our teacher education students over the years have responded with 104 as being the correct answer to the above expression. A rule needs to be learned here in that operations pertaining to multiplication must be completed first prior to any operation in addition. The correct answer would then be 89 instead of 104. If a parenthesis is in evidence, then the operation is performed first pertaining to what is expressed therein, such as–$3\times(7+5)\times4=$. The answer here is 144. In many cases then in mathematics, one does not read from left to right in sequence. There are definite rules to follow in performing operations on numbers. As additional examples, notice the following whereby generally most would start the operations from the right and move to the left:

$$\begin{array}{r} 134 \\ \times\ 84 \\ \hline \end{array}$$

Pertaining to the learning of rules, Kapoor (1996) wrote:

The use of the phrase, "learning to think mathematically" in mathematics is rather broad. There is no consensus on the precise definition of this phrase. Mathematics is a living subject which seeks to understand patterns that permeate both the world around us and the Mind within us. Although the language of mathematics is based on rules that must be learned, it is important for students to move beyond rules and express things in the language of mathematics. The transformation suggests changes in curricular content and instructional style. It involves renewed effort to focus on:

1. Seeking solutions, not just memorizing procedures.
2. Exploring patterns, not just memorizing formulas.
3. Formulating conjectures, not just doing exercises.

Mathematics instruction should provide students with a sense of discipline–a sense of scope, power, uses, and its history. It should give them sense of what mathematics is and how it is done, at a level appropriate for the students to experience and understand. As a result of their instructional experiences, students should learn to value mathematics and feel confident in their ability to do mathematics. ....mathematics instruction should help students to develop mathematical power, including the use of specific mathematical modes of thought that are both versatile and powerful, including modelling, abstraction, optimization, logical analysis, inference from data, and use of symbols...

Mathematics teachers need to provide a variety of rich learning opportunities when pupils encounter objectives pertaining to abstract symbols. Concrete materials should be used to guide pupils in understanding abstract symbols, such as in using markers (sticks, pencils, and seeds, among others) to show meanings attached to the concept of addition – Three pencils and four pencils. are how many pencils all together? This could be shown also in the semiconcrete with pictures of three pencils and four pencils, among other illustrations. In the abstract, this would read 3+4. With the use of concrete and semiconcrete materials of instruction sequentially, learners tend to understand the abstract better in order of learning activities applicable in teaching-learning situations. When viewing the number sentence 3+4=7, primary grade pupils should read the contents as the teacher points to the words in a left to right sequence. Being able to read mathematics content with understanding is of utmost importance. Otherwise, a pupil might have wasted his/her time in reading subject matter.

It would be ideal if a teacher could always provide developmental learnings for pupils. Teachers are human beings and do have to make numerous estimates as to where pupils are presently achieving. Thus diagnosis and remediation are necessary be it in reading mathematics content or solving problems involving numeracy. Pertaining to remediation and intervention, Schmidt (1995) wrote:

In planning intervention for students, the connection between assessment and instruction can provide useful information to remediate students' concepts and skills. This action research study suggests some classroom strategies to assist in providing intervention. They are: build on students' conceptual and skill understandings, use developmentally appropriate games and activities, and organize classroom learning centres to manage group and individual intervention experiences in the classroom.

The above guidelines should provide guidance and direction to teachers to help pupils achieve sequentially. Whenever pupils are not achieving well in reading content in mathematics, the teacher needs to determine why. There are numerous causes here. The point is to determine cause or causes and then provide learning activities in reading mathematics content which provides for optimal progress.

Some probable causes are the following:

1. Lack, of knowledge and skill in phonics. Here, the pupil is not able to associate sounds (phonemes) with symbols or letters (graphemes).
2. Not being able to divide a word into syllables for ease of recognition of the unknown word. Thus a word becomes familiar to the learner when dividing the unknown word into component parts so it is recognizable.
3. Failure to use context clues. A word supplied within a sentence must make sense in relationship to the rest of the words in mathematics content. Any pupil may be

guided to think of a word being supplied in place of the unknown word to notice if it makes sense in a meaningful way.

4. Ignoring picture clues. In mathematics textbooks, for example, there are illustrations, at intervals, which aid in understanding how a problem is to be worked. These illustrations may also provide direct clues as to what an unknown word is in reading mathematics content.

The mathematics teacher does become a teacher of reading since much content for pupils to learn from and study involves identifying abstract symbols such as words, phrases, sentences, and sequential paragraphs.

One-on-one approaches in teaching reading are being emphasized. A rather recent approach here is called Reading Recovery. If a teacher has time, this procedure may be used in reading mathematics content. With aid service, a Reading Recovery philosophy of mathematics might well be stressed even though it is an approach for peoples who have problems in the reading curriculum. Stimson (1995) wrote:

> Some children– in spite of good first teaching–fall behind their peers. For these children, early supplementary teaching and intervention is essential. Davidson's strongest intervention is Reading Recovery–an intense, one-to-one tutoring program for the neediest first graders.
>
> A specially trained Reading Recovery teacher uses a formal approach to tutor a student for thirty minutes, usually for a period of 12 to 20 weeks. The Reading Recovery teacher tailors each student's lesson to build on the child's individual strengths, no matter how meager, showing him or her how to broaden those skills and use them to master others.

An important point to make here is the Reading Recovery philosophy of instruction can definitely be transferred to mathematics. A one teacher and one pupil approach is excellent for those learners who have problems in word recognition and comprehension of content or subject matter. That one teacher or aid should have a relatively easy time in securing the pupil's attention when mathematics content is being read. This approach may be used on any grade level in mathematics. The amount of time given for this activity depends upon what is needed. There are many adjustments that may be made when using Reading Recovery philosophy of teaching in mathematics. The one teacher for one pupil procedure should make for more optimal achievement.

Cross age tutoring has been used successfully by some schools in assisting pupils in reading. Thus an older pupil may guide those pupils who need help in reading mathematical content. Peer tutoring may also be involved. It may not take much time per pupil to pronounce individual words or larger units in reading subject matter in mathematics if cross age or peer tutoring is used in the classroom. The point is that the mathematics teacher needs to use procedures and methods that provide learners with the needed assistance in reading when the time is there.

Pertaining to reading and writing numbers, Reys, Suydam, and Lindquist wrote:

> Reading and writing are symbolic activities and should follow much modelling and talking about numbers. That's why the NCTM Standards (1989) recommended that less attention be given to 'reading, writing, and ordering numbers symbolically." The key word is symbolically. This recommendation alerts us to the danger of a premature focus on symbols. A sustained development of number sense should precede the reading and writing of numbers. This approach ensures that the symbols the students are reading and writing are meaningful to them.

Now let's consider some ways in which understanding place value helps develop the reading and writing of numbers. Let us again take the example of the number 123. We can identify the places (hundreds, tens, and ones) as well as the values of each (1, 2, 3). We know that the one means 1 hundred. We also know that 23 is both 2 tens and 3 ones and 23 ones, and that 123 is 1 hundred, 2 tens and 3 ones; 12 tens 3 ones; and 123 ones.

The writer above does not minimize the writing and reading of abstract numbers. Rather they are concerned that pupils experience an understanding of the value of each place in a number such as 123. Manipulative materials represent the concrete phase of learning. This is the easiest to understand on the pupil's part. The learner may also experience the semiconcrete or pictorial form. Both the concrete and the pictorial forms of instruction provide readiness for learners in reading and writing in the abstract. Starting with the abstract violates pupils' understating of what is taught. The abstract consists of symbols that in and of themselves are meaningless. These symbols such as +, –, ×, and% become meaningful only with the concrete and the semiconcrete phases of learning. Pupils need to see the connection between the concrete and pictorial with the abstract. Retention in learning is hastened when comprehension is attached to each activity presented in ongoing lessons and units of study.

Children's Literature in Mathematics

There are numerous excellent library books for pupils to read in mathematics. In our work as university supervisors of student and cooperating teachers, we have noticed much enthusiasm for reading mathematical content. There are several reasons for this occurrence:

1. Pupils have selected their very own books individually to read.
2. Pupils choose library books that are interesting to the reader.
3. Pupils feel little compulsion to read, but read due to intrinsic motivation factors.
4. Pupils read for enjoyment and for its own sake.
5. Pupils are motivated to share in small groups that which has been comprehended from reading.

The teacher needs to be on the lookout for good children's literature in mathematics. These purchased library books may be housed at one center in the classroom. The mathematics teacher should periodically introduce selected library books to learners. The purpose in making these introductions is to whet the appetites of learners for reading mathematical content. A quality bulletin board display may also encourage pupils to read and learn more mathematics. At parent/teacher conferences the latter should tell parents about selected library books which a child might wish to read. Parents should be encouraged to read orally library books, at home to their offspring in an interesting manner. There are parents who are not aware of children's literature in mathematics. We have observed parents who really became fascinated with literature in mathematics for children. It almost appeared as if parents enjoyed the library books as much as or more than the offspring.

A reading table with accompanying chairs adjacent to the center with library books may assist pupils to do an increased amount of reading.

Library books should be written on diverse reading levels of pupils. Each pupil should be able to locate sequential library books to read on his/her reading level. Generally pupils individually select library books to read that they can comprehend and understand. Books written on the frustrational level of reading are generally not selected by pupils. On the frustrational level, there are too many words that the learner may not be able to identify. The content might also be written on a level which is too complex for the reader to understand. There should be large illustrations in library books written for young pupils in particular, although there are older elementary pupils who also like to view and discuss pictures with others. The teacher should observe which books pupils tend to read and assist in word pronunciation and identification as needed. Good readers may also assist in pronouncing unknown words to individual learners.

If time is available, it is good to have conferences with individual pupils pertaining to what has been read. Veatch (1959) was a strong advocate of individualized reading; her textbook is still a classic today for individualizing a reading program for pupils. She recommended the following:

1. The pupil choosing a library to read from, among others, at a reading center.
2. The teacher having a conference with the learner after the latter has completed reading the library book.
3. The teacher may discuss possible answers with the learner to questions raised pertaining to the involved library book.
4. The pupil reveals comprehension when participating actively in the discussion.
5. The pupil may read orally to the teacher a selection from

the library book that has just been read. The learner then indicates skills possessed in reading as well as interest in the content.

The teacher may assist the pupil in any skills that are lacking in reading mathematical content. By discussing the related subject matter in the library book, the pupil elaborates on the content which might involve creative and critical thinking as well as problem solving. The basic tenets of individualized reading might well be applied to pupils reading library books on mathematical content.

A few examples will be given here of library books for pupils that stress mathematics. Clare (1992) in her book entitled *AGrain of Rice* has a farmer saving the life of an emperor's daughter. The farmer's reward was a grain of rice the first day; the amount of rice to be received was to double each succeeding day. How much rice would the farmer receive the 25th day? There are numerous problems that may be identified and solved from content in *A Grain of Rice*.

McMillan (1991) wrote a children's book entitled *Eating Fractions*. Pupils see fractional parts of different foods such as halves, fourths, eighths, and so on. Recipes, easy to make, are located in the back of the book; here pupils may assist in measuring ingredients for food preparation.

A third library book, among others, pertaining to mathematics, discussed here is by Rod Clement (1990) and entitled *Counting on Frank*. There are numerous humorous situations mentioned in the book such as a boy calculating how many humpback whales would fit into his house.

There are numerous library books written on the developmental level of pupils when reading about content in mathematics. These library books can fascinate learners in wanting to do more reading and become highly interested in mathematics.

A Mathematics Glossary

Pupils with teacher guidance should have ample opportunities to become independent in attaching meaning to words read. With the use of context clues, the learner may ascertain the identification and meaning of a word by noticing the surrounding words within the sentence. If a pupil, for example, does not identify and know the meaning of the underlined word, the rest of the words in that sentence might take care of the unknown: "The word pi is pronounced the same way as the pie that you eat. *Pi* has an approximate value of 3.1417." We truly believe that most pupils would be able to attach meaning to the Greek symbol "pi" in context in these two sentences. The teacher then needs to assist learners to use context clues in reading mathematics subject matter. The use of context clues is a powerful means of recognizing new words as well as determining their meanings.

We suggest that teachers assist pupils to develop a mathematics glossary individually or within a committe. This activity indicates that pupils can be authors and be empowered with their very own writing. Arranging words alphabetically is involved here as well as the correct spelling of words. Relevant terms need to appear in the glossary. Definitions for each word must be clear. Examples may clarify meanings of mathematics terms sooner than definitions. It would be good to use each term in a sentence within a contextual situation. If a learner forgets the definition/use of a term, he/she may refer to the glossary. The glossary should be in loose-leaf form so that entries may be added as necessary. Pupils need to become independent in recognition of words and their respective meanings. It also saves the teacher's time when a Pupil does not need assistance. The teacher might then provide help to those who need it to progress more sequentially. The mathematics glossary should assist pupils to become increasingly better readers than would otherwise be the case. Diagrams might be added to a term if this makes the meaning more clear and distinct. Mathematics does have its own unique vocabulary as well as words that intersect with other academic disciplines and yet the word may have a separate meaning pertaining to mathematics. As an example one of the authors has noticed the following words in a glossary developed by four pupils in cooperative learning: cross products, ratios, scale drawings, similar figures, tangent/cosine/sine, proportion, and fractional. The learners with teacher guidance determine which words go into a mathematics glossary. It is obvious that a glossary will reflect the present unit being studied in mathematics. Definitions written for each word need to be clear, each word should also be written within a sentence in order that pupils perceive contextual use of a vocabulary term.

Pupils Write Their Own Problems

Some very successful classrooms in the teaching of mathematics that one of the authors has observed stress pupils writing mathematics problems. There are learners who do an excellent job of writing mathematics problems. Numerous educators emphasize the importance of writing across the curriculum. When pupils are actively involved in writing in mathematics, increased skills in written work are then being emphasized. One of the authors copied down several word problems that pupils have written in observational visits made to diverse schools. These are following:

1. A_1 had three shirts and his parents bought him two more. How many shirts did A_1 then have? This problem was dictated to the first grade teacher who in return wrote what was stated.
2. Tony's father had fifty-two dairy cows. Six were sold. How many were left? This problem was written by a third grader who lives in a rural area.
3. During vacation time, Mary's parents drove 612 kilometres the first day, 386 the second day, 456 the third day, and 511 the fourth day. How many kilometers were driven all together? This problem was written by a fifth grader pertaining to an imagined number of days driven.
4. Bill has a circular garden. If the radius is seven metres, what is the area of the garden? This problem was written by a sixth grade pupil.

Pupils can assist each other in proofing the final written product. Problems may be written individually or within a committee. If a pupil cannot spell words well, this should not hold back a learner from active participation in writing in mathematics. Learners should assist each other in correct spelling of words. Reading of problems written by learners can be very satisfying to many pupils. When proof reading is done, pupils tend to read critically and creatively with the intent of solving problems and that is to write clearly stated content. Pupils need to experience a variety of reading situations in mathematics. The teacher may present a mathematics situation and have learners write the problem and also solve it. A teacher had sixth grade pupils look at a cylinder, a large empty fruit container, and ask for the volume of this container in cubic centimetres. An example of the final written problem as provided by a committee was the following:

An empty fruit can is shaped like a cylinder and is 45 centimetres high. The radius of the base or circle is 10 centimetres. How many cubic centimeters does the can hold?

For early primary grade pupils, the teacher may write what learners have given pertaining to a mathematics situation. Thus if the teacher shows two spoons in a set followed by two more spoons in a second set, how many are there altogether? We have observed pupils who provided the necessary information clearly to the teacher. The teacher printed in neat manuscript letters that which the learners had presented orally for the mathematics problem. The problem in its final form can be printed in large manuscript letters on suitable paper and put away for future reading by learners. Pupils tend to like to read that which was completed previously.

When pupils write to inform or have a third party respond to written work, Evans (1984) indicates that learners do more critical thinking and are more specific in writing than would otherwise be the case in mathematics. He also advocates that pupils be involved in trouble shooting. Here, pupils explain in writing why errors were made in homework assignments. The pupil then reveals why errors were made. The teacher has more feedback from the learner as to why errors were made. Davidson and Pierce (1988) believe that pupils' writing experiences assist them to do a better job of summarizing content as well as reflecting upon mathematics vocabulary and concepts. They also advocate that pupils engage in journal writing. In this way, pupils identify new questions pertaining to what had been learned or reflect upon previously acquired subject matter in mathematics. It is difficult to separate writing activities from the mathematics curriculum. A quality writing curriculum within mathematics assists pupils to retain, review, and think about processes and procedures involved in ongoing lessons and units of study. Stix (1994) emphasizes pupils see a relationship between manipulative materials being used in a lesson and the related numbers or symbols when being involved in journal writing. Journal writing may be the best way to assist pupils in using mathematics symbols in ongoing lessons and unit of study.

Diagnosis in Reading and Writing in Mathematics

The teacher needs to diagnose weaknesses that pupils exhibit in writing. The specifics diagnosed should then be remedied. Which errors may learners then make in written work?

1. Numerals that are reversed frequently are 3, 7, and 2.
2. Words or sentence parts that are reversed such as "was" for 'saw" or "He/she the numbers added" for "He/she added the numbers."
3. Improper agreement of subject and predicate in writing word problems such as "He ride the bicycle" instead of "He rides the bicycle."
4. Lack of proper arrangement of numerals for column addition such as the one's, ten's, and hundred's columns not aligned appropriately, thus making for errors in adding.
5. Not copying a problem correctly from the basal text in order to solve it at the learner's desk.
6. Failure to rename the minuend in subtraction when compound subtraction is being emphasized.
6. Incorrect regrouping in compound addition when any column has a value of ten or more.
7. Not identifying geometrical figures and shapes correctly so that areas and perimeters can be determined with the use of formulas.
8. Incorrect Procedures used in the basic four operations.
9. A general lack of neatness which hinders in responding correctly in written work in mathematics.
10. Accuracy in written work not being in evidence.

There are many additional areas of diagnosis that can be mentioned here such as not writing the whole and counting numerals correctly; not using the commutative, associative, and distributive properties correctly in writing; being unable to regroup and rename in the basic four operations on number: not being able to count in writing by two's, three's, five's, and ten's; not writing negative numerals correctly; and inability to attach meaning to content written.

The teacher of mathematics needs to observe daily work of learners carefully to notice errors made. Each error should be corrected unless it is minor in consequences. Accuracy, creativity, and interest are salient factors in reading and writing in the mathematics curriculum.

Diary Entries in Mathematics

Pupils individually or in committees may write diary entries pertaining to sequential days of instruction in mathematics. These entries might then be read and shared with others in the classroom setting. The following are examples of specific diary entries which are dated:

October 10. We worked on multiplying a fraction by a fraction. This appeared meaningless until the teacher showed the meaning of 1/2 times 1/2 = 1/4 . The teacher showed 1/2 of a circle. Then the 1/2 was divided into two equal parts to show the answer as being 1/4. Pupils were asked to think of how fractions can be used in everyday life. Everyone agreed that pies were divided into parts within a family and the portion size depended upon the number of family members. Then, too, there are times when a part of the pie is left over for the next meal and needs to be divided among the number in the family whereby each may get a small slice indeed.

October 11. The teacher guided the class to review selected operations on fractions that had been learned previously. Thus the teacher showed pupils a cardboard pie divided into five parts. Each part was a fifth of the pie. The fifths were added to show a value of one. So one pie divided into five parts is equivalent to five-fifths. This was very clear when viewing the whole pie being divided into fifths. There would then be five equal parts.

October 12. The teacher assisted us to understand that a mixed number can be changed to an improper fraction. If 1 and 1/2 circles are being considered, how many halves are there? The single circle was changed to 2/2's. Two halves and one-half can be seen as 3/2's with the use of the paper pie parts. The teacher assisted us to see practical application of division with fractions. Thus if there are five candy bars to divide among ten pupils, what fractional part does each receive? The actual candy bars or some other food items could actually be used to have learners attach meaning to the abstract fraction.

In addition to diary entries, pupils individually or in committees may read and write log entries. Logs cover a longer period of time as compared to diary entries. A log could cover one week's amount of time given to the teaching of mathematics. The diary entries might then be used to write the log. Thus a summary of what has been learned will accrue. Logs are valuable to write due to the following:

1. Main ideas need to be written to summarize content.
2. Higher levels of cognition must be used by learners when writing main ideas which cover much content. For each day's recordings, one main idea should be adequate. A main idea may even summarize a week of school work in mathematics activities.
3. Specifics in written work may be stressed such as legibility in handwriting, correct spelling of words, proper paragraphing, quality sequencing of ideas recorded, and neatness of the final product being in evidence.
4. Logs, as well as diary entries, may be saved for future reading by pupils.
5. Committee skills may be developed by learners if rules are developed prior to group endeavors. The rules need to be enforced.

The teacher should have pupils read and write for a variety of purposes in mathematics. Mathematics content is retained for a longer period of time if it is used such as in written work. Learners tend to forget that which is not or rarely used in everyday life. Pupils tend to remember what has been learned if it is used in diverse ways.

Reading and Writing Test Items

Pupils can use what has been learned through the reading and writing of test items in mathematics. Multiple choice test items might be written when pupils reveal readiness factors. Each multiple choice test item usually has a stem and four responses, one of which is correct. The stem together with each of the four responses should be grammatically correct. The following model of a multiple choice item may be used by pupils:

Which of the following shows the intersection of two or more circles?

(a) the formula for the area of a circle.
(b) Venn diagrams.
(c) the commutative properties.
(d) the property of closure.

Each response must be plausible in the multiple choice test item. For example, if Mickey Mouse had been listed as a response, the concept of being plausible would have been violated. We believe the above test item makes it so that learners need to differentiate each response. Pupils should learn to write test items in mathematics to be exchanged with others to notice achievement. Learners need to be assisted to notice when trivia gets in the way of developing *quality* in test item writing.

Essay test items may be written by learners for others to respond to. Essay items need to be adequately delimited so that a general, clear-cut answer can come from the learner. The other extreme is to write the essay test item so that it is completely factual and involves little in terms of higher levels of thinking. Notice the following essay item which is too broadly stated: Discuss addition. This item is so broad that an entire book could be written on the concept of addition. It does not delimit what a pupil is to write about addition. The following is so delimited that a fact is wanted instead of a discussion: What is the answer to 269 plus 186? This number pair could be written in a computation section of the test. The following is adequately delimited and permits higher levels of cognition: Discuss the differences in finding the area of a circle and the volume of a rectangular solid. Determine at least five differences.

Additional test items that learners may write in mathematics include matching, true-false, and completion. Peers may assist each other in proofing test items written. Improvement in clarity and meaning of each test item is vital. Improvement in reading and writing in mathematics is a salient end-result.

Reading to Solve Word Problems

Word problems, also called story problems, in textbooks may provide selected difficulties to pupils. In solving word problems, a first step is that pupils comprehend the abstract symbols which make for words and sentences. Being able to read with meaning is a very first step in solving word problems. Second, pupils need to possess background experiences in solving these word problems. Background experiences provide readiness for problem solving in mathematics. Third, pupils need to understand what is being asked for in the word problem so that problem solving can come about. Fourth, learners need to view the problem in a holistic manner in that salient ideas are needed from the entire word problem in order that solutions may be found. Fifth, mathematical operations need to be performed to arrive at an answer. The answer should be perceived as being tentative, not an absolute. Sixth, the pupil needs to reflect upon the tentative solution(s). Thus the learner looks at weaknesses that might be inherent in the solution. Peer study of the tentative answer has many benefits. Pupils must be able to explain why they did what was done in securing the necessary answer.

There are pupils who seemingly have fears pertaining to the solving of word problems in mathematics. To minimize these fears, Fairbairn (1993) made the following suggestions:

1. Mathematics teachers should refer to these kinds of problems as being story problems. The content herein should be read interestingly and orally to learners.

2. Local information should be placed inside of the story problems instead of content contained initially in these problems. The numerical data should be left the same: however, the names, places, and products should be given familiar names.
3. Committee work on the part of learners need to be stressed so that pupils may learn from each other.
4. Pupils should write their own story problems for peers to solve. This will take away much of the anxiety in working with these kinds of problems. Why? Pupils will realize that they too can write story problems.
5. Teachers should use interesting subject matter inside the story problems so that basic mathematics skills are learned. Positive attitudes should be an important end-result of this activity.

Computer Use in Mathematics

Computer use should be an inherent part of learning opportunities for pupils so that objectives might be attained more effectively. Carefully selected programs which emphasize simulation may benefit learners much in the area of problem solving in mathematics. Tutorial programs can guide pupils to achieve new facts, concepts, and generalizations sequentially in ongoing units of study. Drill and practice programs should assist learners to review what has been acquired previously. Diagnosis and remediation programs attempt to pinpoint that which has caused difficulties for learners in ongoing lessons and units of study. Remedial work should follow the point of diagnosis. Games in terms of mathematics programs provide enjoyment in learning in mathematics as well as extend content studied previously. Each program should assist pupils to attain sequentially and meaningfully. Interest in learning mathematics is vital and salient. Certainly, the mathematics teacher needs to be a good organizer of instruction to have pupils use technology effectively along with other materials of teaching and learning.

When readiness is in evidence, pupils need to experience the use of the word processor in writing as well as in reading of subject matter in mathematics. Pupils individually and in committees may write and solve problems appearing on the monitor or screen. These problems have been composed by pupils. If pupils do not possess keyboard skills, the teacher may do the typing for pupils. It is good practice for pupils to be actively engaged in writing mathematics problems for others to solve. Perhaps, these problem areas come from the real world of buying and selling of a learner. Life-like problems stated by individual pupils when we have visited classrooms as supervisors of student teachers have been the following:

1. A pupil bought a cap for 4-99 plus 6% sales tax. How much did the cap cost? The pupil gave a ten dollar bill to pay for the cap. How much change should he receive?
2. A pupil who grew sweet corn in the family's garden plot had thirty corn ears to sell. Each was priced and sold for 12 cents, how much the corn sell for?
3. A pupil in a small town sold lemonade on a hot day in summer. Ingredients for the lemonade cost 3.10. Paper cups cost a total of 70. Forty-five cups of lemonade were sold at 20. How much money did the pupil make selling lemonade?

Mathematics problems do not always, of course, need to come from the real world. We have observed pupils who do a good job of simulating problems from the real world using a word processor. These pupils individually or in committees appear to be creative and can write realistic problems in mathematics. We have observed others who solved these problems to engage in critical thinking and reason logically in order to solve problems.

In Closing

Pupils need to experience a variety of reading activities in mathematics. There are commercially published materials for pupils to read. These should be on the understanding levels of individual learners. If the reading level therein is too complex, the pupil will not comprehend the contents. Feelings of frustration and failure may be an end-result here. Should the commercial reading materials be too easy to read, boredom and a lack of challenge may enter in. With individualized reading, a pupil may choose which books to read and which to omit.

There are numerous opportunities to read what pupils have comprehended from a variety of concrete and semiconcrete experiences and put in written form. Here reading and writing become one, not separate entities. What has been written may be saved for future reading by learners. Adequate background experiences assist pupils to be able to record ideas in written form. Learners need to practice the skill of reading so that it is continually refined. Mathematics has its very own terms that are unique to this academic discipline. It also has its own areas of concern, such as problem solving, which makes it imperative that learners learn to read mathematics content with meaning and understanding.

Mathematics textbooks are not good nor bad in and of themselves. How good a basal text is depends upon the quality of teaching that is going on. We have observed student teachers and cooperating teachers who have done an excellent job of teaching mathematics using the basal textbook, along with other materials used to clarify and extend experiences. The mathematics teacher needs to be certain that each pupil can read and understand the content in an adopted single or multiple series of texts. Readiness activities should be provided for pupils prior to their reading abstract subject matter. Thus the teacher may use several approaches here. One being to read over with the pupils mathematics content before pupils work exercises contained therein. Second, a peer or an older pupil might assist the learner who had trouble reading the inherent content. A tape recording may also be made of the word problems so that those who have difficulty reading may listen to the tape and follow along in word recognition from their basal mathematics textbook. One pupil-one teacher in tutoring may be necessary to have pupils individually read the subject matter with adequate comprehension.

Mathematics teachers and aids may need to assist pupils during time devoted to reading instruction with phonics, syllabication, pictorial clues, context clues, and configuration clues (viewing the shape of form of a word in comparison to other words) in order that unknown words can be identified by the learner. What happens beyond that is of utmost importance and that being learners

1. comprehending what has been read.

2. applying and using information as needed in school and in society.
3. analyzing to separate relevant from irrelevant information useful in a given situation.
4. synthesizing content after analysis so that application can be made in more specific situations involving mathematics.
5. evaluating the solution to a mathematics problem after analysis and synthesis.

Selected References in Mathematics

Carlo, Marie (1996). Recorded Books Raise Reading Skills, *The Education Digest,* 61: 56.

Clare, Helena (I 992). *A Grain of Rice.* New York: Bantam Doubleday.

Clements, Rod (1990). *Counting on Frank.* Milwaukee, Wisconsin: Gareth Publishers.

Davison, D. M., and D. L. Pearce (1988). "Using Writing Activities to Reinforce Mathematics Instruction," *Arithmetic Teacher,* 36: 42-45.

Ediger, Marlow (1988). The Elementary Curriculum, Second Edition. Kirksville, Missouri: Simpson Publishing Company, 13.

Ediger, Marlow (1985). *Teaching Mathematics in the Elementary School (A Collection of Essays),* ERIC Clearing House– Resources in Education.

Evans, C. S. (1984). "Writing to Learn in Math," *Language Arts,* 61; 828-835.

Fairbairn, D. M. (1993). "Creating Story Problems", *Arithmetic Teacher,* 41: 140-142.

Kapoor, Don (1996). Mathematical Power–Mathematization, Saskatchewan Mathematics Teachers' Society Journal, 31: 25 - 26.

Kennedy, Leonard M. and Steve Tipps. *Guiding Children's Learning of Mathematics.* Seventh Edition. Belmont, California: Wadsworth Publishing Company, 1994.

McMillan, Bruce (1991). *Eating Fractions.* New York: Scholastic.

National Council Teachers of Mathematics. *Curriculum and Evaluation Standards for School Mathematics,* Reston, Virginia, 1989. National Council Teachers of Mathematics. *Student Math Notes,* Reston, Virginia. 1989.

National Council Teachers of Mathematics. *An Agenda for Action,* Reston, Virginia, 1980.

National Council Teachers of Mathematics. *The Mathematics Education of Exceptional Children and Youth, An Interdisciplinary Approach,* Reston, Virginia, 1981.

Ripley, William H., and Timothy R. Blair (1983). Reading

Diagnosis and Remediation: Classroom and Clinic. Boston: Houghton Mifflin, 15.

Reys, Robert, Marilyn N. Suydam, and Mary Montgomery Lindquist (1995). *Helping Children Learn Mathematics.* Boston: Allyn and Bacon, 139.

Schmidt, Mary Ellen (1995). "Mathematics Intervention: Second Grade Place Value Concepts," *Education,* 116:229-231.

Stix, A. (1994). "Pic-jour math: Pictorial Journal Writing in Mathematics, *Arithmetic Teacher*, 41-264-269.

Slavin, Robert (1990). "Student Team Learning in Mathematics", in Neil Davidson (Editor), *Cooperative Learning in Mathematics.* Menlo Park, CA: Addison-Wesley, pp. 89-97.

Stimson, Janet (1995). "At-Risk or At-Promise," *Thrust for Educational Leadership,* 25:16.

Veatch, Jeanette (1959). *Individualizing Your Reading Program.* New York: G. P. Putnam's Sons, 242 pages.

9

Technology in the Mathematics Curriculum

There is strong emphasis placed upon use of modern technology in the elementary school curriculum. Technology is very strongly used in all facets of society, and elementary schools should not lag behind what is stressed in the societal arena. The elementary pupil of today will be expected to achieve in a heavily endowed work place involving technology. Many factories and farms have been strongly automated. Fewer workers are continually needed in these work places. Machines automatically do work that was formerly done with the use of human muscles and physical work.

Personal Beliefs About Technology Use

There are selected criteria from the psychology of learning that needs emphasis in having pupils work with technology. We believe that technology should capture pupil interests in learning. Activities here should be fascinating to engage pupil interaction. These interests should provide for effort in pupils desiring to achieve, grow, and develop. There is little time for misbehavior if pupils are interested in the task at hand. We have noticed, for example, first graders who had little interest in drill and practice in arithmetic using paper and pencil. And yet when a hand calculator or computer program was emphasized, these learners truly showed interest and fascination in learning. Interest is a powerful factor in learning since attention to the task at hand makes for increased achievement.

Second, we believe that technology may assist learners to perceive purpose in learning. If purpose is lacking, there will be little incentive for pupils to learn. Goal centered pupils achieve more than those who fail to perceive objectives in learning. We have observed many pupils who did not like to check long division problems using paper and pencil. Again, when the checking was done rapidly and accurately with the calculator or computer, there seemingly was even joy in doing the checking to see if the long division problem had been worked correctly. It appeared that pupils saw purpose, not drudgery, in checking these long division problems.

Third, we believe technology can assist pupils to attach meaning to ongoing lessons and units of study. What pupils learn then should make sense, not be nonsense tasks. There are numerous programs in computer use which guide pupils to achieve an objective. These numerous ways stress if one procedure is not understood, there are other approaches which will guide pupils to attach meaning. It is so important that pupils understand what is being learned. Many of us have learned that to divide fractions, we need to invert the divisor and then multiply. This mechanical procedure made no sense to us in grade school and in high school. There should be meaning in why 'the divisor is inverted and then multiply.' With clear illustrations together with the abstract numerals on the monitor, pupils may well understand and attach meaning as to why to "invert the divisor and multiply." What is learned should make sense and not merely be committed to memory.

Computer programs should assist pupils to perceive knowledge as being related, not in isolated bits. We noticed a delightful program on a monitor with high pupil enthusiasm working on the Egyptian system of numeration when studying a social studies unit on the Middle East. Here, pupils were fascinated to learn that individual strokes represented the numerals from one through nine. Further interests were shown in the following features of the Egyptian system of numeration:

1. Each heel bone of an ox, shaped like an arch, represented a value of ten. Nine heel bones represented a value of ninety.

2. Each coiled rope represented a value of 100. There could be as many as nine coiled ropes to represent a value of 900.
3. Each lotus flower represented 1,000. The pattern is that nine lotus flowers represent a value of 9,000.
4. Each bent finger represented a value of 10,000. Nine bent fingers represent 90,000.
5. Each tadpole represent 100,000; thus nine tadpoles represent 900,000.

We present this information, as an example, to show that computer programs along with other technologies can definitely assist pupils to perceive that knowledge is related. In this case, social studies and mathematics can definitely be related so that the learner perceives the interrelationship of subject matter. Morris and Pai (1976) wrote the following pertaining to Jerome Bruner's thinking on the relationship of knowledge:

> ...since human beings seem to be able to store more information than they can spontaneously recall, the main problem in human memory is that of effective retrieval. Bruner is convinced that the key to effective retrieval is organization of information. He contends there is sufficient evidence to support the assertion that, in general, any information organized around the interests and the cognitive structure of the learner can be most efficiently recalled. Hence, the only means by which we can reduce the quick rate of loss of human memory is to organize facts according to basic principles and concepts from which they were inferred. Further, "the very attitudes and activities that also seem to have the effect of conserving characterize figuring out or discovering things for ourself also seem to have the effect of conserving memory". In addition to these effects, the learning experiences resulting from self-discovery give us an increased awareness of the connections and continuities between what we learn and what we do. As a result, we are likely to see our activities in a broader context and thus gain more control of our acts in relation to an end in view. In learning by discovery, knowledge already possessed by the learner is used to gain new insights, and in the process old knowledge

becomes reconstructed.

Being very strong on learning by discovery, Jerome Bruner stresses organizing information around the interests and cognitive structure of pupils. Discovery conserves or saves what has been learned previously. Pupils need to use knowledge to obtain new insights thus connecting what we learn and what we do. There are many key ideas Bruner presents here for learners to relate knowledge and increase memory/recall. The use of technology such as video-tapes and software programs can and do assist pupils to relate knowledge inductively and thus retain content for a longer duration of time.

Fifth, the use of technology can certainly assist to provide for individual differences among pupils in terms of achievement in diverse academic areas. When pupils work on computer programs, they can definitely work at their optimal rate of achievement individually. Thus, in a tutorial program, for example, pupils need to possess readiness factors such as having adequate background information. The learner then may move forward on that program at an as optimal rate as possible. Comparing this learning situation with viewing a video-tape, the contents in the latter may move forward too rapidly or too slowly.

Sixth, technology and its use might well guide pupils to develop wholesome attitudes toward learning. Pupils seem to be fascinated with interacting with technology. We have observed pupils in classrooms with interest in achieving in mathematics, as an example, until it is time for the learner to work with the computer. Here, the pupil interacted with drawings and abstract related numerals on the monitor. Problem solving was stressed here for a fifth grade pupil emphasizing finding the volume of a cone. The drawings were excellent and the hints given in finding the volume were sequential to permit the learner to determine the needed answer. Later, another pupil also came to the computer to solve additional problems cooperatively. The interest was high and the two learners worked together harmoniously. The joy that comes in working with others truly has its values for pupils.

Philosophy of Education and Technology

We are strong believers in teachers, not only stressing the

psychology of learning, but also the philosophy of education in technology use. There are selected philosophies that teachers need to understand and use in teaching-learning situations.

A first philosophy and its use we would like to discuss is experimentalism. Experimentalists believe strongly in a changing environment. Changes occur in all facets of the social/natural environment. Rather rapid changes have occurred such as in technology.

With change, new problems arise. These problems need identification and delimitation so that they can be solved. An hypothesis is developed in answer to the problem. The hypothesis is tentative, never an absolute. Each hypothesis is to be tested in a life like situation. Problems, hypotheses, And tests of hypotheses are done in context within a practical situation. Experimentalism is utilitarian, not obstract nor theoretical. Pertaining to John Dewey and his beliefs on change, Ediger (1995) wrote the following:

John Dewey (1859-1952) lived during a period of rapid change. When he was born and even until the early 1900s, the automobile basically did not exist. When he died in 1952, manufactured automobiles, as a whole, were very dependable with hydraulic brakes. Heaters, and even a few with air conditioners. Electricity had its beginning in home and factory use in the early 1890s and was highly refined with its uses in 1952, with electric ranges, dishwashers, clothes washers, and driers. Changes have occurred from zero automobiles in 1859 to more highways and intestates being built to take 1859 of horse drawn farm equipment was utilized to plow, harrow, disk, and seed the farm land. By 1952 farm tracters had electric lights hydraulic brakes, and could pull a plow with four to five shears in plowing the land. Tremendous changes then occurred from 1859 (year of birth) to 1952 (year of death of Dr. Dewey).

With these and many other changes problems arise. Problems need identification and careful delineation in the school curriculum, as well as in society. Each problem is vital. Information acquired in school needs to be utilized to solve problems. Knowledge is not attained for its own sake, but is instrumental to the solving of identified problems. In society also, information is secured from a variety of reference sources, useful to solve each chosen problem.

From the data gathered, directly related to the problem, a hypothesis is developed. A hypothesis results for each identified problem. The hypothesis is tentative and subject to change through testing. Testing is done in a life-like situation. The results of the test may confirm or refute the hypothesis. Minor revisions of the hypothesis may also be needed. Generally, change will occur-rather continuously.

Experimentalists believe that one can only know experience. One cannot know the real world in whole or in part as realists advocate nor does one know ideas only of what exists out there in society, as idealists stress. With the world of experience as experimentalists believe, one identifies and solves necessary problems. Eichelberger (1989) wrote the following pertaining to pragmatism, also called experimentalism:

> The relationship between knowledge and reality (truth) that is used by researchers today is that of the pragmatist, which states that all knowledge is produced by human beings and that we can never distinguish between knowledge and truth. In empirical research, this means that if something works in practice then it is true, or we can assume that it is true. A truth (knowledge) that is not supported by further empirical study will be modified or discarded.

How does any philosophy of education relate directly to the use of technology? We have noticed several computerized programs that are excellent for pupils to use in problem solving. Thus pupils in context have identified a problem for which they wish to have or find a solution. A software program carefully selected might well provide data to test a hypothesis. Generally, additional technological sources will be used to evaluate an identified hypothesis in answer to a problem. However, there are numerous programs which may provide information in the problem solving arena. Then, too, there are simulated programs which tend to be life-like and real. These entire software programs go through flexible steps of problem solving.

Changes in technology abound. Rose and Fernland wrote:

> During the 1980's, computer assisted instruction (CAI)

> was an important part of classroom use. Teachers, department chairs, and district technology coordinators purchased commercial and public domain programs in the subject areas, stored on one or more floppy disks, including drill and practice programs, tutorials, simulations, and games. During the next decade there were four major changes that improved CAI: (1) the decline of the use of floppy disks, replaced by the enhanced storage capability of CD-ROM and videodisc, (2) enhanced interactivity in software in which students play a more active role, (3) sophisticated graphics, video clips, colour and sound, creating multimedia presentation no longer dominated by screens of text; and (4) the growing marriage of CAI and telecommunications, allowing a seamless transition from single computer use to collaborative work with distant partners and access to internal- based sources.

The use of CAI in the social studies classroom continues to be strong, although such use is being eclipsed by the tool uses of computers; word processing; communications, research, and multimedia production, CAI is available on the internet, a helpful tool for teachers who want to review the product and consult other teachers who have used the program with their students. CAI has greatly improved in creativity and quality; many programs offer motivating experiences for students in analysis, problem solving, and decision making.

Idealism as a Philosophy of Education

Previously, it was mentioned that experimentalists believe we can know experiences only from the physical and social world. Idealists state that we receive ideas only, not experiences; nor can we know what the real world is like in whole or in part as realists indicate. Idealism is an idea centred philosophy of education. Mind is real and needs to receive nourishment through quality ideas in different academic disciplines. There are numerous tutorial programs with computer use that stress learners achieving important concepts and generalizations. Knowledge objectives predominate, according to idealism as a philosophy of teaching and learning. Ediger (1986) wrote the following:

> Idealism is a more traditional approach in making decisions as compared to experimentalism and existentialism. According to idealists, individualists cannot know the world as it truly is in terms of a objective reality. Each person, however, obtains ideas pertaining to objects and items in the environment. The mind brings order to what is observed and seen. Thus, of all facets of human development that is significant to develop, the mind or intellectual achievement must come first. Rich learning experiences will need to be in evidence to guide pupils to achieve maximum development mentally. Thus experiences may well be selected in terms of leading pupils to attain universal ideas...

From the thinking of idealists, the following implications apply for teaching and learning:

1. Broad generalizations need emphasizing that have much use to the learner in terms of mental and moral development.
2. Quality ideals for pupils to emulate need adequate emphasis in the school curriculum.
3. Intellectual objectives should receive primary stress in the curriculum.
4. Quality academic coursework should guide pupils to achieve worthy generalizations.
5. Abstract ideas are more important to emphasize as compared to the concrete and the semiconcrete.

Key ideas in understanding idealism in teaching and learning are written by Bigge (1982) in the following statements:

> The heart of idealism is the belief that basic reality consists of ideas, thoughts, minds or substantive selves, not physical matter. Since priority is given to minds, minds have bodies, but bodies do not have minds.. The universe is an expression of intelligence and will; its order is due to an external, spiritual reality. For idealists, people are just good-active substantive minds; they are absolutely real selves endowed with free will or genuine moral

choice. This philosophy has ancient roots; it dates back to Socrates (469-399 BC) and Plato (427-347).

Idealism is really idea-ism. The source of this title is based on Platonic thought. For Plato ideas alone were genuinely real; they consisted of immaterial essences. That which people perceive is a shadow of reality; each thing that they perceive gets its existence from its Thingness; an idea. A book is a book because of its being more or less an imperfect replica of Bookness. A woman is a woman because she is a replica of Womanness. Plato's assumed world of 'eternal verities' consisted of the True, the Good, and the Beautiful.

We can trace the development of idealism by listing some of the leading philosophers who contributed to this position and stated a leading idea that each has contributed to the philosophy. Socrates believed that children are born with knowledge already in their minds, but they need help to recall this innate knowledge. Plato contributed the idea of ideas, which are the universal forms of all existing things and are the essence of reality...

What then are the implications of idealism for teaching and learning in the classroom involving computer use? I have seen selected excellent software packages which stress an idea centered curriculum.

It seems as if for each academic area, there are tutorials which might well assist any pupil to achieve subject matter knowledge.

These software packages should assist pupils to

1. achieve abstract content which is challenging and yet attainable.
2. learn content in depth with emphasis placed upon mental development of pupils.
3. acquire subject matter which makes sense and has meaning.
4. relate relevant content from an academic centered curriculum.
5. attain vital facts, concepts, and generalizations in each academic discipline.

An idea centered curriculum might also guide pupils to use what has been learned in problem solving. This belief assists in relating idealism with experimentalism.

Existentialism and the Curriculum

Existentialists are very much concerned about the everyday life and its anxieties of individuals. Individuals are concerned with choices that needed to be made regardless if the desire is there to make these decisions. There is dread, fear, anxiety, and uncertainty in making choices. Many existentialists believe life to be absurd and ridiculous. There is dread in choosing when so many alternatives are available in the making of these choices. People do not live in a subject centered world, nor in a world of science. Rather they live in an openended world where there are no standards in and of themselves. These standards, rules and regulations need to be developed. Human beings make their own world; there are no absolutes nor are there given rules to live by. People, past and present, have developed standards to go by in life, but these are human made in an open environment where people, individually and collectively, develop the kind of society they wish to have. Pertaining to existentialism, Ozman and Craver (1990) wrote:

> Because the individual human is so important as the creator of ideas, existentialists maintain that education should focus upon individual human reality. It should deal with the individual as a unique being in the world, not only as a creator of ideas, but as a living, feeling being. Most philosophies, existentialists charge, tend to focus upon only as a cognitive being. The individual is this, but he is also a feeling, aware person, and existentialists think that this side deserves attention.

Which implications in the curriculum might follow some of the tenets of existentialism?

1. Pupils individually need to choose freely, from among alternatives, those learning activities which are purposeful and meaningful.
2. Content in the curriculum should reflect human feelings of loneliness, alienation, anxiety, and tension.
3. Personal feelings of the pupil should be reflected in ongoing lessons and units of study. These feelings might

well be expressed in art and construction projects as well as of personal writings of learners.

The pupil needs to realize that choices do need to be made. If others make decisions for the personal self, choices are still being made, but the individual has abdicated responsibility in the decision making arena. Choices made do involve dilemma decisions, but authentic decisions must be made. Coercion is definitely not a part of the decision making philosophy of existentialists. Quality decisions made do not always make for good human relations. Alienation may also be an end-result. The individual always needs to consider the consequences of choices made. Moral decisions made in a free environment is the goad of existentialists. Individuals should remember they are responsible for choices made; no one else can assume this responsibility. Choices are subjective, not objective by any means.

With technology in the curriculum, existentialism advocates:

1. Individuals selecting from among others computer programs to complete. The individual should also choose which tasks to engage in when additional forms of technology are used.
2. The human condition with all of its uncertainties and anxieties should be stressed in the technology curriculum.
3. The pupil needs to have ample opportunities to study situations in which dilemmas are present. Decision making is not clear cut nor an absolute. Content in technology can emphasize these ideas.
4. The learner needs to express his/her feelings in diverse projects and activities. Thus a variety of writing experiences, fine arts and practical arts activities, speaking and reading learning opportunities, as well as listening may be stressed as evaluation techniques as well as enrichment activities in the technology curriculum.
5. Heavy pupil involvement and choice in the technology curriculum should always be in evidence with existentialism as a driving philosophy in education.

Realism and the Technology Curriculum

Realists are strong advocates of individuals knowing in whole or in part what the real world is like. Their model comes from the world of science and mathematics. Precision and extreme accuracy are major tenets of realism as a philosophy of education. Thus the realist is strongly interested in having pupils achieve precise, measurably stated objectives in each curriculum area. With these kinds of objectives, carefully chosen by teachers and other educators, pupils do or do not attain each objective as a result of instruction. Learning activities selected by the teacher harmonizes with what pupils are to learn as contained in the stated objective(s). Evaluation techniques need to be aligned with the stated objectives. Validity is then in evidence in testing and measurement. Reliability needs to stress test-retest, split half, and/or alternative forms of appraisal. Results from pupil tests should indicate numerical data such as percentile ranks, per cent of items correct, standard deviations, quartile deviations, and standardized scores. Subjectivity in testing is definitely not wanted. Rather objectivity in testing is advocated to determine what any one pupil has learned as a result of teaching.

Pertaining to realism, Wild (1955) wrote the following:

The child, of course, should be interested in what he is learning. But it does not follow that whatever the child is interested in is, therefore, valuable. This is absurd. The skill of the elementary teacher "lies in eliciting the interest of the child in the right things, especially in grasping the truth for its own sake. At the early stages no psychological or rhetorical technique should be neglected which is capable of strengthening this urge. When a mathematical principle has been understood, the child's attention should be drawn at once to the problem this enables him to solve. No opportunity should be lost to point out the principles of pure science which underlie modern technology. Language and grammar should be taught at essential phases of that mysterious process of apprehension by which the actual structure of things is mentally reflected and expressed, and by which such knowledge is achieved.

Realists do place very stong emphasis upon the following in teaching and learning situations:

1. Carefully selected ends for pupils to achieve need to be written in precise, measurable terms.

2. Learning opportunities chosen by the teacher align with the ends or objectives mentioned in number 1 above.
3. Pupil achievement in having attained the precise objectives are measurable and presented in numerical terms.
4. The models of mathematics and science with its accuracy and specificity should be incorporated into the curriculum.
5. Research studies can provide much data on what learners sould study such as, for example, which words pupils should master in spelling. Many excellent studies have been made which indicate the words pupils use most frequently in functional writing. Words that are misspelled in these writings provide a scientific basis for determining practical words to be chosen by the teacher for pupil mastery.

Technology needs to be matched with the chosen objectives of instruction in lesson plans and units of study. After the use of technology in teaching and learning situations, the teacher may measure what pupils have learned. The results are given in numerical terms, not vague subjective data. The objective results may be reported to parents to indicate learner achievement in the school curriculum.

Leadership in Technology Use

Teachers need to be and are leaders in curriculum development. They select objectives, learning activities, and appraisal procedures. Teachers organize the classroom for instruction. Organizational work includes grouping pupils for instruction, disciplining pupils, as well as devising a schedule for teaching. Technology is definitely involved in making curricular decisions. For example, there should be an ample number of software programs in the learning activities section to guide pupils to achieve objectives. Definite leadership skills are necessary here. In addition to the classroom teacher, the principal plays a vital role in curriculum development.

Ritchie (1996) wrote the following pertaining to reasons why the use of technology is minimal in schools:

* A lack of administrative support

* Inadequate staff development and technological support
* Low quantity, quality, and access of technologies in the classroom
* Non-existent or cursory plans for adopting and implementing technology into a school.
* The failure to allocate a technology coordinator to help train teachers and coordinate the technologies
* A lack of funds and personnel to maintain equipment
* Continual assessment of content acquisition through traditional methods
* Establishment of a broad participatory clientele to establish a technology culture (Hoffman, 1996).

From the above statements, it is quite clear that school administrators need to understand and value technological use in the classroom. School administrators should perceive the necessity of implementing technology use in the classroom so that pupils may achieve more optimally. No doubt, there are school administrators who lack quality experiences with technology and therefore do not see the need for pupils experiencing learning activities involving technology. Each principal and supervisor should avail themselves in learning more about technology and how to integrate its use into the school curriculum. Talking to and learning from classroom teachers should assist the school administrator in realizing the importance of technology in a modern elementary curriculum. Staff development programs in using technology in the curriculum should be in the offing. Teachers and administrators need to realize the importance of an updated curriculum. The school of today and the work place of tomorrow should not be in isolation from each other, but rather become integrated entities. Definite goals in inservice education using technology are musts! These goals and experiences for participants need to be chosen carefully. Relevance and importance are two concepts that need careful consideration when inservice education programs are developed and implemented. The goals of the workshop need to be clearly stated and should be cooperatively developed by workshop participants. There should be a large group session to hear a speaker or two who introduce vital inservice education goals. In the large group session, participants need to identify problem areas pertaining to the use of technology.

Cooperative endeavors and committee work should follow to solve identified problems from the large group session. Consultants need to be available to assist in clarifying ideas and raising important questions to consider. A hands-on approach should be in the offing. Individual endeavors need also to be pursued in the inservice education program. Participants individually have concerns that need addressing with consultant assistance. There should be opportunities to try out what has been studied in the inservice education program to the level of application in the regular public school classroom. Feedback from the classroom to participants in the inservice education program is a must!

There need to be definite plans to integrate technology into the school curriculum. This should not be left to chance, but rather quality goals and plans have been developed to use technology to its fullest in teaching and learning situations. Teachers need to have easy access to technology in lesson plan and teaching unit construction. A trained and educated coordinator of technology use can assist teachers to educate children for more optimal achievement. The coordinator of technology needs to develop good human relations with teachers with the latter having access readily to technology.

Adequate money needs to be budgeted and used to develop a curriculum with technology as a guiding principle. The lay public needs to be informed continuously about the merits of using technology in the classroom to assist each pupil to achieve as optimally as possible. The school culture reflects the importance of technology use with pupils, teachers, and administrators indicating its importance to child growth and development in the school setting.

Maskin (1996) wrote the following:

> Promoters of computers in the classroom claim that exposing pupils to websites, e-mail, and news groups promises more than the means at securing a job in the next century. Technology boosters also predict that the use and mastery of the internet and the world wide web will produce affective changes that can be measured to

> produce increased student self-esteem and confidence. Whether working at home or in school, an individual or in a cooperative learning or team setting, students will become "infotectives", i.e. independent thinkers, researchers, inventors, inquirers, capable of solving problems that often required the active direction of a teacher or supervisor...

In expanding the learning environment to include data bases, computer networks, and other library resources throughout the world, the internet makes it possible for students to shape their own education. Once the easy accessing protocols are learned, the student can dive into these resources in the comfort of his or her home and or library without the constant supervision and intervention of the teacher. Lao Tzui's dictum, "He who teaches least teaches best," describes a student centered teaching, learning, and assessment environment in which the student can access information from multiple perspectives and learn to use this information to solve complex problems.

Freedom, however, also opens up the possibility of choice. The emerging information technologies can just as easily be used to access "sports trivia as they can explore issues being debated in Congress or at the World Bank. Many students, if left to their devices, might choose to spend hours surfing the net for their own enjoyment rather than using it to complete a school assignment. The job of the teacher, therefore, is to involve students, individually or in teams, in internet projects that are fun to do and skill enhancing. Students exposed early on to such educational endeavors are more likely to feel comfortable and confident in Drucker's knowledge based society...

I am convinced that internet connectivity empowers students, gives them a research advantage, and generally gets them excited about learning.

We are truly in an information age in which there are so many outstanding sources of content for pupil acquisition. Pupils need to have ample opportunities to secure a variety of subject matter on a topic. It does cost money to have the latest of technology in our schools. But can we afford to be without it? Pupils today, in a few years, will be in the work place where the information age will even more be clearly defined as compared to today. Pupils of every race, creed, and religion must have the chances in an equitable manner to be able to use the latest in data securing sources. The upper income level pupils will have these opportunities of obtaining information through world wide web and internet in the home setting. Other pupils also should have equality of opportunity to use state-of-the art sources to obtain information.

Pertaining to the future of technology, Mehlinger (1996) wrote the following:

> Without going into detail regarding specific pieces of hardware, I can say with confidence that schools should expect more *integration. Interaction, and intelligence,* from future technology. In their early days in school, computers and video were regarded as separate entities, and it was assumed they would stay that way. In fact, we can expect a continuing ir tegration of these technologies. Voice, data, and images will be brought together into one package. One current example of this process is desktop video. In a single, relatively inexpensive unit, one has telephone (voice), computer (data storage and manipulation), and video (sending and receiving moving images) capabilities. Those who use the machine can talk to people at a distance, exchange documents, work collaboratively, and even see collaborators on the screen.

Technology will also become more interactive. In the field of distance learning, rather than strictly rely on one-way video and two-way communication, teachers and students will see another simultaneously, thereby making distance learning more like face-to-face classroom interaction. Computer based instruction will also be designed to respond to learners' interests and abilities, giving them greater control over what they need to learn and the pace at which they will learn it. And computer searches, which can be bewildering to the casual observer, will become easier and more responsive to what a user needs. Greater interactivity will make instructional programs even more powerful than they are today.

Finally, technology will have greater intelligence. This

intelligence will be displayed in several ways. First, the technology will have more features and greater capacity. Second, it will have the capability to learn from the user, so that it can customize its services to fit the user's learning style and interest. Future technology will provide not only data bases but knowledge bases. And technology will be able to stay abreast of that information most valued to the user and alert him or her to its availability.

Integration, interaction, and intelligence. These are three features we can expect of technology in the future. And they will change the way technology is employed in schools.

In Summary

From the psychology of learning, there are numerous criteria recommended for teaching pupils. These are that interest needs to be developed within pupils for learning, purpose should be there on the learner's part to achieve, meaning should be inherent in ongoing lessons and units of study, relationship of knowledge is salient in the instructional arena, individual differences among pupils need to be provided for, and good attitudes need adequate emphasis.

Four philosophies of education were discussed and need to be appraised so that the best one(s) are used to meet individual pupil learning styles. These philosophies are experimentalism with its stress upon pupil problem solving; idealism with its emphasis upon an idea centered curriculum advocating learner's achieving abstract subject matter, existentialism with values placed upon the individual pupil selecting, from among alternatives, learning opportunities to pursue; and realism with its stress upon pupils achieving measurable stated objectives.

The future seemingly looks bright for use of technology in the classroom. The use of world wide web and internet, e-mail, faxing, and the electronic bulletin board, among others, will guide pupils to attain vital objectives of instruction. Desktop videos, as a truly modern device in technology, integrate voice, sound, and the pictorial.

Selected References

Bigge, Morris L. (1982). *Educational Philosophies for Teachers.* Columbus, Ohio: Charles E. Merrill Publishing Company, pp. 25 and 26.

Choice or Chance (1984). Chicago, Illinois: Rand Mc NEA and company.

Ediger, Marlow (1995). *Philosophy in Curriculum Development.* Kirksville, Missouri: Simpson Publishing Company, pp. 86-87.

Ediger, Marlow (1986). *Social Studies Curriculum in the Elementary School.* Third Edition. Kirksville, Missouri, p. 241.

Eichelberger, Tony R. (1989). *Disciplined Inquiry: Understanding and Doing Educational Research.* White Plains, New York: Longman, Inc., p. 11.

Hoffman, Bob (1996). "School Technology Integration: An Automated Needs Assessment and Planning Tool," in *Technology and Teacher Education Annual,* edited by Robin, Price, Willis, and Willis, Charlottesville, Virginia: Association for the Advancement of Computing in Education.

Maskin, Melvin (1996). "Infotectives on the Infobahn: Designing Internet-Aided Projects for the Social Studies Classroom, *National Association of Secondary School Principal's Bulletin,* Vol. 80, No, 582, pp. 59-69.

Mehlinger, Howard D. (1996). "School Reform in the Information Age," *Phi Delta Kaplan.* Vol. 77, No. 6, pp. 405-406.

Morris, Van Cleve and Young Pai (1976). *Philosophy and the American School.:* Houghton Mifflin Company. p. 378.

Ozman, Howard, and Samuel Craver (1990). *Philosophical Foundations and Education,* Fourth Edition. Columbus, Ohio: Merrill Publishing Company, p. 249.

Ritchie, Donn (1996). "The Administrative Role in Integration of Technology," *Bulletin of the National Association of Secondary School Principals,* Vol. 80, No. 582, p. 43

Rose, Stephen A., and Phyllis Maxey Fernlund (1997), "Using Technology for Powerful Social Studies Learning, *Social Education,* Vol. 61, pp. 161-162.

Wild, John (1995). *Modern Philosophies of Education.* Chicago, Illinois: The National Society for the Study of Education, p. 31.

10

Gifted Students in Mathematics

Gifted students in mathematics need to have a curriculum which provides for their unique developmental needs. These learners must not experience the same subject matter as is true of average achievers and slow learners. Gifted students being members of a team in cooperative learning may lack challenge and motivation. With cooperative learning, heterogeneous grouping is in evidence and can well include the gifted. Situations such as these indicate the gifted are there to assist students of lesser attainment largely. No doubt, selected opportunities should be given to the gifted to work with average and slow students. However, as a whole, gifted students need to experience their very own scope and sequence in mathematics. Individual upper limits of achievement of the gifted need to be stressed and encouraged by teachers, supervisors, and administrators.

The Gifted Mathematics Curriculum

Each gifted student needs to achieve optimally in mathematics. A carefully designed curriculum must be in evidence. Each objective chosen for learner attainment must be relevant. Thus, objectives need to reflect those experiences that emphasize critical thinking. Here, the student learns to analyze what is useful and not useful in problem solving. Life-like problems require that students break down subject matter into component parts in order to separate what is vital to solve the problem as compared to that which is more trivial. Analysis involves thinking critically. If students are to solve word problems from a basal mathematics textbook, the salient from the non-salient needs to be analyzed so that solutions are in the offing. The mathematics curriculum then must emphasize critical thinking as a major objective.

Creative thought is a significant goal to stress in ongoing units of study. Not always do tried and true methods of dealing with problems work. Thus, life demands that individuals become creative beings. New solutions are necessary to solve problems. Novelty is involved as well as originality. Mathematics teachers need to encourage new, novel, and original means of solving problems. Creative learners perceive gaps in knowledge. They like to use their very own methodology in mathematics to close these gaps or perceived loop-hooles in problem solving. Numerous approaches may be used in solving problems. Learners individually must determine which methods of problem solving meet personal needs best. Brain teaser problems should be a part of the mathematics curriculum for the gifted. The teacher is a guide and stimulator, not a dispenser of information.

Gifted students should be involved in determining what is to be learned in the curriculum. These learners tend to be challenged where an open-ended approach is in evidence in teaching-earning situations. Ongoing lessons and units may then stress the contract system of instruction. With the contract system, the learner is heavily involved in determining what to learn (the objectives) . Through teacher-student planning, the latter assists in selecting that which should go into the contract for completion. The due date and signatures of both student and teacher appear on the contract. A learner being highly motivated may suggest a very challenging contract to complete.. Thus, the involved student may put into the contract that which emphasizes higher cognitive objectives in the mathematics curriculum. Humanism as a psychology of instruction emphasizes that the learner select and choose what is to be learned within a framework of a quality mathematics curriculum. The teacher here assises and encourages, but does not lecture to students. The mathematics teacher then encourages, helps, and assists each learner to attain optimally. Humanists would also stress that stations of learning be planned and implemented in mathematics. The teacher plans each station.

Students may also be involved in planning what is to acquired at each station. For gifted learners, each station must have tasks for students to complete that guide in attaining as much as possible. Generally five tasks are listed on a task card. Gifted may choose which station to work at as well as which tasks to complete. The student selects the sequence of activities to encounter at the diverse stations. Sequence here resides within the learner. If selected tasks do not meet the needs of learners, they may plan with the teacher of gifted mathematics students other learning opportunities. Student involvement in determining scope and sequence in mathematics emphasizes learners enjoying and appreciating this curriculum area. Quality attitudes guide students to achieve more optimally. Tasks that lack perceived relevance may be omitted by the student.

Teachers advocating behaviorism as a psychology of education may wish to write precise objectives which implement measurement driven instruction (MDI) in teaching and learning situations. With MDI the mathematics teacher writes precise objectives for students to achieve sequentially. These objectives need to be on the attainment level of gifted students which guide each to learn as much as possible. The teacher may announce prior to instruction what the gifted are to learn as a result of participating in carefully chosen activities and experiences. Students then understand what is to be learned as a result of instruction. The teacher with MDI is ends orientated in that he/she teaches so that students may achieve the objectives stated in measurable terms. With precise objectives, no guesswork is involved when determining if a student has/has not attained a specific objective. The mathematics teacher can test students to ascertain if goal attainment is in evidence. If not, a different teaching strategy may be needed. A logical curriculum results when teachers order objectives for students to attain sequentially.

Computer programs have much to offer gifted learners in terms of a challenging mathematics curriculum. To stress worthwhile goals, the teacher may choose tutorial software which emphasizes where each gifted student is presently and then assists him/her to make continuous progress. Also, simulated materials have much to offer in software use. Simulation advocates an attempt to have students solve life-like problems in mathematics. Reality and realness are key concepts emphasized in quality simulated programs. A third kind of software program for gifted learners in goal attainment is the use of games. Games played by the gifted tend to possess intrinsic interest. Programs selected here should have definite educational values and assist learners to attain challenging goals in ongoing units of study.

Wholesome competition among learners is necessary when games are played in computer learning. It is always worthwhile to stress attitudinal objectives in the mathematics curriculum whereby the gifted student develops respect and acceptance of other people. Being able to work well with others is so necessary in school and in society. Another goal to emphasize in mathematics is to have learners appreciate and enjoy mathematics. Mathematics may be appreciated for its own worth as well as for its utilitarian values. The desire to learn, grow, and achieve are intrinsic values to the gifted and aid in attaining optimally.

Project methods of teaching mathematics tend to stress utilitarian objectives in the curriculum. Gifted students then apply what has been acquired previously in a new, practical situation. These learners then may be involved in determining the cost of putting in a new carpet or tile in school when the need to do so is reality. Comparing costs and quality becomes a part of installing the carpet or the tiles. With project methods, the student has a goal in mind (carpet and tile installation in school), plans to achieve the goal (how the work is to be done in selecting a carpet or tile), works in the direction of completing the task (shopping and comparing prices as well as the quality of the merchandise), and appraises what has been done in the finality of the activity (quality criteria need to be developed and used in the evaluation process). The mathematics teacher becomes a helper and consultant when project means of instruction are used. Gifted students must experience the practical as well as the theoretical in mathematics.

The mathematics laboratory has excellent strategy and goals to emphasize in mathematics. Here, a hands–on procedure of instruction is in evidence. Concrete materials must be located at a center for learner use. Gifted students then largely determine how to use the materials such as meter sticks, centimetre tapes, liter containers, metric scales, and teaching aids containing bases other than base ten. Thus students may estimate the length of the classroom, which is recorded, and compare it with the real length through actual measurement.

Gifted learners must experience a mathematics curriculum which contains vital content, is useful in the societal arena, stresses higher levels of cognition such as critical and creative thinking within the framework of problem solving, and guides in developing quality attitudes.

Learning Opportunities for Gifted Students

Activities and experiences to attain objectives should capture learner interests and thus develop motivated gifted students in mathematics units and lessons of study. Mathematics textbooks have previously provided much subject matter as learning opportunities to guide optimal student attainment. Gifted students should be protested on each unit in the textbook to determine a suitable starting place. These learners must begin where adequate background information is in the repertoire and yet challenge is inherent. The gifted learner must feel that the content to begin with in the basal mathematics has opportunities for acquiring new subject matter and yet is not overwhelming. New content to be acquired is sequential and meaningful. Zest for learning by the gifted student is in evidence. Achieving in mathematics is viewed as an opportunity to grow, develop, and attain. The gifted should perceive the mathematics curriculum as presenting opportunities in life rather than the routine and the limited. Opportunities to learn possess endless possibilities. The sky is the limit for learner achievement.

A second possible learning opportunity for gifted students stresses the teacher choosing activities and experiences based on behaviorally stated objectives developed by the local school district or the state level. Each learning opportunity must align with the specific measurably stated objective. With behaviorally stated objectives in evidence, the mathematics teacher may select those activities which match up with and are valid for each specific end. The precise objectives provide guidance to the teacher in choosing those experiences which harmonize with each objective.

Subject matter in the basal textbook may have some of the content; however additional sources will need to be used including the teacher's very own ideas to implement in teaching-learning situations.

Third, units of instruction may be developed by the teacher. To write a challenging mathematics curriculum, the teacher of the gifted must be creative and originality needs to prevail to truly develop an exciting, relevant unit of study. Too frequently, the teacher has not leaned upon the self to come up with learning opportunities for the gifted that guide each to attain optimally. A competent, responsible mathematics teacher needs to use his/her talents to develop the best curriculum possible.

Fourth, students may bring empty cereal boxes, soap wrappers, and other containers such as empty fruit and vegetable cans to determine unit prices for such brand of cereal, soap, fruit and vegetable. Here, learners need to concentrate on the useful the utilitarian and the functional. Gifted students are consumers of goods and services presently as well as in the future.

Fifth, gifted learners need ample opportunities to develop positive attitudes in mathematics. Quality attitudes should be achieved by students in each lesson and unit of study. There are excellent trade books from which learners may select to enjoy content on mathematics. These books should stress diversity of topics including the history of mathematics, development of the metric system, The Egyptian system of numeration, the Roman numeration system, base five and twelve, and futurism in mathematics. Trade books tend to fascinate gifted students. The books may be housed at a center; the teacher periodically needs to introduce selected books to students. Learners may volunteer to share content read with others in the classroom setting.

Sixth, students should have ample opportunities to work at computer terminals. Selected programs should emphasize students attaining definite objectives in mathematics units of study. Other programs chosen by the learner should stress appreciation and enjoyment. Learners must have chances to explore, discover, and use computers in creative ways, including the writing of programs. Gifted students should feel the endless opportunities for growth and achievement in computer use.

Seventh, at selected intervals gifted students should write their very own word or story problems. The written products must be edited for clarity, feasibility, and rationality. The paper containing the problems may be exchanged with other learners to complete. The responder to the problems should write comments on the paper if vagueness in the problems is in evidence. He/she may also indicate how the written product may be improved upon. Creativity is a vital element in writing word or story problems for others to complete. Further creative written products of the gifted should include diverse forms of poetry such as diametres, quatrains, septolets, limericks, free verse, haiku, and tanka. Mathematics content contained in poetry moves in the direction of stressing the integrated curriculum. Gifted learners for enrichment activities should be challenged to write folk-lore based upon subject matter acquired in ongoing units of study in mathematics. Thus tall tales, fairy tales, myths, legends, among others, may be written by gifted students. Learners here may wish to collaborate on writing poetry and/or folk-lore.

Students may wish to use selected content learned through pantomime. With pantomime, no spoken words are emphasized by those participating. Creative dramatics involving subject matter acquired may be emphasized as a learning opportunity. With creative dramatics, the parts for each participant are not written down, but recalling subject matter as the need arises is important in these drama situations. Formal dramatics are also stimulating to use for gifted learners. Here, the parts for each to dramatize are written down. Much planning is involved in doing a pantomime, creative dramatics presentation, and/or formal drama. Cooperation is a key element in planning. All need to participate and no one dominate the planning session. Respect for the thinking of others is vital. Accepting each other's ideas within the planning and implementing sessions is important.

A variety of material in instruction should be used in the mathematics curriculum. Video-tapes, CD ROMs, slides, cassettes, filmstrips, illustrations, study prints, video-disks, single concept film loops, and the internet should be added to the use of materials which may provide learning opportunities for gifted students. Students individually should attain as much as possible.

Evaluation at Achievement

Different means need to be used to determine gifted student progress in mathematics. Methods to appraise should be valid and reliable. Criterion referenced tests harmonize with MDI procedures of instruction. Norm referenced tests may be used when comparing one's own students with those of a pilot study in which the test was standardized. Teacher observation of learner attitudes, interests, and love for mathematics in its diverse manifestations should be assessed continuously. Quality criteria must be used by the teacher when observing gifted student progress. The ultimate objective in teaching mathematics is to assist each gifted student to achieve as much as possible.

11

Vital Issues in Teaching Mathematics

Mathematics teachers need to be well versed in issues involved in teaching-learning situations. Issues must be resolved if possible. If this is not possible, then diverse procedures should be used to assist students to attain as optimally as possible. A quality library should be available in the school setting to guide mathematics teachers in reading content emphasizing the improvement of the curriculum. Teachers need to be encouraged to read journal articles and teacher education textbooks which stress restructuring the mathematics curriculum. Attending professional meetings pertaining to the teaching of mathematics is a must. It is important for teachers to share their ideas obtained with others in the school setting. Which issues then are salient for mathematics teachers to be knowledgeable about?

Relevant Issues

Should teachers focus on teaching for outcomes or should processes receive major stress? Most states emphasize a strong outcomes based mathematics curriculum. The outcomes are written within the behaviorally stated objectives, also called measurably stated objectives. Each objective is precise and leaves little or no leeway for interpretation in terms of what is to be taught. Learning opportunities are selected by the teacher and implemented so that learners attain each sequential objective. The teacher may then evaluate if pupils individually have been successful in goal attainment. If the pupil has achieved the outcome, the teacher has taught well and the learner has been successful in goal attainment.

Toward the other end of the continuum, selected educators advocate that process objectives should receive major stress in mathematics. Process objectives are difficult to write in measurable terms. It is complex to write process goals which measure sequential progress. Generally, general objectives are written as process ends for student attainment. Process objectives emphasize that students sequence the order of content acquired. For example in using a problem solving strategy of instruction, students with teacher guidance identify a problem within a life-like situation. Students then brainstorm hypotheses of answers to the proposed problem. Generating ideas in a brainstorming session can be time consuming, but is worthwhile since it tends to move toward higher levels of cognition. After the first four or five hypotheses have been given, it becomes increasingly difficult to think of additional, new responses. Each hypothesis must be tested to see if it can be substantiated. Screening of untenable hypotheses will soon become an observable fact. Testing each hypothesis then is an important part of problem solving. As a result, a hypothesis is accepted, refuted, or modified. Flexible steps of problem solving represent not ends in and of themselves, but rather a process to use in operating upon subject matter. The involved subject matter is mathematics and its societal use.

Inductive versus Deductive Methods of Teaching

Inductive methods of instruction emphasize that students learn by discovery. A minimal amount of teacher lecture and explanations are involved here. The mathematics teacher, as well as leaners themselves, must be good askers of questions to guide learners to find out on their own in the curriculum. Students need to be stimulated to learn using a variety of activities including concrete, semiconcrete, as well as abstract materials. When learners respond to questions, they need to be guided by the teacher to ultimately formulate a generalization or conclusion. It takes time to use an inductive procedure in teaching. The teacher must not be in a hurry to assist students in inductive learning. Rather, the mathematics teacher supervises learners to stay on task in responding to questions and securing necessary information. Depth understanding of mathematics subject matter is salient. From the specific to the general is a key concept to use in stressing inductive learning on the part of students.

With deductive methods of teaching the teacher clearly and concisely explains content meaningfully to students. The teacher continually observes learners to notice if they have questions or comments. Subject matter not understood needs to be clarified. A variety of activities should be used in teaching deductively, as was true of inductive procedures. Teaching aids and needed materials must always be used to stress meaning theory in mathematics. Learers should understand what is taught so that retention is increased. When students tend to forget quickly that which has been learned, the tendency might have been that learners attempted to memorize what was taught rather than attach meaning to salient facts, concepts, and generalizations. Teachers stressing deductive teaching must provide opportunities to students to use what has been learned and demonstrate that acquisition of subject matter is definitely in evidence. There needs to be evidence that students individually achieved and attained with deduction as a methodology of instruction.

Homogeneous versus Heterogeneous Grouping

Advocates of heterogeneous grouping of students for instruction believe that mixed achievement levels of learners should be in one classroom. With heterogeneous grouping, students are able to learn from those who attain at a lower and higher level of achievement. Elitism is then minimized among students within a classroom. Equality of individuals is a major objective in a democracy. Mathematics teachers need to provide for individual differences in achievement among learners in heterogeneous grouping.

Homogeneous grouping advocates also are numerous. They stress that a set of students in the classroom should be as uniform as possible in achievement in the classroom setting. The teacher can provide better for individual differences when uniformity of mathematics achievement is in evidence among students in a classroom, according to advocates. The chances are that all students can be reached in instruction when uniformity in student attainment prevails in the learning environment. The gap in achievement is then greatly minimized and the teacher can focus more on mathematics instruction for a somewhat uniform group instead of teaching a wide range of student attainment in the classroom arena.

Cooperative Learning versus Individual Endeavors

Cooperative learning emphasizes students working within a committee in ongoing lessons and units of study. Three to four learners may then pursue learning opportunities within a lesson to its completion. Sharing of ideas and techniques could aid in social development but more so in the intellectual dimension, according to advocates of cooperative learning. Students participating in cooperative learning would be of mixed achievement levels within a committee. They would learn from each other and use talents as each student's abilities permit. The person with the most abilities would need to assist the others on the committee or team. Team efforts rather than individual attempts would be in the offing. Harmonizing the work of team members becomes a major goal of instruction. Team members need to attain optimally.

Toward the other end of the continuum, each student would attain as much as possible on an individual basis. For example, if instructional management systems (IMS) are used, students individually achieve sequential behaviorally stated objectives at their own optimal rates of attainment. Individually, the learner is to achieve as much as possible in ongoing units of study in mathematics. If basals are used in mathematics, the teacher would guide students to achieve as much as individual abilities permit within the framework of the basal mathematics textbook. The same could be said of any other material of instruction used in mathematics.

State Mandated Objectives versus Local Decision Making

Numerous states have mandated specific objectives that students are to achieve. These precise objectives have been developed on the state level and are available for local teachers to implement in teaching- learning situations. The state mandated objectives generally are required to be implemented by different school districts within the prescribed state. A few exceptions may be made if a school district has an outstanding perceived plan of instruction which is deemed to be highly innovative. State mandated objectives reflect a hierarchically arranged method of implementing instruction. Those who wrote the objectives are rather far removed from where they will be implemented in instruction. Teachers on the local level are held accountable for student achievement in goal attainment. Criterion referenced tests (CRTs) are developed on the state level and given in the individual schools to notice student achievement. Newspaper reports publish how well the local school district did as far as student results on the state mandated tests are concerned. CRTs are supposed to be valid in that they measure student learning in terms of stated mandated objectives.

Somewhat opposite of state mandated approaches of determining objectives emphasizes the mathematics teacher in the classroom determining what the objectives of instruction should be. The capable classroom teacher with much knowledge about each student to use in planning objectives, learning opportunities, and appraisal procedures should be able to do a professional job of developing the mathematics curriculum. Individual differences in achievement must be considered to guide optimal individual progress. A well trained, educated mathematics teacher can do much to assist each student to learn as much as possible in mathematics.

Evaluation of Achievement

Criterion referenced tests, discussed previously, are one approach that presently is enjoying considerable popularity. Standardized, norm referenced tests (NRTs) continue to be favorably received in many states. These tests are criticized for not having the highest validity in measuring student progress. Thus the NRTs do not have related objectives for teachers to follow in teaching- learning situations. However, standardized tests do permit local comparisons of student progress in mathematics with that of the norm group upon which the test is based. Teacher written tests can also be used to determine student progress.

Toward the other end of the continuum, student achievement in mathematics may be revealed through a portfolio approach. Within a portfolio, the learner shows tests results, snapshots, cassette recordings, daily work, among other data, to show achievement in mathematics. The portfolio is broader in scope than test results only to show progress in mathematics. Items contained in a portfolio should show student progress that is representative of the involved student. More time is needed by the examiner to review what is in a portfolio as compared to looking at numerical results obtained from test results only. A more comprehensive system of evaluation is in evidence when evaluating a portfolio as compared to viewing test scores solely. The following issues have been discussed;

1. outcomes or products versus processes stressed in teaching learning situations.
2. inductive versus deductive methods of instruction.
3. homogeneous versus heterogeneous means of grouping students in the classroom.
4. cooperative learning versus individual endeavors.
5. state mandated objectives versus local decision making of the mathematics curriculum.
6. test results versus portfolios to show student progress to others. Whichever point of view is emphasized in the mathematics curriculum, the focal emphasis should be upon assisting students to attain optimally.

12

Content in the Mathematics Curriculum

Debate has always been in evidence as to what should be taught in mathematics. Content taught should be relevant. Thus pupils should learn what is significant. Useless, inert subject matter has no value for learners in the mathematics curriculum. Rather, pupils should achieve that which has use and is achievable. There is much that pupils need to learn in mathematics. The teacher then must carefully evaluate which objectives learners must attain.

Using the Textbook

Mathematics textbooks and their use in the curriculum has a long history. Warren Colburn, author of "First Lessons in Arithmetic on the Plan of Pestalozzi" published in 1821, was a very reputable writer for his day. He stressed pupils using objects in teaching-learning situations. Thus role learning was emphasized; learners used markers (objects) when performing the basic operations of addition, subtraction, multiplication and division. Pupils then should understand what had been learned. Warren Colburn's text was a huge success in that it was used as a basal for more than a half century.

The popularity of using a single or multiple series mathematics textbook has continued since Colburn's time. There are definite reasons why this happens to be the case. Scope or what is to be taught is contained in the text that the teacher follows in teaching-learning situations. Sequence in content to be learned has also been determined by the textbook writers. A considerable amount of faith in reputable textbooks is in evidence. The mathematics curriculum has then been planned for the teacher. Truly, it would be much work if the teacher would start from scratch in developing a mathematics curriculum on his/her own. Time would need to be spent to choose what is vital for pupils to learn. Sequence in learning is salient. If content is not sequential to the learner, the content may be too easy making for boredom and a lack of challenge. If the subject matter is too complex, Pupils may tend to fail and believe they cannot understand the content being taught by the teacher. In using basal textbooks in teaching mathematics, the teacher must

1. assist each pupil to understand and attach meaning to ongoing activities.
2. attempt to secure the attention and interests of each learner.
3. guide pupils to perceive value in the objectives being stressed in teaching-learning situations.
4. diagnose and remedy where pupils do not progress continually.
5. adjust the curriculum to the present achievement level of the learner.

Supplementing the Textbook

Mathematics teachers using the basal as a framework for the curriculum may supplement instruction by developing worksheets and teaching aids. These supplementary materials may be used by the teacher to assist pupils in filling gaps in sequence where the adopted mathematics series has not been adequate. Thus a worksheet exercise may be completed by learners when more practice is needed on a new operation or process that has been taught. A teaching aid can be used to assist pupils to perceive subject mater taught in a more meaningful way. Audio-visual aids such as video tapes and video disks may be used by the teacher to remedy that which was diagnosed as causing a problem in learning. Computer programs in drill and practice, tutorial, games, and simulations guide learners to achieve in a more optimal manner. These programs relate directly to ongoing lessons and units in the mathematics curriculum. Learning opportunities should guide pupils to experience mathematics as being comprehensible and having reasons for learner participation. Improper sequences in the textbook require additional activities that supplement and enrich. Pupils need to be successful learners in ongoing units and lessons in the mathematics curriculum.

Utilitarian Mathematics

Pupils tend to like what is useful and has value in everyday situations in life. A practical curriculum is then in the offing. What is learned in school can then be used in society. In 1922, Guy Wilson came out with a series of textbooks in mathematics that stressed the utilitarian only. Pupils would then learn to determine the price of selected items purchased from a grocery store or how much a given quantity of coal would cost for heating a house. Mathematics content learned for its own sake was not emphasized. Nor was drill and practice stressed unless learners would be helped to solve textbook problems.

Utilitarian problems within a textbook framework soon become outdated due to prices of items changing in value in just a few weeks or even days. Then too society changes rather rapidly in that an item such as coal may become outdated in heating a house.

John Dewey (1859-1952) stressed a curriculum of problem solving. These problems needed to be real and life-like. Dewey's philosophy stressed that pupils with teacher guidance identified problems that were perceived as having utilitarian values. Useful problems were those that contained content applicable in the societal arena. School and society were not to be separated but be integrated entities. Mathematics taught and learned in school, then, must have utilitarian values in the real world. Problems chosen for solution need to relate those experienced by learners. Once problems have been chosen, a hypothesis or answer is developed. The hypothesis is tentative and subject to testing. Testing the hypothesis is done in a life-like situation. The hypothesis is subject to change and modification if needed. A variety of reference sources are used to test each hypothesis. These reference sources include realistic situations, reading, and non-reading sources.

Problem solving in mathematics is useful presently and in the future for the learner. It also cuts across different curriculum areas and boundaries. An integrated curriculum may then be in the offing. With reality being stressed in mathematics, the pupil is an active participant in society and does not have to wait until adulthood to be involved in problem solving. Interest in the problem, since it was identified with active pupil involvement, makes for effort in learning. Interest and effort become one and not separate entities. Purpose is inherent in the mathematics curriculum due to learners being heavily involved in selection of problem areas. Thus, problem solving is quite different from "word problems" contained in textbooks. The latter contains situations written by textbook writers who imagine the real and the life-like in devising and writing, but they are not problematic situations faced by pupils. A problem solving mathematics curriculum stresses continual change since pupils differ from each other in time and place as to what is salient and personal to the life of the learner.

The teacher in problem solving approaches in teaching must be flexible in thinking and support learner involvement in the mathematics curriculum. The teacher becomes a guide, resource person, motivator, and helper. The teacher is not a lecturer nor a dispenser of information. The role of the teacher becomes one of emphasizing the real, the concrete, and actual experiences in society.

Developing Appreciations in Mathematics

Quality attitudes need to be achieved by learners in mathematics. Positive feelings, values, and beliefs pertaining to this curriculum area are vital. Learner's lack of attainment in many cases is due to faulty attitudes toward mathematics.

Mathematics can be valued for its own sake. Throughout the centuries, there have been educators who have argued knowledge being important for its own intrinsic worth. One early philosopher who believed in achieving knowledge for its own sake was Aristotle (364- 322 B.C.) in ancient Athens. As pupils progress through the formal years of schooling, good teachers have always stressed the importance of positive learner affect toward mathematics. Ultimately, pupils perceive the intrinsic values of studying mathematics. Thus mathematics has patterns that are regular such as the ten digits needed to show any amount numerically in base ten system of numeration. Five digits show any value or amount in base five (0, 1, 2, 3, and 4), twelve in base twelve, and two in base two, among other bases. Structural ideas also show its regularity such as the commutative property of addition and multiplication, the associative property of addition and multiplication, the distributive property of multiplication over addition, the property of closure of addition and multiplication, the inverse operations of addition and subtraction as well as the inverse operations of multiplication and division. Mathematics has its structure and order. Learners also need to develop quality attitudes toward harmony and beauty in mathematics. The latter is especially noticed in geometrical designs that learners construct and notice in the world of aesthetics.

Too frequently, pupils are left out completely in helping to determine objectives, learning activities, and appraisal procedures in mathematics. Certainly, there is room for pupils' involvement here. Input from learners assists the pupil to perceive purpose or reasons for learning. If learners do not perceive purpose for learning, achievement no doubt will go downhill. Thus at intervals, pupils should assist the teacher in choosing topics or areas of personal interest in mathematics. A major goal here is to guide learners to achieve positive attitudes toward mathematics with its order, beauty, and self fulfilment.

National Goals in Mathematics

There are numerous national study and professional groups that have studied long and hard that which should be emphasized in mathematics. Thus the National Council Teachers of Mathematics (NCTM) in 1989 developed standards for implementation in public school mathematics. These standards when achieved by learners should assist pupils to be knowledgeable, have appropriate skills, and to use mathematics in everyday functional situations.

America 2000 represents a national attempt in improving the curriculum. Goals in America 2000 were established by the National Governor's Conference in 1989 by selecting six broad objectives for students to attain. One of the six emphasized US pupils being first in mathematics and science on international tests by the year 2000. Selected states have established specific objectives pertaining to each broad goal. Means of measuring achievement on these specific objectives is also important. Having national study groups attempt to upgrade the mathematics curriculum is not new. One of the writers is very familiar with the modern school mathematics movement of the later 1950's an extending into the 1970's. During that time the National Defense Educational Act (NDEA) of 1958 furnished funds to national study groups to devise a new program of mathematics for public school pupils. Sputnik had been sent up as the first satellite in 1957 by any nation, and this nation was the USSR. With fear and competition between the US and the USSR, the former felt threatened and challenged to send up a satellite also. Much criticism was leveled against the public schools and their perceived weak curriculum areas of mathematics and science. Many articles in educational journals and in news reports stressed how the schools in Russia were much superior in mathematics and science compared to those in the US. The NDEA then provided federal funds to schools on a matching basis to purchase materials of instruction to improve mathematics and science teaching. Leading national study groups, federally funded, came out with a new mathematics curriculum. Among these national groups were the School Mathematics Study Group, the Greater Cleveland Mathematics Project, the Illinois Mathematics Study Group, among others. The findings and recommendations of these study groups were incorporated into leading basal mathematics textbooks. Mathematics teachers received stipends to attend seminars, courses, workshops, and lectures on improving the content and methodology of instruction. There was even a stipend for family members who went along with the parent teacher for the summer months of on campus instruction on the university level.

The new NCTM standards have much to recommend themselves as do the goals of America 2000. Hopefully pupils will achieve sequentially and optimally.

In Conclusion

There are many recommendations, approaches, ideas, and philosophies available to teachers to guide pupil achievement in mathematics. Teachers need to assist each pupil to achieve sequentially and make continuous progress. Motivated learners who perceive reasons for learning can achieve more optimally.

13

Learning Activities and Teaching Methods in Mathematics

Pupils need to experience mathematics in an interesting way. The teacher must choose worthwhile objectives for learners to achieve. Each objective should be selected with great care. Learning activities to achieve the objectives need to capture pupil purpose or reasons for learning. Evaluation techniques to determine pupil progress must be valid and reliable. These approaches to evaluate should ascertain if each pupil has attained the stated objectives.

Learning Activities to Achieve Objectives

The mathematics teacher needs to start with concrete materials in teaching- learning situations. Concrete materials are represented by such items as objects, realia, and things. Concrete materials may then stress a hands-on approach in learning. If early primary grade pupils are studying addition of a single digit plus a single digit addend (4+3), they may use four sticks and three sticks to be joined together to make a set of seven. The order of addends may also be changed to show that three sticks and four sticks joined together also make a set of seven. The commutative property of addition states that a+b=b+a. This property is highly valuable for pupils to understand and use since two addends of any value can be ordered in any direction and the answer will be the same in addition. As learners progress through continually higher levels of schooling, they can use the commutative property of addition. The commutative property also holds true for multiplication in that 4×3=3×4.

It is good to have pupils perceive quantity using diverse examples such as four pupils and three pupils in the classroom make a total of seven.

The semiconcrete facet of learning should follow sequentially from the concrete. In the previous example, if early primary grade pupils were studying the value of 4+3= , pictures may be shown of four dogs and three dogs joined together to show the concept of seven. Again, the commutative property may be shown with the illustrations in that the order of the addends could be changed to show that 3+4=7. Pictures/ illustrations should be changed to cats, boys, girls, toys, among others, so that learners truly understand that 4+3 and 3+4=7, and not that the four dogs and the three dogs alone make a sum of seven. The abstract can be printed next to the concrete and semiconcrete representations, i.e. 4+3 and 3+4= .

With the abstract phase of learning being the ultimate goal of instruction, the mathematics teacher may revert back to the concrete and the semiconcrete. Thus if pupils are to reveal that 4+3=7, they may show this understanding with checkers, chess pieces, and other materials. Meaningful learning must occur and become a part of the repertoire of the pupil.

In sequence, the pupil may understand the associative property of addition. The associative property states that a+b+c= c+b+a or any other arrangement of the addends. Three or more addends can be ordered in any direction and the sum will be the same. The associative property also holds true for multiplication.

With appropriate order, pupils may generalize that subtraction undoes addition. Thus if there are seven dogs and three run away, four will remain. Seven minus three equals four. Pupils should notice the number names such as "four", "three", and "seven" as readiness permits. Concrete and semiconcrete materials may be used in subtraction as was true in addition. Ultimately the abstract becomes salient such as 7 – 4 = 3. With practice on the concrete and somiconcrete materials, learners can become quite proficient in the use of the abstract. The abstract is used in society and is convenient to use as compared to continual referral to the concrete and semiconcrete. Early primary pupils should not be hurried in using the abstract, but should have quality, ample experiences with concrete and semiconcrete materials.

Methods of Teaching

The mathematics teacher must experiment with a variety of methods to understand which approach works best with individual pupils. Pupils differ from each other in so many different ways. Thus the learning style for one pupil may not be the same or similar as compared to another learner.

Many pupils like an inductive procedure. Here the teacher needs to be a good asker of questions. Responses come from pupils in answer to these questions. Practical questions may be asked of pupils such as the following :

1. How many pupils are in our classroom today?
2. How many are absent?
3. How many pupils are in each reading group? The assumption here is that pupils are in different reading groups for instructional purposes.

Questions may also be asked of pupils pertaining to the following contained in a lesson plan;

1. If I place three sticks next to the four sticks as you can see here, how many sticks do we then have all together?
2. Suppose I have these three sticks and join four sticks to this set, how many are there then?
3. If I take three sticks away from the seven sticks, how many are left?

If a pupil responds incorrectly, a tactful approach is to merely ask for another answer. Pupils should be permitted to hypothesize freely without restraints. Should the classroom become disruptive, the mathematics teacher may then call upon specific pupils for an answer. Learners may also raise their hands and be recognized by the teacher prior to giving an answer. It is important to praise pupils for answering correctly as well as for behaving in a positive manner.

It is always important to diagnose why a response is incorrect. Should a pupil say that five sticks remain when three sticks are taken away from the seven sticks, a pupil or the teacher should count in one-to-one correspondence the number or remaining sticks.

There are pupils who learn best with the use of a deductive procedure of teaching. With deduction, the teacher needs to explain clearly how to work correctly a given problem such as 4+3 =7. Within the explanation, the teacher, for example, shows pupils how 4+3=7 using concrete and semiconcrete materials. The explanations must be clear, concise, and meaningful. The teacher needs to observe that pupils are attentive and listening. After using explanations to present content clearly to pupils, the teacher needs to determine what each has learned. Many approaches can be used by pupils to reveal that which has been learned including showing with sticks a set of four and a set of three seeds. The two sets are joined together to show the sum. Pencils, erasers, and pieces of chalk may also be used to represent that which was explained by the teacher.

A third way to teach is to have pupils engage in problem solving. For example, the teacher may show seven cookies and have a pupil take three away. The problem is "How many are left?" Learners may speculate in this life-like situation on the number of cookies that are left over. With problem solving, social use is made of what is being learned. It is very important for pupils to see how one can use mathematics in the real world. Perhaps, this is the ultimate test of pupils being able to apply mathematics in a functional situation. Best it is if pupils are stimulated by the teacher to identify problems. Learners might then perceive purpose or reasons for learning. The number of cookies left in the above example can then be divided among pupils for each to eat.

Mathematics textbooks may have selected excellent addition and subtraction number pairs for pupils to work. Working at each of the number pair in addition and subtraction, pupils receive practice in what the teacher had presented in the classroom. Learners have a better chance to retain that which has been learned if meaningful practice is in evidence. Accompanying workbooks contain exercises which provide further practice to pupils. With the use of textbooks and workbooks, the teacher must follow the following guidelines;

1. Use a variety of materials of instruction beyond that of textbooks and workbooks since pupils possess diverse

learning styles.

2. Do not overemphasize drill and practice to the point where pupils lose interest in learning.
3. Make content meaningful so that pupils understand what has been learned.
4. Guide learners to perceive reasons for learning.
5. Provide for individual differences so that each pupil learns as much as possible.

Sequence in Learning

Mathematics teachers need to evaluate where each pupil is presently in achievement. It is important to find this starting point. Otherwise if content taught is too difficult, pupils cannot learn the new subject matter being emphasized. Content that is too easy promotes boredom on the part of pupils. Thus the teacher must attempt to teach that which is new to the learner and at the same time is challenging, not the trivial nor the routine. There are several approaches in sequencing learning opportunities for pupils.

First, a logical sequence may be implemented. With a logical sequence, the teacher writes measurably stated, also called behaviorally stated objectives, for pupil attainment. These objectives are highly precise and leave little or no leeway in interpretation as to what will be taught. Prior to implementation, the mathematics teacher may even announce to pupils what they are to learn from the lesson presentation. Pupils then have security as to what is to be learned. Guesswork here is eliminated. Teachers have developed a teaching strategy with appropriate learning opportunities so that each learner may attain the stated objectives. After instruction, the teacher appraises pupils to notice if objectives have been attained. Objectives not achieved need a differed teaching strategy. In a logically developed mathematics curriculum, the teacher selects and writes the objectives, chooses the learning opportunities, and uses quality evaluation procedures to ascertain pupil progress. Logically then the teacher arranges the order of objectives, activities and experiences, as well as appraisal procedures to the best possible to optimalize learner achievement. Advocates of a logical mathematics curriculum believe that properly educated mathematics teachers are in the best position to choose objectives, learning opportunities, and evaluation procedures due to training, education, and maturity.

A second procedure in sequencing activities is to use a psychological mathematics curriculum. Pupils themselves are heavily involved, in degrees, when choosing objectives, learning opportunities, and evaluation procedures. A learning stations approach may well be stressed here. The teacher sets up the learning stations with appropriate materials of instruction at each station. Again, the materials should consist of the concrete, somiconcrete, and the abstract. Approximately four or five tasks or learning opportunities should be listed on a card at each station. Pupils individually may then choose the order of tasks to be completed. There should be more tasks in total than any one child can complete so that choice is involved as to what to complete and what to omit. Time on task is very important for each pupil. The teacher assists pupils with questions and problems so that pupils individually might attain optimally. A psychological sequence stresses pupils individually being involved in choosing ordered tasks. Advocates of a psychological mathematics curriculum believe that sequence resides within the pupil, not within textbooks, work books, or predetermined measurably stated objectives for learner attainment.

The writer recommends the selection of an appropriate sequence, be it logical or psychological, which assists pupils to learn as much as possible on an individual basis. Mathematics teachers must provide for individual differences so that optimal attainment on the part of each learner is possible.

In Closing

Rather than stress one procedure only as compared to another in teaching mathematics, the teacher must always keep in mind to select the best methodology possible in teaching- learning situations. That best method should benefit each pupil to attain as much as is possible.

14

Sequence in Mathematics

A major task of the mathematics teacher is to provide quality sequence in the curriculum. Pupils need to experience sequential learnings or achievement will go downhill. Thus the teacher initially must determine where each pupil is attaining at the present time. Otherwise good sequence cannot be in the offing. If learning opportunities are too easy, pupils might experience boredom. Should the experiences be too complex, learners may well feel failure. In either case, a lower self concept could be an end-result.

Determining Present Achievement Levels

Where is each pupil achieving at the present time? This is a vital question for teachers to answer. A good mathematics teacher attempts to answer this question to the best of his/her abilities. A strategy must be in the offing to ascertain where each learner is at in mathematics achievement. There are numerous ways of determining this. One approach is to use the pre-test that accompanies the basal textbook series presently being used in mathematics. The manual section will state how many items or which per cent of the test items need correct responses for the learner to proceed with the sequential tasks in that ongoing unit of study. The pupil may even score high enough on the pre-test so that he/she skips that unit of study and goes on to the next sequential mathematics unit. Generally, an eighty per cent rate of correct responses is needed, as a minimum, in order for the pupil to test *out* of taking that unit of instruction. The mathematics teacher might wish to have learners score at a higher per cent in order to pass out of taking that unit of study. Mastery of content is important.

The teacher might wish to write his/her own pre-test to determine if a pupil is ready to begin a new unit of study in the basal mathematics textbook. He/she then determines which rate of correct responses are needed for a learner to pursue the related unit of study. If teachers write their own tests, they must be certain that the test is valid. To be valid in this case, a test must cover what will be taught in the new unit of study. Predictive validity is then necessary.

For a third procedure in determining readiness for studying a new unit in mathematics, the teacher could observe where learners are presently in achievement. Observational methods here stress using quality criteria and accurate observations made of each pupil's present attainment. Comments could be written down by the teacher pertaining to observations made. Comments made of each learner that are recorded should be dated. Comparisons may then be made of earlier as compared to later pupil performance. When making these comparisons, the teacher may appraise the quality of the sequence of instruction. If a learner is not making continuous optimal progress, the teacher must take careful notice of this situation. Learning opportunities need selection which guide pupils individually to attain as much as possible.

Fourth, behaviorally stated objectives may be written, prior to instruction. Careful deliberation must be in evidence for each objective so that worthwhile, vital objectives are chosen for learner attainment. All objectives are clearly stated and leave no leeway for interpretation. A pre-test may be written and administered to pupils based on these precise objectives. Results from the test will indicate the starting point for each learner in a new mathematics unit of study. Those goals already achieved from pre-test results can then be omitted from an individual pupil's curriculum. The reason for attempting to find an appropriate starting point is to have learners progress continuously from then on.

The writers have supervised student teachers (ST) in the public schools for approximately thirty years. A middle school ST developed learning stations for her classroom of pupils. Thirteen stations were developed for the twenty-six learners. At each station there were five tasks on a task card. Easier and more complex tasks existed at each station. Learners then individually could choose which sequential tasks to pursue and complete. The choices were up to the pupil. Thus the pupil chose the starting point of departure in a mathematics unit. Sequence resided within the learner. A psychological curriculum is in evidence when pupils sequence their very own learning opportunities. Humanism is then in evidence when pupils individually perceive order in activities and experiences. The learning stations philosophy worked out well in this situation for the ST. How responsible pupils will be when working independently at learning stations depends upon several factors. When learners want to choose their own activities and experiences, intrinsic motivation is in evidence, a desire for independence is wanted, and pupils enjoy making decisions. A psychological sequence will now be compared with a logical sequential mathematics curriculum.

Sequence in the Curriculum

Quality sequence or order of activities and experiences are needed after it has been determined where a pupil's starting point is. A logical curriculum may be stressed. With a logical curriculum, the learner experiences objectives to attain which are predetermined. Thus the teacher may select the sequential order of objectives for pupil attainment. He/she has determined which the best arrangement is for learners to attain the ordered goals. From the simple to the complex, emphasizing the teacher's own thinking, is the proper way for pupils individually to achieve the stated objectives. Each objective is written with precision so that no leeway exists in deciding upon what should be taught. Either the learner does/does not achieve the objectives as a result of instruction. Learning opportunities are chosen by the teacher to assist pupils to achieve each sequential objective. The sequence of learning opportunities is also determined by the mathematics teacher.

The teacher may develop the logical mathematics curriculum. However at the district level, an instructional management system (IMS) might be developed logically by teachers with supervisory and principal guidance. The state may also develop and mandate its logical mathematics curriculum. Pupils are to achieve each objective as sequenced by the teacher, district, or state. Criterion referenced tests (CRT's) are used here to measure pupil's progress. These tests are valid in that they measure against the stated objectives. If the CRTs measure each pupil's progress consistently, then reliability is in evidence be it split-half, test-re-test, and/or alternative forms.

Writers of mathematics textbooks also stress a logical curriculum. Thus the writers emphasize what pupils should learn first, second, and so on, in mathematics. The writers may have written tests that are valid and reliable to measure that which pupils have learned from working exercises in the textbook. The test results may pinpoint where a pupil needs more assistance to achieve well. If teachers use supplementary materials, they will be emphasized as the need arises within the framework of sequence in the basal textbook. Improved sequence may result when using the supplementary materials at specific points in teaching and learning to assist each learner to attain optimally. Thus the supplementary materials fill voids in sequential experiences in the textbook.

Teachers might set up learning centers in the classroom which contain tasks at each center to help motivated pupils achieve more optimally. To work at the centers may be voluntary. There are teachers that also require learners to pursue certain tasks at the center when having completed their regular assignments in mathematics. The tasks at the centers should possess interest, challenge, and fascination for pupils. Only then will learners desire to do extra work. The teacher may appraise learner attitudes when observing how many pupils do work at situations which are truly voluntary. When pupils select sequential tasks to complete, they order their very own experiences in a psychological sequence.

Learners need to experience a logical or psychological sequence which provides for individual differences. The sequence emphasized must help pupils individually to attain as much as possible. Adopted textbooks, supplementary materials of instruction, and learning centers, among other approaches, should be used to guide each pupil to understand, feel challenge, love mathematics, and become skillful in using subject matter effectively in school and in society.

15

Mathematics—Social Studies, Making the Connections

Much is written and spoken about the interdisciplinary curriculum. Thus educators are recommending that more and more subject matter from diverse academic disciplines be taught as being related, rather than as isolated entities. Toward the beginning of the twentieth century, pupils were taught in a manner whereby each academic discipline remained as being separate, not integrated. There were an increasing number of educators who recommended that content be correlated whereby two academic disciplines were taught in an integrated manner. Later, about the 1930's, more and more educators were recommending that borders and boundaries be minimized among different subject matter areas. John Dewey (1859-1952) was a strong exponent of problem solving in the curriculum. Here, pupils guided by the teacher would identify a problem, gather data or information in answer to the problem, develop a tentative answer to the problem, and test the answer in a life-like situation. Problem solving did not emphasize a specific subject matter area. Rather whatever was needed to solve that identified problem was used as information. John Dewey was a very early advocate of the interdisciplinary curriculum. Already in 1896, he established a laboratory school connected with the University of Chicago. Pupils in this school used problem solving procedures continuously as learning activities. The teacher assisted learners in problem solving. Teachers did not lecture to pupils nor did the latter sit at desks in a passive manner. Rather pupils were actively engaged in selecting and solving life-like problems. Dewey emphasized that problems be life-like and related to what exists in society.

Problem solving strategies are difficult to emphasize in teaching, but these approaches do stress an interdisciplinary curriculum. Whatever content is needed to solve problems is used, regardless of the academic discipline involved. What does a complete interdisciplinary curriculum do to scope and sequence in mathematics? Mathematics educators seem to have considerable agreement on what should be taught in the curriculum. Thus scope and sequence can be spelt out more clearly and with considerable agreement among educators as compared to the other academic areas taught in school. On the other hand, educational psychologists have long recommended that pupils perceive knowledge as being related, not as isolated entities. Thus if a pupil perceives the relationship of knowledge among diverse academic disciples, he/she might be able to recall content better due to one known idea being related to another idea, and so on. A learner perceiving knowledge as being isolated may not be able to think of related content in a lesson or unit of study. He/she perceives content in terms of isolated entities, unrelated to the larger whole.

Relating the Mathematics and the Social Studies Curriculum

We have supervised student teachers and regular teachers in the public schools for thirty years. These teachers have tended to work as a team. Many of the ideas we will be presenting here come from supervising teachers in the public schools. Teachers we have supervised have used slides and other visual aids to relate mathematics and the social studies. We will now explain a few examples of slide content to the world of mathematics.

1. The wall around old Jerusalem is two and one-half miles in length and is forty feet tall. Here, teachers have had pupils mention landmarks that are two and one-half miles from the local school building. Sometimes teachers have checked pupil reponses by driving to the landmark mentioned after school hours. Since the wall of Jerusalem is about forty feet high, comparisons are made with the height of the local school building. The height of the local school building is generally available in the principal's office.

Proportion has also been used to determine the height of the local school building such as noticing the length of its shadow and comparing it with the height of a stick and the length of its shadow.

2. A second slide shows the city of Jerusalem which has an elevation of 2,500 feet. Learners find out the elevation above see level locally. Comparisons are then made of the elevation of Jerusalem with the local area. Many times pupils have wanted to compare the degrees in latitude and longitude of Jerusalem with the local area.

A third slide shows the city of Jericho with its luscious fruits and vegetable crops grown. Pupils wonder why Jericho can grow an abundance of garden crops and yet be classified as a desert with less than eight inches of rain per year. Research is done by pupils with teacher guidance to notice that the rain has fallen in Jerusalem from the clouds by the time it reaches Jaicho. Jerusalem being 2,500 feet above sea level and Jericho being 800 feet below sea level, in a distance of eighteen miles, has the Judean hills in between. The winds blow westward from the Mediterranean Sea to Jerusalem and most of the rain is deposited near Jerusalem before reaching Jericho eighteen miles east. The moisture laden winds leave the Mediterranean Sea (at sea level) and rise to an elevation of 2,500 feet at Jerusalem. As the moisture laden winds rise, cooling occurs and rain falls. Cool air cannot hold moisture as well as does warm air. As the wind goes further to Jericho, there is very little moisture left in the winds that originated in the Mediterranean Sea.

Here, pupils have studied the affects of elevation and the amounts of rainfall in a given area of the world by discussing and solving problems such as the following:

1. How does elevation affect rainfall amounts in the Dead Sea area as compared to nearby Jericho?
2. Why are these two areas desert in nature with less than eight inches of rainfall per year?
3. How is irrigation water secured for making Jericho a beautiful garden spot?
4. What landmarks do you know that are eighteen miles apart, such as is the case of Jerusalem and Jericho? Estimation is involved in hypothesizing and each

hypothesis may be checked out if necessary.

There is much emphasis placed upon using arithmetic when solving these problem areas.

To bring it closer to home base, numerous pupils have been on Pike's Peak, just outside of Colorado Springs, Colorado. This peak is 14,500 feet in elevation above sea level. Learners have studied and solved problem areas such as the following pertaining to Pike's Peak:

1. How does the temperature reading on this peak compare to its base? Why does this occur?
2. What happens to animal life as the atitude increases when going upward to Pike's Peak on the cog railway or by hiking?

A fourth slide on the Middle East area of the world stresses the Crusaders capturing the Holy Land area, especially Jerusalem and Bethlehem. This occurred in 1099 AD during the First Crusade. Pupils are fascinated with determining how many years ago that was. There are other relevant dates that interested pupils in finding out the number of years that have since elapsed such as:

1. Constantine and his mother Queen Helena building the first Church of the Holy Sepulchre inside the walled city of Jerusalem in 330 AD.
2. Justinian the Great building the Church of the Nativity in Bethlehem in 529 AD, which still stands today.
3. The building of the present wall around Jerusalem in 1542 by the Ottoman Turkish Empire.

Pupils individually become fascinated in comparing their very own age with the number of years that have gone by since the inception of each of the above incidences.

A fifth slide shows gasoline prices as indicated by Israeli currency and the liter unit used to sell gasoline. Learners wrote story problems involving the purchase of a certain number of liters of gasoline purchased involving shekels, the currency used per liter purchased.

A sixth slide shows population of the following nations of the Middle East: Jordan, Egypt, Israel, Lebanon, Saudi Arabia, Iraq, and Iran. Here, pupils in committees developed a bar graph showing the population of each of these nations. Statistics can be taught at an early age and not at the graduate level of instruction only.

A seventh slide shows the capital city of each Middle East nation mentioned above with the related population. Respectively, these capital cities are Amman, Cairo, Jerusalem, Beirut, Riyad, Baghdad, and Teheran. Pupils used these data to make a line graph in comparing population figures of capital cities in the Middle East area of the world.

An eighth slide shows the number of people in the Middle East who belong to the following religious groups: Sunni Muslim, Shia Muslim, Judaism, Christianity, and Alawite Muslim. Learners in committees developed a circle graph showing the per cent of members in each group of the total number for the entire set of members. This activity is suitable for talented fifth and sixth graders as well as those who are highly motivated to learn in mathematics. All pupils should be challenged to achieve as much as possible in mathematics.

An eighth slide shows a map of the West Bank, Jordan, and Israel. Pupils were to ascertain the number of kilometres as well as miles between the following given cities:

a). Hebron and Jerusalem
b). Bethlehem and Nablus (ancient Samaria).
c). Beersheba and Nazareth.
d). Petra and Amman.
e). Tel Aviv and Eilat.

A ninth slide shows replicas of people, buildings, and religious symbols made of olive wood, mother of pearl, and different metals. Prices are given in shekels. Learners computed the price of each item in US currency.

A tenth slide contained the Mosque of Abraham in Hebron, the Church of the Holy Sepulchre, as well as the Western Wall of the ancient Jewish Temple in Jerusalem. Pupils were given the following dimensions:

1. An inch equals four feet. Each committee of pupils determined the length, width, and height of the Mosque of Abraham, using the actual size of the building on the slide.

2. A centimetre equals one metre. Pupils in cooperative

learning were to find out how long, how wide, and how high the Church of the Holy Sepulchre and the Western Wall are, using the size of the buildings/structures on the slide to obtain dimensions for the scale drawings.

For each of the tasks above, pupils felt motivated and encouraged to pursue and achieve. We did not see any wasting of time on the pupils' part. Pupil purpose appeared to run high in perceiving connections between mathematics and social studies.

Interest was also extremely high when pupils studied the ancient Egyptian system of numeration when studying Egypt in the Middle East. The Egyptian system emphasized the following:

1. A single tally mark or stroke for a value of "one". There could be as many as nine tally marks to show units or values of one each. For example, a value of two would have two tally marks, three would have three tally marks and so on.
2. For a value of ten, one arch, also called a hoof of a cow, would be drawn. Nine arches had a value of ninety.
3. A coil of rope had a value of 100. Thus two coils of rope equalled 200; three coils =300; and four coils of rope equalled 400, and so on. Ten coils of rope equals a lotus flower.
4. Each drawn lotus flower had a value of 1,000. Two lotus flowers had a value of 2,000 whereas three lotus flowers had a value of 3,000, and so on. Ten lotus flowers equal a bent finger.
5. Each drawn bent finger had a value of 10,000. For each 10,000 value, one bent finger was drawn. Ten bent fingers equal a tadpole.
6. Each tadpole had a value of 100,000; thus in showing a value of 700,000 seven tadpoles need to be drawn. Ten tadpoles equal an astonished man.
7. Each astonished man had a value of one million, the number of millions that needed to be shown on paper were the number of astonished men drawn.

Pupils enjoyed activities pertaining to the Egyptian system of numeration when provided with a certain number of drawings and then asked to provide the base ten equivalent. For example, a drawing consisting of two astonished men, six tadpoles, three bent fingers, five lotus flowers, one coded rope, eight arches, and four tally marks has what value in base ten? The answer is 2,635,184. Learners felt that much thinking went into the determinations of the value of the drawings when using the Egyptian system of numeration. Certainly, pupils need to be ready for activities such as the Egyptian system of numeration before being actively engaged in these kinds of experiences. If pupils are ready, they do appear to have much interest in other numeration systems than base ten.

The Roman system of numeration is more practical as compared to the Egyptian system in that the former is seen at selected places today. There are clocks, corner stone blocks in buildings, and wristwatches that contain the Roman system of numeration. Pupils read time in the school hallway, from a clock with Roman numerals. The local school building contained the date of the corner stone laying CMLXI or 1961. To be sure the Roman system as we know it has changed a little since the days of the Roman Empire, approximately 2,000 years ago. However, we recommend using the symbols as are commonly shown in society. We believe pupils appreciate base ten more so after studying a system which does not have the order or patterns that base ten has. Learners realize from a study of the Romans system of numeration that

1. it uses an additive system in writing values such as a value of three has 3 tally marks; 3 X's have a value of thirty with each X having a value of ten.
2. it has a subtraction system in writing numerals such as CM=900. The symbol "M" equals 1,000 and the smaller C value of 100 indicates subtracting the latter amount from 1,000.
3. there is no place value in the Roman system of numeration.
4. it is difficult or impossible to add, subtract, multiply, or divide, as is done in base ten, using the Roman system.

Pupils should be challenged to make as many discoveries as possible involving different systems of numeration.

In Closing

It is possible to have pupils relate mathematics to social studies. Pupils might well be encouraged to achieve objectives in mathematics when perceiving that it is related to social studies.

We believe strongly that interest in learning is a powerful factor in learning in mathematics. Thus the attention of pupils needs to be secured in order for learning to take place. Teachers need to choose those learning opportunities which will guide learners to perceive knowledge as being related. Learners need to apply what has been learned to new situations. The level of application in learning assists pupils to perceive reasons or purpose for learning. Thus what is/has been learned can be used in diverse situations. Generally, knowledge that is related can be applied sooner than that which is unrelated.

16

Objectives in the Mathematics Curriculum

Objectives need to be selected carefully since they provide definite direction in terms of what the mathematics teacher will be teaching. There are states that mandate the objectives for pupils to achieve. Pupils are then tested, based on these objectives, at selected intervals as they progress through the diverse school years. When the objectives are stated in measurable terms, the teacher needs to make certain that learning activities are provided which harmonize with the stated objectives of instruction. The criterion referenced tests will then attempt to measure if learners have been successful in goal attainment. They are generally aligned very carefully with the stated objectives to make for increased validity of instruction. If the state mandated objectives are more broadly stated, the mathematics teacher has more leeway in choosing learning opportunities which harmonize with the general objectives. With these general objectives, it may not be as certain then what pupils will be tested on if state mandated criterion referenced tests are used to ascertain pupil achievement. When the writer started teaching in a rural school in the early 1950's, he chose his own objectives to stress instruction. There were no state mandated objectives to guide instruction. In 1989, the National Council Teachers of Mathematics (NCTM) came out with a carefully designed set of objectives for teaching and learning situations. The NCTM objectives provide voluntary guidelines for teachers to use in developing instructional strategies. The

NCTM Curriculum Standards for School Mathematics: Grades K- 4 (1989) emphasized the following, among other objectives of instruction:

1. Mathematics as problem solving: Students will use problem solving approaches to investigate and understand mathematical content, formulate problems
   * develop and apply strategies to solve a wide variety of problems
   * verify and interpret results
   * acquire confidence in using mathematics meaningfully
2. Mathematics as Communication: Students will
   * relate physical materials, pictures, and diagrams to mathematical ideas
   * reflect on and clarify their thinking about mathematical ideas and situations.
   * relate their everyday language to mathematical language and symbols.
   * realize that representing, discussing, reading, writing, and listening to mathematics are a vital part of learning and using mathematics

More will be discussed here pertaining to these NCTM standards. It is important to notice that problem solving as an objective is considered to be very important for mathematics teachers in designing the curriculum. In society, people in many of life's situations are solving problems using mathematics. Thus individuals or groups identify a relevant problem, gather needed information as possible solutions, test the answer or hypothesis, and revise the hypothesis if necessary. Problems in mathematics arise when buying goods and services as well as when selling goods and services. Pupils in class need to think of solving their own personal problems in mathematics such as when items are actually purchased and change is needed from the currency used in the transaction. They might also devise simulated problems to solve in the classroom setting. There are excellent simulations in computer use which pupils might engage in actively in solving problems involving virtual reality. It is important for pupils to try different algorithms in the solving of problems in mathematics. Thus there are different ways of solving problems in mathematics.

Pupils individually need to discover which algorithm works best in any given situation. Accuracy in working on problems is of utmost importance. Certainly, pupils need to test the accuracy of solutions to problems. Estimating if an answer is reasonable is a recommended procedure here. When being able to provide reasonable estimates, the learner checks his/her response with that which appears to be plausible. It is always good to be able to estimate, for example, the cost of a given set of items purchased even if a calculator has been used in ascertaining the sum. One can, of course, punch in the incorrect values in addition when using a calculator. Hopefully, pupils will ultimately and continuously develop feelings of confidence in doing mathematics. Success in mathematics breeds more success. Quality sequence in mathematics will increase pupil's chances of growth, achievement, and progress in mathematics.

Each person communicates ideas in society pertaining to the world of mathematics. Communication may take the form of being oral, written, and/or pictorial, among other ways. The world of reality presents concrete materials such as goods and services purchased. What is real needs to be communicated in mathematical terms, symbols, and words using numerals, such as the counting or whole numbers. The proper operation symbol needs to be used such as plus, minus, multiply, or divide. Thus the concrete or real may be expressed in the abstract.

It is always good if pupils think about or reflect upon what has been done or learned in mathematics. If pupils do not reflect upon mathematics used in problem solving, the chances are that forgetting will occur. The reflection can provide review opportunities in which there are opportunities to look for new algorithms to be used or alternative ways of perceiving a problem, as well as rehearsal of that which has been learned previously.

Learners need to think of ways of using what has been learned. Too frequently, pupils separate what has been learned in the classroom with what is needed in the real world in society in making transactions. This separation should not be made. After all, mathematics teachers need to guide pupils to use and apply the concrete (objects, items, realia), semiconcrete (pictures, illustrations, drawings, diagrams), and the abstract (numerals, numbers, and operational signs) to functional situations in real life. The dichotomy between classroom and society needs to be avoided. Rather, school and society become one in learning and applying that which has been and is being learned.

A variety of procedures need to be used in guiding pupil learning so that optimal achievement in mathematics may occur. Reading, discussing, writing, listening, observing, drawing, and dramatizing are methods of instruction that may be used as learning opportunities in guiding pupils to achieve more optimally in realizing NCTM standards of instruction.

Mathematics as General Education

Each pupil needs to experience quality in the mathematics curriculum. Mathematics lessons and units of study are for all pupils. Carefully chosen objectives, learning activities, and evaluation procedures need to be in evidence. Ralph Tyler (1949), late professor of the University of Chicago, raised four questions that all teachers need to ask and determine answers in teaching and learning situations. These questions are the following:

1. Which objectives should pupils achieve?
2. Which learning activities should be chosen so that pupils might achieve the stated objectives?
3. How should the curriculum be organized for pupils?
4. How should pupil achievement be evaluated to notice learner progress?

The above-named questions are vital to ask and to plan carefully for their implementation so that each pupil might realize optimal achievement. Thus each pupil needs the best of objectives, learning activities, organization of the curriculum, as well as evaluation procedures in the mathematics curriculum. In determining objectives of instruction in mathematics, the teacher needs to have pupils engage in higher levels of cognition. The lowest level, role learning is not to be completely discarded. However, pupils need to attach meaning to what is being taught in ongoing lessons and units of study. Thus if pupils do not understand what is taught, forgetting may well occur rapidly. Purpose or reasons for learning may be hindered. Motivation to learn is closely related to pupils understanding facts, concepts, and generalizations. The cognitive levels of objectives must go beyond that of rote learning. A higher level pertains to pupils using what has been learned. There are numerous practical activities whereby pupils may use subject mater acquired. Primary grade pupils might use what has been learned by "buying and selling" in a miniature grocery store with prices marked on the empty food containers. Pupils may then "shop" for groceries by using toy money to pay for the food items purchased.

Interest in achieving vital goals can go downhill. Certainly, pupil interest in learning in mathematics is also of utmost importance. Interest in learning sustains pupils to attend and persevere in ongoing tasks in mathematics. Learning activities to achieve objectives should be on the pupil's understanding level. Individuals do possess different levels of achievement and interest in a topic in mathematics. Mathematics teachers then need to meet individual needs of pupils. Each activity needs to possess vital subject matter so that relevant objectives might be attained.

Equity in Mathematics

Pupils need to experience equity in the mathematics curriculum. Individuals then should achieve optimally regardless of race, creed, sex, or national origin. Pupils individually should be guided to experience quality in ongoing lessons and units of study. Too frequently pupils of lower socioeconomic levels, for example, have been limited in their experiences with computers. Schools in low income levels do not have the technology that better financed classrooms have. With less financing, the number of computers become more limited. These computers might also be older and possess fewer capability advantages. Lower income level homes certainly will not have the number of computers that higher income levels have. In a rapidly expanding information age, pupils from poverty level homes will certainly be disadvantaged as compared to their counterparts in suburban public schools and higher income level pupils attending private schools. Equity in funding of schools and equity in opportunities to learn must be the lot of all pupils. Money does not solve all problems to be sure, but it does buy a lot of advantages that poverty cannot attain. With twenty-five per cent of United States pupils coming from poverty level homes, it behooves school leaders to see to it that pupils individually experience equity in the mathematics curriculum. If pupils from poverty level homes do not experience equity, they will be further and further behind in mathematics achievement as compared to learners from more favorable levels of home incomes.

A quality mathematics curriculum is needed by all elementary school pupils so that further sequential learning will be their lot on the secondary school levels. If pupils do not experience a quality kindergarten through high school mathematics curriculum, selected pupils will be held back from entering certain fields of science and engineering, among other endeavors. It takes a good mathematics curriculum for all pupils so that each can make the best vocational choices possible. The best objectives, learning opportunities, and evaluation procedures need to be available to all learners. Equity is a salient concept to emphasize in developing the mathematics curriculum.

Memorization in Mathematics

Mathematics teachers need to be careful about pupils memorizing subject matter in the curriculum. Too frequently, pupils have been required to memorize basic addition, subtraction, multiplication, and division facts without understanding what has been learned. To be sure, pupils ultimately need to respond quickly to these basic facts. However, meaning and understanding always come first. Memorizing is the lowest level of cognition such as being able to recall answers to basic addition, subtraction, multiplication, and division facts. Mathematics educators always state the importance of pupils attaching meaning to what is being learned. Learners first need to comprehend subject matter acquired. For example, a first grade pupil should be able to show comprehension to the value of $3+4=\_\_$ when this is being studied in an ongoing lesson or unit of study. How might the pupil be taught as well as how may the learner show meaning and understanding in achieving objectives? Teachers might have pupils discover the answer by showing a set of three sticks and asking how many there are here. If pupils can count rationally, they will respond with "three." Next the teacher should show a set of four sticks and ask pupils how many there are in this set. The two sets are then joined together to have pupils respond with what three sticks and four sticks are in number when joined together. Using sticks and other manipulatives, the pupil individually should attach meaning to a basic addition fact. Understanding the meaning of 3+4=_ is very important for further sequential learning to occur. It may be necessary for a pupil to memorize later what 3+4=__, if manipulate experiences continually need to be used when responding to answer what this basic number pair equals. However, meaning and understanding come prior to rote learning and memorization. Pupils can apply and use what has been learned much better if meaning is there as compared to committing content to memory without the needed understanding.

Rapidity of Learning

There are teachers who feel that pupils should complete problem solving and computation exercises with great speed. Generally, pupils will work at optimal speed if understanding is there in work performed. If they do not do so, then the mathematics teacher needs to emphasize time on task for individual pupils. There are pupils who waste time in getting to work as well as during the time the mathematics activity is in evidence.

Learners here need assistance to persevere in mathematics. Learners should set high goals for themselves and attempt to achieve them. They need to build confidence in their very own abilities. Pupils tend to develop a good self concept if success is experienced in ongoing lessons and units of study. Teachers should sequence learning opportunities so that pupils individually achieve new challenging objectives and are successful in doing so. Once pupils are successful learners, they tend to develop an inward desire to learn, grow, and develop in mathematics. Emphasizing speed in computing or solving problems, generally, is not a part of a quality mathematics curriculum.

Cooperative Learning

One of the writer when being an elementary pupil remembers all work and assignmenta being completed in mathematics on an individual basis. It was considered cheating to work together with others. John Dewey (1859-1952) advocated pupils working in committees or small groups when learning. He believed that pupils achieved more when working cooperatively than individually. Dewey felt that pupils did not like working by the self, but preferred to work collaboratively with other learners. Today much stress is placed upon pupils working harmoniously together to solve problems. When working together, pupils learn form each other, as well as from the teacher. They assist each other as well as challenge the thinking of committee members, leading to higher levels of cognition.

Committee membership should be small such as three to five members so that all can participate freely when interacting with each other. It is good procedure to start with one committee first in order that the teacher can learn to work with a group. If all pupils in a classroom started working on committees immediately, the teacher may not be able to move from committee to committe in order to provide guidance and direction. Once a single initial committee is able to proceed with minimal assistance from the mathematics teacher, a second committee may be formed. The second committee needs to assume more and more responsibilities before additional committees are in evidence. The mathematics teacher is not a lecturer or dispenser of information but one who motivates, encourages, and challenges committee members to stay on task. He/she helps pupils to confront and solve problems within the framework of committee endeavors. The mathematics teacher also guides pupils to use proper procedures in committee work in which

1. all participate and no one dominates committe endeavors.
2. learners stay on task and not waste valuable time.
3. each respects the thinking of other participants.
4. ideas are presented clearly.
5. pupils discuss and learn from each other, leasing to higher levels of cognition.
6. processes and products of mathematics are equally important.
7. goals and objectives of instruction are being realized.
8. active involvement of learners in a hands-on approach is

being stressed.

9. emphasis is placed upon critical and creative thinking.
10. application of subject matter is emphasized.

Should committees and cooperative learning be emphasized throughout the day or should there be time also for individual work by pupils in the mathematics curriculum? There needs to be rational balance between the two approaches. In society individuals work collectively as well as individually. People need to use time wisely be it in groups or on an individual basis. Also there needs to be time for the class as a whole to be taught together. Thus there are common learnings in mathematics which all pupils in a classroom can experience. Here, the teacher must be careful that all pupils are attending and achieving when large group instruction is being emphasized. Flexible grouping is necessary so that individual, committee, and large group instruction is emphasized when needed to guide each pupil to achieve adequately in mathematics.

Using Mathematics Textbooks Excessively

Well selected textbooks in mathematics add much to the mathematics curriculum as learning opportunities. These texts tend to be well written and provide a guide to the teacher in selecting objectives, learning opportunities, and evaluation procedures. Much time is saved by the teacher when using a basal or multiple series of mathematics texts in planning the curriculum. One of the writer reads in journal articles periodically that a teacher teaches well since he/ she is not using a mathematics textbook in teaching pupils. When not using or using heavily a basal text says nothing about the quality of teaching. One can teach well with or without the use of basal textbooks in mathematics. If content therein is made meaningful, interesting, and purposeful for pupils, it might well be that a good job of teaching mathematics is in evidence when using a quality mathematics textbook.

There are exceptions, however, to the use of mathematics basal texts and teaching effectively. Many pupils do require a hands-on approach in learning. Pupils do possess diverse learning styles and stressing the concrete or enactive phase of learning assists many pupils to achieve more optimally. Thus blocks, seeds, pop bottle caps, sticks, models, toys, and other objects are necessary to engage pupils actively in learning. It is also wise in teaching to stress the iconic or semiconcrete facets of learning such as use of pictures, films, filmstrips, videotapes, video disks, software packages, and other modern technology in teaching and learning situations. These materials are one step removed form real-life situations as are indicated in the concrete/enactive materials. Too frequently textbook content stresses the abstract phase of learning largely. Thus reading of content in story or word problems as well as strict computation in addition, subtraction, multiplica-tion, and division emphasizes the symbolic and the abstract to the near exclusion of the concrete/enactive and the semiconcrete, iconic materials of instruction. Pupils might then lack meaning and understanding of what is taught. One of the writers believes very strongly in pupils attaching meaning to what is being learned. Learners also need to attend and pay attention to ongoing lessons and unit objectives as well as learning opportunities. A way of learning opportunities must be provided to pupils so that each may learn as much as possible in mathematics. A teacher must truly provide for individual differences among learners. If content presented is too difficult, pupils cannot achieve and learn. If it is too easy, boredom and a lack of challenge to learn might will be an end-result.

The nature of mathematics has helped to determine what is taught and when it is taught in the elementary grades. Whole numbers are the basis for many mathematical ideas; moreover, experiences with them arise long before children come to school. Thus whole number work is stressed first. Work with rational numbers logically follows work with whole numbers. Such seemingly 'natural' sequences are the result of long years of curricular evolution. This process has involved much analysis of what constitutes a progression from "easy" to "difficult" based in part on what is deemed to be needed at one level for the development of ideas at later levels.

Once a curriculum is in place for a long time, however, people tend to consider it the only "proper" sequence. Thus to omit a topic or to change the sequence of topics often involves a struggle for acceptance.

Sometimes the process of change is aided by an event, such as when the Soviet Union sent the first Sputnik into orbit. The shock of this evidence of another country's technological superiority speeded up curricular change in the United States. The "new math" of the 1950s and 1960s was the result, and millions of dollars were channeled into mathematics and science education to strengthen school programs.

The problem remains continually as to *what* should be taught elementary school pupils in mathematics. Teachers, principals, supervisors, parents, and curriculum directors need to study and appraise continuously what knowledge has most worth for pupils in mathematics. One early statement of objectives on what knowledge has most worth was advocated by Herbert Spencer of whom Brubacher (1966) wrote:

> In mid-nineteenth century England a somewhat different approach was being made to educational aims by Herbert Spencer (1820-1903), the social philosopher. Perturbed by the confusion in educational aims in his day, Spencer looked about for a standard by which to determine their relative value. This he found in the contemporary emphasis upon utilitarianism and on science, especially evolutionary thought, to which he was quite sympathetic. Answering his own question on how to live completely, he arranged the aims to education in the order of their survival value to the individual and to society. First of all, education should aim to teach the art of self-preservation; second, it should teach one how to earn a living; next, it should ensure survival by teaching about rearing and disciplining children; fourth, education should fit one for social and especially for political duties; and last, though most of Spencer's predecessors put this aim among the first, education should equip one for enjoyment of the refinements of culture of art, literature, and the like.

Spencer's objectives stressed the practical and the useful in mathematics, among other utilitarian curriculum areas. Abstract knowledge, theories, and learning for its own sake would not be advocated by Herbert Spencer. The seven cardinal principles of education were developed by the National Education Association

(NEA) and stressed what is useful in society, not self development nor knowledge for the sake of knowledge (1918). These broad goals were the following: command of fundamental processes, health, citizenship, worthy home membership, vocations, worthy use of leisure time, and ethical character.

Problems arise when the mathematics curriculum is viewed from either a subject centered or a problem centered approach in teaching and learning. A subject centered mathematics curriculum may not stress what is practical or useful. It might emphasize a textbook/workbook approach in teaching pupils. Perhaps, a few other materials are involved in learning activities provided to provide for meaning and understanding. The goal is to have pupils learn subject matter, not necessarily application of content acquired. Toward the other end of the curriculum is a more utilitarian centered mathematics curriculum whereby pupils learn to identify and solve life-like problems. In the subject centered curriculum, the teacher does more direct teaching of content to pupils whereas in a problem solving approach the teacher is a guide and encourages learners to identify and solve problems. Perhaps, the issue may be clarified further when stressing the basics in mathematics as compared to a practical curriculum in mathematics. The basics have never been identified although there is much talk about its importance. These essentials, it is believed, are needed by all pupils regardless of ability and achievement levels of learners. The basics have their very own scope and sequence arranged ahead of time prior to instruction. In contrast, the practical is emphasized in sequence when the problem(s) have been chosen and need solutions. A practical curriculum cannot be determined specifically prior to instruction. Generally, as the need arises, practical learning will be needed by involved learners.

Using a Variety of Methods of Instruction

Too frequently, teachers fail to use diverse methods of teaching mathematics. The same or similar methods are used over and over again. Thus a teacher may lecture and explain each new lesson to pupils rather continuously for sequential days of instruction. The chalkboard might be the major material of instruction used here. Would pupils in most cases become bored in these situations. Why not change methodology in teaching so that pupils are more attentive and achieve more optimally?

There are numerous methods of teaching that may be used. Learning by discovery has many advantages in its use. Pupils individually or in committees may discover on their own answers and procedures to problem solving in mathematics. The teacher then asks questions and probes so that pupils find out on their own, rather than the teacher lecturing/explaining how to proceed in securing an answer to a problem. Pupils tend to be fascinated in learning by discovery and finding out on their own. Higher levels of cognition are stressed in these types of learning activities.

Much has been written pertaining to mathematics anxiety on the part of women in the public schools as well as in higher education. A hypothesis to examine is if discovery learning assists in minimizing anxiety in mathematics. Each pupil needs to learn as much as possible in terms of knowledge, skills, and positive attitudes in ongoing lessons and units of study in mathematics.

Somewhat toward the other end of the discovery learning continuum is a hierarchical approach in teachers teaching mathematics. In a hierarchical manner, the teacher determines the objectives for pupil achievement which includes state mandated objectives. He/she decides upon the sequence or order of learning opportunities for pupils in mathematics. Additionally, the mathematics teacher here decides upon which evaluation techniques to use to determine pupil progress.

One of the writers believes strongly that pupils should be involved in determining which objectives to achieve in mathematics. Learners also need to have a voice in which learning opportunities need to be emphasized as well as appraisal procedures to use in the appraising process. Why should pupils be involved in decision-making?

1. Life consists of deciding between and among alternatives. Thus learners need to have opportunities to make choices from among alternatives.
2. Pupils need to become increasingly independent as they progress through the public school years of schooling. There is no other alternative since parents become older and eventually have to cease having control over their

offspring. Pupils continually and gradually need to lean upon themselves for ideas, problem solving, and responsibility.

3. Higher levels of cognition involving critical and creative thinking as well as problem solving very frequently go along with decision-making skills.

There are numerous ways in which pupils can be involved in determining the mathematics curriculum. These include the following:

1. Planning with the teacher what to complete for enrichment/extra credit work.
2. Deciding with teacher guidance what needs to be retaught, reviewed, as well as remediate in terms of subject matter taught previously.
3. Working problems using diverse algorithms. The algorithm decided upon works best for the involved learner.
4. Choosing sequential tasks to complete when using learning centers in mathematics in the classroom.
5. Selecting from among alternatives, for example, as to which problems to complete when the teacher stresses that any five out of eight problems needs to be finished.

Pupils differ from each other in numerous ways such as in interests, abilities, achievement, and learning styles. The mathematics teacher then needs to make provisions so that each pupil learns as much as possible. Thus selected learners may learn more through a teacher/pupil planned curriculum than using other approaches.

The interdisciplinary curriculum is receiving much emphasis in printed educational materials as well as at teacher education conventions. Thus the teacher may organize the curriculum in terms of teaching arithmetic largely in ongoing lessons and units of study. A separated subjects curriculum is then in evidence. Certainly, higher levels of cognition such as cortical and creative thinking as well as problem solving may be emphasized in a separate subjects curriculum. With higher levels of cognition, the chances are that geometry and algebra will increasingly be included in the mathematics curriculum, resulting in a correlated or fused curriculum. Adding in an integrated manner, probability and statistics, graphing, and trigonometry, among others, goes beyond the correlated mathematics curriculum and may be called the broad fields design for instruction if taught in a related manner, not as separate subjects. The interdisciplinary curriculum goes beyond the broad fields curriculum and might include science, social studies, the fine arts, and physical education. Mathematics may well be the language of science since the latter stresses precision and accuracy of measurement. One of the writers has given numerous talks on relating social studies and mathematics such as at National Council Teachers of Mathematics (NCTM) meetings at Springfield, Missouri; Knoxville, Tennessee; St. Johns, Newfoundland, Fall of 1995. As a former teacher on the West Bank of the Jordan for two years, the author used slides to indicate what his student teachers and cooperating teachers, whom he supervised, stressed in a social studies unit on "The Middle East Area of the World."

Among other items, the two teachers stressed

1. pupils determining the distance around the walled city of Jerusalem in the English as well as the metric system of measurement. This distance was related to some landmark near to the local school.
2. pupils finding a city or other area eighteen miles from the local school in comparing Jerusalem and Jericho which are the same distance apart.
3. pupils comparing elevations among selected cities in the United States. This was compared with the elevation differences between Jerusalem and Jericho, 2,500 feet above sea level and 800 feet below sea level respectively.

Pupils might also study the Roman and Egyptian system of numeration as examples in relating history in the social studies with mathematics. There are numerous questions that need to be asked pertaining to the interdisciplinary mathematics curriculum. These are the following:

1. How much of the interdisciplinary/integrated curriculum should one emphasize in mathematics? To be sure the language arts areas of listening, speaking, reading, and writing are an inherent part of the mathematics

curriculum. These areas of the language arts are musts in mathematics and cannot be omitted. NCTM (1989, page 78) Standards that Pertain to Communication, Reasoning, and Connections emphasize the following, among others, for grades five through eight

* model situations using oral, written, concrete, pictorial, graphical, and algebraic methods;
2 Reflect and clarify their own thinking about mathematical ideas and situations;
3 Develop common understandings of mathematical ideas, including the role of definitions;
4 Use the skills of reading, listening, and viewing to interpret and evaluate mathematical ideas;
5 Discuss mathematical ideas and make conjectures and convincing arguments;
6 Appreciate the value of mathematics notation and role in the development of mathematical ideas.

Teachers should place high priority upon pupil communicating ideas in mathematics. Thus pupils are able to listen carefully to ongoing expression of ideas in mathematics. Learners need to listen for diverse purposes such as listening for directions, sequence of subject matter presented, facts, concepts, generalizations, main ideas, processes and solutions to problems, as well as critical and creative listening. In the area of oral communication, learners should speak clearly and accurately. They need to be able to explain a process or procedure with meaning and understanding. It is important to convey specifics, conclusions, applications, unique ideas, and analytical content to others in school and in society. The importance of quality oral communication cannot be overemphasized. Listening is related directly to oral communication when interacting with others in the mathematics curriculum. In the area of reading mathematical content, pupils should learn to read fluently and independently. The skills of phonics, syllabication, structural analysis, use of picture and context clues are important in mathematics. Learners need to understand content read so that progress and achievement are continuous and optimal. Reading to obtain knowledge and meaning in mathematics, as well as be able to use information secured are salient goals in mathematics. Also, pupils need to become analytical readers, interpreting content in novel ways. Learners should be able to appraise subject matter read. Realizing the worth and value of subject matter in problem solving is salient. The reading of symbols such as +, − , x, among others presets subject matter that truly is unique to the mathematics curriculum.

Being able to write legibly to communicate ideas clearly is very necessary for achievement in mathematics. Legibility in writing numerals, operation signs, words, and sentences as well as paragraphs are salient goals to achieve for all pupils in mathematics. Proper spacing, alignment, proportion of letters and symbols, and neatness of work must become a part of the repertoire of each pupil. Clarity in communication of ideas in mathematics is important if pupils are to become proficient in critical and creative thinking as well as problem solving.

Pertaining to correlating language arts and mathematics, Kolstad and Briggs (1996) wrote the following:

> Research on including reading, writing, and oral language in math is very positive. Not only do the students benefit as mathematicians, they develop as readers, writers, and speakers from the additional opportunities to practice these skills. Practicing language arts skills across the curriculum is in line with the whole language movement, as well as with the integrated curriculum approach. The benefits of including literature and reading experiences throughout the curriculum have been expanded upon by whole language researcher. Research by Grossman, Smith, and Miller (1993) and Evans (1994) strongly supports the benefits of using writing for improving student performance in mathematics. In order to uphold the NCTM recommendations, students must learn to communicate mathematically, in writing and through oral language (Capps and Pickreign, 1993).

Research supports the benefits of incorporating reading, writing, and oral language into mathematics instruction to help students convey mathematical information in familiar words and to assist them with their thinking processes, as they work through math calculations and problem solving situations. Another reason writing is a valuable asset in mathematics instruction is that the teacher is better able to evaluate students, understanding of math concepts and processes based upon what the children have written. A teacher can also evaluate students by what they say. By including oral language activities in math lessons, students' abilities to communicate mathematically will improve. Thus, a teacher will be better able to evaluate and clarify students' thought processes, while building students' confidence in their own abilities to discuss mathematics. Therefore, based upon the many benefits and the number of emerging strategies for implementing language arts into mathematics, the teacher should begin incorporating reading, writing, and oral language activities into mathematics lessons on a regular basis. Despite the valuable strategies and teaching techniques now being used, more research needs to be conducted on the benefits of incorporating language arts into the math curriculum and teachers need more suggestions and additional resources to ensure the success of a language-rich math program.

Responsibility of the Teacher

Mathematics teachers have salient responsibilities if pupils are to attain vital objectives of instruction. Pertaining to being model teachers in the classroom, they should stress (Ediger, 1994)

1. meaningful lessons and units of study. With meaning, pupils understand and comprehend that which was contained in ongoing learning opportunities.
2. interesting content and skills in the curriculum. With interest, the pupil and the curriculum become one, not separate entities. Pupils should attend and achieve from ongoing lessons and units of study.
3. purpose in learning. With purpose for learning, pupils accept reasons for attaining relevant facts, concepts, and generalizations presented. Purpose development by the teacher may take little time indeed. With deduction, the teacher explains clearly and concisely why pupils should achieve the objectives to be stressed. With inductive approaches, the teacher raises a few questions about the new lesson whereby the pupil responds and perceives purpose and reasons for learning. Extrinsic rewards can

be emphasized. Here, the teacher announces prizes and awards that pupils can secure if they attain the objectives of the lesson. Pupils need to know precisely what is to be learned to obtain the rewards.

4. sequence in learning. With quality sequence, pupils relate newly acquired information with that previously achieved. Previous knowledge attained provides readiness for the new objectives to be achieved. Pupils need guidance to perceive relationship of knowledge in teaching- learning situations.
5. balance among objectives stressed. Thus knowledge, skills, and attitudes–three kinds of objectives need to be achieved by students. These objectives interact and are not in isolation from each other. For example, if pupils possess positive attitudes, they should achieve needed knowledge and skills more readily.

Selected References

Brubacher, John S. (1966). *A History of the Problems of Education.* New York: McGraw- Hill Book Company, Second Edition, 16.

Capps, L. R., and J. Pickreign (1993). Language Connections in Mathematics: A Critical Part of Mathemaitcs Instruction, *Arithmetic Teacher,* 41, 8-12.

Ediger, Marlow (1994). Early Field Experiences in Teacher Education, *College Student Journal,* 28, 302.

Evans, C. S. (1984). Writing to Learn in Math, *Language Arts,* 61, 828- 835.

Kolstad, Rosemaire, and L. D. Briggs (1996). Incorporating Language Arts into the Mathematics Curriculum: A Literature Survey, Education, 116:431.

National Education Association (1918). Commission on the Reorganization of Secondary Education, *The Cardinal Principles of Secondary Education.* US Bureau of Education Bulletin 35.

National Council Teachers of Mathematics (1989). *Curriculum and Evaluation Standards for School Mathematics.* Reston, Virginia: NCTM. NCTM (I 989), 78.

Reys, Robert L., Marilyn N. Sudydam, and Mary Montgomery Lindquist (1995). *Helping Children Learn Mathematics,* Fourth Edition. Boston: Allyn and Bacon, page 3.

17

Organizing for Instruction in Mathematics

There are numerous decisions that the mathematics teacher needs to make when organizing for instruction. Generally, the school principal/supervisor and the mathematics teachers have made decisions as to which pupils are to be placed specifically in a classroom. Numerous criteria are used in making these kinds of decisions. Thus there are issues here that need resolving in terms of the following:

1. Homogeneous (uniform achievement levels in mathematics of pupils) versus heterogeneous grouping of pupils (mixed achievement levels within a classroom).
2. self contained (a single teacher teaching most curriculum areas in each school day) or departmentalized grouping of learners. The latter stresses a specially trained and certified mathematics teacher that teaches the one curriculum area only.

There are additional issues in organizing for instruction in mathematics that will be discussed.

Grouping for Instruction

Which is more nearly the ideal, homogeneous or heterogeneous grouping for instruction? This debate has been going on for sometime. In 1920, Detroit, Michigan public schools stressed an X, Y, Z plan in grouping pupils for instruction. Thus pupils with the highest IQs were taught in one room as compared to the average and the slow learners being taught in their respective rooms. It was not long before the XYZ plan was no longer in operation. Why? IQ test results did not divide pupils adequately in terms of high, average, and low achievers in mathematics. Each roomful of pupils then were highly heterogeneous.

Presently, the trend is to place pupils in heterogeneously grouped classrooms in mathematics. There are several reasons for doing so. These reasons include the following:

1. It is more democratic for learners of all ability and achievement levels to be taught together rather than segregating pupils.
2. Pupils should interact with others of all ability levels since society is organized in a way in which this is done.
3. Pupils achieve at a higher level or just as well when mixed achievement levels of learners are taught in the same classroom as compared to homogeneous grouping.
4. Pupils of lesser achievement levels need a role model in learning and those more talented can provide this model.
5. Pupils of higher ability levels ran assist those of lesser achievement levels and thus attain more optimally.

There are dissenters to having heterogeneous grouping of pupils in a classroom. They present the following reasons for their beliefs:

1. talented and gifted pupils are held back in achievement if they are taught to the levels of progress of slow learners.
2. Pupils may attain more optimally if they are grouped, regardless of their achievement, which stresses continuous progress in a homogeneous group.
3. Slow learners will not be looked down upon by faster achievers if the former are grouped homogeneously.
4. Talented and gifted learners will be frustrated by the slow pace of achievement whereas slower achievers may be frustrated with tasks they cannot attain.
5. Teaching truly becomes difficult when the teacher has a very wide range of achievement to provide for in the classroom.

Perhaps, a compromise may be stressed in the homogeneous/ heterogeneous controversy in terms of grouping pupils for instruction is concerned. To be sure, pupils need to learn to work effectively and harmoniously with others regardless of achievement levels. In society, people interact with others of truly different achievement levels. Problems at the work place result when people fail to respect and accept others. Thus heterogeneous grouping is a must at selected times in the teaching of mathematics. When markers and other concrete materials are used in teaching, all pupils can benefit here regardless of present achievement levels. Then too, there can be individual and committee projects in mathematics in which pupils are homogeneously grouped. Why? Perhaps, the content is best learned when likenesses in achievement are inherent in the committee project. When a pupil pursues a project individually, he/she may attain as rapidly as individual abilities and interests permit.

Reys, Suydam, and Lindquist (1995) provide the following guidelines when using large group, small group, and individual instruction:

1. Use large-group instruction:
   * If the topic is one that can be presented to all pupils at approximately the same point in time (that is , if all pupils have prerequisites for understanding the initial presentation)
   * If pupils need continuous guidance from the teacher in order to attain the knowledge, skill, or understanding
2. Use small group instruction:
   * If pupils can profit from pupil- to- pupil interaction with less teacher guidance
   * If explorations and communication about mathematics are being encouraged
   * If cooperative learning skills and affects are being fostered
3. Use individual instruction :
   * If pupils can follow a sequence or conduct an activity on their own
   * If individual practice for mastery is the focus

The kind of teaching envisioned by the NCTM Professional Standards is probably quite different from the kind of teaching you experienced. The emphasis is shifting from a teacher directed classroom to one in which students are actively involved in learning. The teacher, of course, is still in control, but involves the students through discussions and activities, usually by incorporating much small group work. Presentations and discussions with the whole class have not disappeared, but we have learned that children learn much more effectively when they work with materials to solve problems and talk about the results with each other.

Mainstreaming of Pupils.

Classrooms of pupils have tended to become increasingly heterogeneous with mainstreaming of pupils PL 94-142, Education for All Handicapped Children Act passed in 1975 by the federal government, more recently called IDEA (Individuals with Disabilities in Education Act). Thus a pupil who is mentally handicapped, hearing impaired, vision impaired, orthopaedically handicapped, and/or a autistic may be taught in the regular classroom. If a parent desires to have his offspring taught in the regular classroom, then this decision must be abided by. Sometimes, parents want their handicapped offspring taught in a special education classroom where the pupil/teacher ratio is low, perhaps one teacher to five to seven pupils. Their thinking might be the child is better served in a classroom in which the teacher can provide more time for each handicapped learner.

Handicapped pupils need to have an Individualized Educational Program (IEP) by law. The IEP is developed cooperatively by the regular teacher, the special education teacher, the principal, and involved parents. The parent, in particular, must approve of the IEP. This lists in measurable terms what the pupils are to achieve. An audit can occur later on to ascertain if the involved learner has achieved the measurably stated objectives in the IEP. Thus a handicapped pupil with an IEP cannot be minimized or shunned, he/she must be taught what is stated in the objectives.

In most cases an aide will assist the regular teacher in providing for a very handicapped mainstreamed pupil. Handicapped pupils need help in achieving objectives of the school and in taking care of the self thus involving the necessity of a teacher's aid. What is important is that handicapped as well as all pupils have vital objectives to achieve in mathematics. Learning opportunities are there to provide for individual differences as well as quality in teaching and learning. Evaluation procedures attempt to ascertian that which pupils individually and in groups have learned.

Team Teaching in Mathematics

A team of teachers may consist of two or more members. If two teachers are on a team, they may engage in cooperative leadership whereby no one is designated as chairperson for planning sessions. Should there be three or more members on a team, one teacher needs to be designated as the leader. The leader may receive increased salary due to having responsibilities of being the chairperson. His/her tasks are to have members work harmoniously and cooperatively in developing the best mathematics curriculum possible for elementary school pupils. If members cannot get along well, the progress of the team will be hurt. Each team member should have a good knowledge of the mathematics curriculum. The team needs to come up with the best plan for teaching mathematics possible. Pupils individually need to learn as much as possible in ongoing lessons and units in mathematics. To do this in team teaching, the members need to develop quality goals, learning activities so that learners may attain these ends, as well as evaluating techniques to notice achievement and progress.

When teaching large group instruction in team teaching, the most capable of the team members should do the teaching. After large group instruction, pupils should work in committees of four or five to clarify that which was learned in large group instruction. Team members need to assist learners in small groups to understand and attach meaning to that which was presented in large group teaching. Individual projects and activities need to be pursued by pupils following large group and committee endeavors. These individual experiences assist pupils to feel purpose and value in what is being worked on in mathematics.

There are pros and cons of team teaching in mathematics. The following questions might be raised pertaining to the team approach in teaching mathematics to pupils:

1. Are team members able to work together effectively in planning and teaching sessions? A lack of harmony can make for a long school year as well as a lack of progress in teaching and learning.
2. Are members well versed in mathematics technology and other methods of instruction?
3. Do team members keep up with the latest trends in teaching mathematics?
4. Is staff development an ideal for team members so that each teacher is abreast on new approaches in teaching mathematics?
5. Do team members read professional materials in teaching mathematics?

When identifying loopholes in team teaching as well as other procedures and methodologies, a principal/supervisor may take out weaknesses and make necessary changes in team teaching. More than one mind is better than a single mind in advocating team teaching as a way to organize for instruction in mathematics. Built in inservice education is available in that teachers may learn form each other in planning sessions as well as when observing each other teach pupils.

The Self-Contained Classroom

Many elementary school teachers teach in self-contained classrooms whereby most of the curriculum areas such as mathematics, social studies, science, and literature/reading are taught by a single teacher.

The teacher then needs to have a broad base of knowledge of each curriculum area so that all areas are taught in a professional manner. There are to be sure definite advantages of the self-contained classroom. These are the following:

1. The teacher has a good chance to integrate subject matter from different curriculum areas when it is good to do so. There are times when pupils need guidance to perceive knowledge as being related from diverse curriculum areas.
2. Flexible scheduling may be emphasized in that more time can be given to one curriculum area for that day if needed;

the borrowed time may be given back at other times as it is important to have balance in the curriculum.

3. The teacher can get to know the individual pupil well since he/she is in the self-contained classroom each day. Information acquired pertaining to each pupil should be used in improving the mathematics curriculum.

There are weaknesses in the self-contained classroom which need removing. These are the following questions which then should be answered:

1. Can teachers be competent in teaching mathematics when so many curriculum areas are taught each day?
2. Will mathematics be slighted in the self-contained classroom if the teacher has a favorite curriculum area to teach which is not mathematics?
3. Might inservice education in mathematics be adequately stressed when there are several other curriculum areas taught?
4. May the methods of teaching mathematics be adequately strengthened if diverse academic areas are to be taught?
5. How might mathematics receive its fair share of attention and assistance in teaching and learning in the self-contained classroom?

The above-named questions need answering since so many elementary school classrooms stress the self-contained classroom concept. Any plan used to organize for instruction needs to strengthen teaching each curriculum area. Thus mathematics instruction should improve if the self-contained concept is stressed in teaching and learning.

Modified and Complete Departmentalization

Numerous elementary school classrooms stress modified departmentalization. Here, a teacher might teach mathematics and science, only as an example to different classrooms of pupils. Thus the teacher may specialize more in the teaching of mathematics as compared to what exists in the self-contained classroom. At times mathematics and science can be correlated as is good to do so in the classroom. A planned series of meetings including faculty meetings, workshops, and staff development programs might then be stressed in mathematics. These meetings might also stress correlating, fusing, and integrating subject matter when it assists pupils to learn more optimally. Intermediate grade levels will stress modified departmentalization more so than will the primary levels of instruction in mathematics. Why? Subject matter becomes increasingly more complex as pupils progress through the different levels of schooling thus necessitating more of departmentalization in mathematics.

If an elementary school has complete departmentalization, a mathematics teacher will teach this one academic area only. This truly gives the elementary teacher opportunities to specialize in teaching one academic area only. He/she may then read journal articles on improving the mathematics curriculum with the intent of implementing quality ideas read. This teacher may attend professional meetings in the teaching of mathematics. Hopefully all these areas of inservice education will guide the teacher to select the best mathematics objectives, learning opportunities, and evaluation procedures possible in teaching pupils. One of the writers hopes this will be true of all teachers who teach mathematics regardless of the plan used to organize for instruction.

If a mathematics teacher an the elementary level is teaching in a departmentalized plan, he/she should seek out other mathematics teachers to discuss new ideas in teaching and to learn from each other. As was mentioned previously, team teaching has built in opportunities for inservice education whereby participants can learn from each other in planning sessions as well as from observing each other teach. Interactions among other plans in organizing for instruction are more difficult to implement. However, mathematics teachers do need to learn from each other and continue to grow and develop. Departmentalization without team teaching necessitates the individual teacher to seek out diverse ways and means of inservice education including planning with other teachers on how to improve upon the teaching of mathematics.

Nongraded Mathematics Instruction

Ideally the mathematics curriculum should be ungraded. Why? Pupils are at different levels of achievement in mathematics. A standard mathematics curriculum does not meet the needs of many pupils. Each pupil needs to be assisted to achieve as much as possible. Thus the mathematics teacher faces the challenge of attempting to provide for individual pupils so that optimal learning on the part of each is possible. The mathematics teacher could individualize instruction so that each pupil is at a different place in achievement in mathematics. A mathematics textbook could be used so that pupils are at different places within the textbook in achievement. Each ideally would then be working optimally. Does this mean that a pupil would always work by the self? No, not necessarily. In cooperative learning three to four pupils might be working together to solve problems, real or virtual situations. Within the cooperative learning setting, the individual pupil may work on more stimulating tasks or assist others to achieve, grow, and develop. The individual pupil who is talented and gifted should not always, by any means, be asked to assist the less able. They need to work on a challenging mathematics curriculum of their own. Perhaps, this challenge is in cooperative learning in mathematics. Or, it might mean working individually on challenging mathematics problems. Optimal achievement and growth for each pupil is a necessity in mathematics. Social growth and development is important also. That is why cooperative learning should also have its rightful place in the mathematics curriculum. Later on as adults, individuals need to get along well with others and work harmoniously at the work place for the good of all involved.

In a nongraded mathematics curriculum, it is important to remember that

1. pupils are working at diverse levels of achievement; grade levels mean little when attempting to provide for individual differences.
2. pupils need to learn to work together in a harmonious manner with respect and acceptance of all.
3. pupils individually need to attain optimally in knowledge, skills, and attitudes in the mathematics curriculum.
4. pupils should develop feelings of motivation, interest, and challenge in ongoing lessons and units in mathematics.
5. pupils should be actively engaged in learning opportunities.

The nongraded mathematics curriculum emphasizes that there are no grade levels for pupils. Shoe horning does not work. Pupils are individuals with diverse interests, talents, learning styles, and abilities. A curriculum needs to be designed which makes adequate provision for barners as human beings having much worth. Ediger (1988) wrote the following:

Teachers, principals, and supervisors need to develop a philosophy of teaching elementary school mathematics which makes ample provision for each individual pupil to realize his/her optimal achievement.

A relevant philosophy pertaining to the teaching of elementary school mathematics will stress the importance of pupils achieving important objectives. Each objective that pupils are to achieve should be weighed against alternative goals in making the final selection so that learners truly learn what is important in the school and class setting.

Selected teachers, supervisors, and principals may wish to emphasize the use of general objectives in teaching-learning situations. Other educators may rather desire to use specific, measurable objectives. What is of utmost importance in teaching and learning is that pupils attain quality objectives which emphasize higher levels of cognition such as critical thinking, creative thinking, and problem solving. Thus the dichotomy between general versus specific objectives may be resolved by selecting those objectives which will guide a learner in becoming a fully functioning member of society.

Stoddard (1961) developed a dual progress plan of grouping pupils for instruction. Mathematics, along with science, was taught as being nongraded. Departmentalization was emphasized here for the intermediate grade levels of pupils. Social studies and language arts were taught on a graded basis by a homeroom teacher.

The nongraded mathematics curriculum has stressed no grade levels but individual pupils worked at optimal levels to achieve as well as possible. The dual progress plan in organizing for instruction had both the nongraded and graded facets of arranging learners for teaching. It also had both facets of departmentalization, such as mathematics and science, as well as the self-contained classroom which included social studies and language arts.

Pupil and Teacher Attitudes

Quality attitudes may make or break achievement of individuals. Too frequently, the attitudes of individuals leaves much to be desired. Negative attitudes hinder learner and teacher achievement. Both lose out when a lack of good attitudes is in evidence.

Respect for others is a must. There needs to be unconditional respect for others regardless of race, creed, religious beliefs, sex, and achievement. When pupils do not respect others, the one receiving the negative feelings is hurt and feels left out. If pupils lack feelings of kindness toward others, these attitudes will, no doubt, remain in the work place later when these same individuals are adults. It is uncomfortable to work in a place where there is hostility and anger toward individuals.

Teachers need to respect pupils regardless of present achievement levels. They then provide for each pupil where he/she is presently achieving and work toward continuous progress in mathematics. The objectives are selected and designed to optimalize pupil achievement in mathematics. Too frequently, pupils come form poverty level homes, something like twenty-five per cent of pupils fit in this category. It behooves schools to accept increasingly the responsibility that homes formerly provided. The school has no choice in this matter if pupils are to attain more optimally in mathematics. A hungry pupil cannot do well in mathematics. In addition to serving nutritious noon meals, the school needs to provide breakfasts which also meet minimum nutrition requirements, as a minimum. Ediger (1996) wrote the following:

I do not believe pupils can achieve well if they are hungry and have inappropriate clothing. The late A. H. Maslow advocated physiological needs (adequate nutrition, proper clothing, and appropriate shelter) as being basic and necessary for each pupil. Generally physiological needs must be fulfilled prior to meeting more complex needs of learners in ascending order of complexity, such as safety and security, love and belonging, esteem, knowledge, and self actualization. Very frequently, educators have tried to improve achievement and learning on the part of pupils through other approaches, even leaving out the taking care of physiological needs of pupils. Approaches that have been used to increase pupil attainment, isolated from meeting physiological needs have been the following :

1. state mandated objectives for pupils to achieve.
2. effective schools' research and their recommendations.
3. Education 2000 as developed by the National Governors' Conference in 1989; their recommendations emphasized development of national goals for learners to attain.
4. standards for pupil achievement as set by national organizations...
5. objectives by local school district such as Instructional Management Systems (IMS).

Attempts at goal setting are admiral, particularly if they

1. perceive pupils as individuals who possess unique interests and talents.
2. are realistic and achievable.
3. are voluntary for teachers to use in developing the best curriculum possible for each learner.

Goal setting by outside agencies and organizations is difficult to do since these groups and individuals are external to the pupils being taught. Thus goal setting groups are impersonal and do not plan teaching and learning of a specific set of pupils to be taught.

It is the teacher then who needs to lean upon these standards to select objectives for pupil attainment in mathematics and personalize them. Objectives then are developed for a specific set of pupils and organized sequentially to provide for each learner so that optimal attainment in mathematics is possible. The teacher as well as school administrators need to realize that the whole pupil needs educating including physiological, safety and security, love and belonging, esteem, and knowledge needs are related and not isolated from each other. Pupils who came for unsafe areas of a city or a rural area might well be hindered from achievement in mathematics due to a lack of security. Child abuse which tends to be rather rampant in the United States will also take its toll of pupils doing well in mathematics. Teachers need to guide pupils to develop feelings of belonging in school and work with parents so that the child feels he/she is a part of the home and needs to be a worthy accepted member therein. The teacher must always accept pupils unconditionally and strive to guide others to accept a pupil. Cooperative endeavors provide excellent opportunities for pupils to develop feelings of belonging. Learners need to experience groups whereby each is highly acceptable of others. Being an outcast in a classroom will not be in the least bit enjoyable. Mathematics teachers then need to arrange groups so that each pupil feels he/she belongs as inherent members therein. The talents of pupils need to be observed and identified. They are there and need to be noticed and nurtured talents of pupils in mathematics are very necessary for the teacher to notice, accept, and guide in further development. These talents can further be developed through enrichment experiences, extra credit assignments, self selection problem areas to be pursued by the learner, learning centers and stations, and contract systems of instruction. Encouragement and challenge are key concepts here in identifying and manifesting pupil talents in mathematics.

Each pupil has a desire to become the kind of person he/she desires. Certainly, the teacher must guide each learner to become the kind of person he/she wishes and this includes achievement in mathematics. One cannot isolate a pupil and desire to develop talents in mathematics only. The total child is involved in learning and needs to have the knowledge, social, emotional and physical domains developed optimally in toto.

Organizing the Room Environment

Pupils love to observe and learn from a stimulating environment. The curriculum area of mathematics has many possibilities for arranging a rich learning environment for pupils. Thus bulletin boards may be developed by the teacher/pupils pertaining to each unit being studied. As supervisor of student teachers and cooperating teachers, one of the another has noticed many bulletin board displays that are highly worthy for use in direct teaching as well as for incidental learning for pupils. The following are examples of these bulletin board displays:

1. Four pupils were flying balloons in which one balloon had the shape of a square, another a rectangle, another a circle, and a fourth a triangle. This display was used in direct teaching of geometrical figures for kindergarten pupils.

2. A pictograph showed in which month each first grade pupil had his/her birthday. Thus for January there were three pictures of children since three first graders had their birthdays during this month. The other months of the year followed with the correct number of pictures for each showing when pupils had their birthdays.
3. A large birthday cake , attractively decorated, was made of different colors of construction paper. Candles made of construction paper were inserted into holes in the cake. The number inserted depended on the day of the month such as a birthday of a child being on January 23, thus necessitating 23 birthday candles in the cake. In this way pupils received practice on the first/second grade multi-age room, in counting the number of days that had elapsed in a month, directly related to the number of candles on the cake.
4. Fourth grade pupils were asked to bring into the classroom pictures from magazines/newspapers or drawn personally to show incidences in which the operation of multiplication by a two or three place multiplier was in evidence. Scenes included eleven head of cattle in a holding pen with a total of twenty-four pens being in the illustration: fourteen red cars being in a lot at an automobile agency. There were twelve of these sets; and seventeen kinds of soft drinks in the supermarket with fifteen of each kind in a set. Learners here were to do homework in relating the semiconcrete to the abstract to determine the products in multiplication. Application of what had been learned was a further goal.
5. Fourth and fifth grade pupils made a bulletin board display consisting of geometry art. Here, there were cutouts of diverse geometrical figures of different colors; these were used to make people, buildings, and machines. An interesting caption appeared on this display reading "Geometry in Our Creative World."

Student teachers and cooperating teachers we have supervised developed numerous centers around the classroom for pupils to work at, either as a part of an assignment or as enrichment experiences. One fascinating center emphasized a laboratory approach in learning mathematics. A hands-on approach was at the heart of learning opportunities at this center.

1. To measure length, width, and area, the following persons/objects were used and the results recorded; sheets of paper of different sizes, pencils and pens, as well as textbooks. Learners also measured the length and width of the door nearby, windows in the classroom, size of desk tops and of the classroom, height of the classroom ceiling and of pupils, among other objects and items. A centimeter tape and a meter stick were used in emphasizing the metric system of measurement.
2. To determine volume, pupils used pint, quart, gallon, peck, and bushel containers when using English measurement. Liter containers were used when stressing metric systems of measurement. Water, milk, and other fluids were measured using both systems of measurement.
3. To measure temperature, a mercury thermometer, a candy thermometer, and an oven thermometer were used for both Celsius and Fahrenheit temperature readings. Learners made comparisons of various liquids, using thermometers, with and without sunlight in the same locality. Temperature of different food items made for interesting comparisons.
4. To measure time, traditional clocks as well as digital watches were used by pupils. A daily schedule was drawn up for one day to show the amount of time spent in each activity.
5. To measure angles in geometrical figures, compasses and protractors were used. Pupils constructed these figures to measure angles as well as measured angles of concrete materials in the classroom, such as the door.

The mathematics teacher needs to be creative in thinking of activities and experiences for laboratory procedures in guiding pupils in learning mathematics. Kennedy and Tipps (1991) wrote the following:

When the mathematics curriculum consisted entirely of number operations and mental calculations, no one required materials more elaborate than a chalkboard and a piece of chalk. Today's curriculum is much more complex and what we know about teaching and learning is more complete. The mathematics program advocated by National Council Teachers of Mathematics, mathematics educators, and many individual teachers is founded on the knowledge that students learn better when tools for learning mathematics are available.... Materials for teaching should be in the school's budget, just as paper and paste, reading supplies, and physical education equipment are. When money is a problem, as it often is in schools, teacher-made materials can substitute for many commercial items. There should be sufficient quantity of both commercial and teacher-made materials for an entire class or for small group work. Not every teacher in the school needs a classroom set of each of the materials. A mathematics closet in the school can be used to store materials until needed by teachers. Materials that are in constant demand may require multiple sets.

Well chosen, properly used manipulatives enhance understanding, generate interest, and promote problem solving and understanding of concepts. They may be used for introducing, reinforcing, reteaching, and extending concepts for small groups, entire classes, or individual students. Materials make even the most difficult mathematics concepts easier to understand. Manipulatives enable students to connect real objects and abstract mathematical concepts.

Sequence in the Mathematics Curriculum

In organizing for instruction, the mathematics teacher needs to think about what comes first, second, third, fourth in learning activities for pupils to achieve objectives. Quality organization is salient here. There are several approaches in determining sequence in the mathematics curriculum. First, the teacher basically chooses which learning opportunities pupils should experience and in which order. The following are provided as an example in the teacher determining sequence for pupils in mathematics:

1. Showing and discussing a video-tape on addition of unit fractions.
2. Using unit fractions pertaining to adding parts of a candy bar, clearly visible to all in the classroom.

3. Putting pieces together of a circle shown on a screen by using the overheads-projector. Here, for example, pupils observe one-third + one-third + one-third, as unit fractions, in adding to show the values of one.
4. Having pupils select from a learning center parts of a geometric figure with values of a unit fraction such as one-half of a square. A second one-half of the square is then joined with the first part to indicate in writing the abstract that one-half plus one-half is equal to one.
5. Letting learners work a practice exercise in which unit fractions are emphasized. The teacher needs to observe and evaluate throughout the sequence of activities if pupils are paying attention to each activity, are actively involved in learning, exhibit interest in ongoing learning opportunities, and generate relevant hypotheses to stimulating questions raised by the mathematics teacher.

In the above example, the teacher chooses sequence in learning activities for pupils. Many teachers use this approach in organizing the mathematics curriculum.

As a second example in determining sequence in the mathematics curriculum, the teacher may believe that pupils do their very own sequencing in learning. These teachers then stress strong involvement by pupils in determining order in experiencing objectives, learning opportunities, and evaluation procedures. Sequence resides within the learner not the teacher nor textbooks or other materials of instruction. Thus the mathematics teacher provides as many chances as possible for pupils to be active in choosing what to learn (the scope) as well as sequence. A learning stations approach might be stressed here. Thus from among diverse stations, the learner chooses which tasks to pursue and which to omit. There are ample tasks here so that selections and omissions are possible with time on task still being a major objective in learning. Thus the pupil may select tasks in mathematics which are on his/ her level of learning. Ideally the chosen tasks are challenging and do provide quality sequence in achievement. A second approach in which a pupil may sequence his/her learning experiences emphasizes a contract system. Pupils with tech guidance may select what to complete sequentially in the mathematics curriculum. The teacher assists, guides, and helps develop the contract. The due date is placed on the contract with signatures of both the pupil and the mathematics teacher. The pupil might then complete tasks in any order in the contract. Sequence then residing within the learner. A third approach would be for the pupil and the teacher to plan which learning activities and in which order should be completed by the former. The involved learner needs to have a strong voice in determining *what* to learn (the scope) as well as *when* to learn the contents (sequence).

Unit Teaching in Mathematics

Mathematics teachers need to plan each unit taught carefully and thoroughly. The following parts need to be placed in the unit of instruction:

1. The objectives section. Here a debate exists in selecting and writing objectives. Should they be stated in measurable terms or should they be stated in a more open ended approach, such as in general objectives? General objective need to be clearly written so that the mathematics teacher knows what is to be taught. Thus vagueness in written objectives has been eliminated.
2. The learning opportunities section. These learning opportunities aid pupils in achieving stated objectives in mathematics. How broad should the scope of learning opportunities be? There needs to be a multimedia approach. Thus carefully selected basal texts, technology, items that are reality based for the mathematics laboratory, computer assisted instruction, video disks and tapes, workbooks, and teacher collected materials are needed to offer a quality mathematics curriculum.
3. Grouping of pupils for instruction. Here, the mathematics teacher needs to think of how learners are to be placed in groups, be it the class as a whole, committees and cooperative learning, and individualized instruction. A guideline that needs to be followed pertains to the conditions under which a pupil may learn as much as possible in mathematics individually as well as collectively.

4. Enrichment experiences for pupils. Here, the teacher needs to develop and implement using learning stations. Tasks at these learning stations provide for stimulating and challenging activities when pupils have completed their regular class work in a mathematics lesson. The tasks need to provide for individual differences in that learners may choose as well as leave out what is not perceived to be purposeful. An adequate number of tasks then needs to be in the offing. With enrichment activities, pupils should experience interest and motivation in working on self selected tasks in mathematics.
4. The evaluation section. Mathematics teachers need to use a variety of procedures to determine pupil achievement. Norm referenced and criterion referenced tests may be used to reveal learner achievement and progress. However, by themselves, this would not be adequate. Pupils' attitudes toward mathematics also must be evaluated. This can be done through teacher observation. The teacher may observe if pupils complete their work on time, if they indicate liking mathematics, if they have an inward desire to do more work such as at enrichment centers, and if they discuss mathematics with others positively in their spare time. Teacher observation can be used to notice everyday deficiencies pupils have in mathematics and work toward remediation. Presently much emphasis is given to constructivism which indicates the mathematics teacher should appraise learners within a situation. The situation or learning activity should be reality based. Portfolios is also a relatively new approach advocated to appraise learner progress. Checklists, rating scales, pupil journal entries, and teacher written test items are further techniques to use in appraising learner achievement. Then too, there should be ample opportunities for pupils as well as teachers to appraise themselves in terms of quality standards of achievement.

Mathematics teachers need to be self organized for each day of instruction. Pupils realize if a teacher is not prepared adequately for teaching a lesson or unit in mathematics. As professionals, teachers must be adequately ready to guide optimal learner achievement in mathmatics. They should

1. read recent articles on teaching mathematics such as from the monthly publications of the Arithmetic Teacher and the Mathematics Teacher.
2. road research studies on teaching such as from The Educational Research Information Center (ERIC) Clearing House on mathematics.
3. visit classrooms where exemplary mathematics teaching is in evidence.
4. attend professional meetings in teaching such as the National Council Teachers of Mathematics (NCTM), annual and regional conventions for teachers. A variety of meetings are held at these conventions to meet personal needs of mathematics teachers.
5. write articles for possible publication on mathematics teaching. Readers are looking for ideas from classroom teachers.
6. become involved in workshops, faculty development, and departmental meetings in the school setting pertaining to improving the mathematics curriculum.
7. share ideas on teaching mathematics with other teachers. Learn from each other.
8. develop a weekly or monthly newsletter in school for teachers in teaching mathematics.
9. read recent professional textbooks on mathematics teaching. Use these ideas to improve the mathematics curriculum where feasible.
10. attend classes on college/university campuses to take courses in using technology in the mathematics curriculum.

In Summary

There has been a long time debate on heterogeneous versus homogeneous grouping of pupils in the school setting. Within a class, the mathematics teacher will wish to use each approach at appropriate times. Generally, a classroom will be heterogeneously grouped with mixed achievement levels of pupils therein. Thus the mathematics teacher may feel that selected pupils need to be placed in a specific group for more practice on a specific process in ongoing lesson or unit of study. These learners may need more time in understanding on computing as compared to other learners in the classroom. At other times, the class as a whole may be taught when introducing a new algorithm using concrete materials of instruction. The entire class of pupils then receives the same stimulating information. Enrichment activities may be designed for the talented and gifted as well as those who are highly motivated to achieve. In these situations, there will be more of homogeneous grouping here. Grouping pupils for instruction needs to be flexible and utilitarian. The mathematics teacher needs to look at the purpose for grouping learners in organizing for instruction.

Most elementary school teachers teach in self contained classrooms, not in departmentalized rooms. In either case, the teacher may use heterogeneous as well as homogeneous grouping for instruction in mathematics. When studying the learner, the mathematics teacher might discern which pupils at a given time need to be placed into special groups within the classroom. At other times, the entire roomful of pupils may be taught at one time, such as when introducing new concepts, a new unit of study, or a new algorithm. Committee work and cooperative learning might stress uniform or mixed achievement levels of pupils. Pupils do learn from each other in small group endeavors. Quality human relations is important here. Conflict management, consensus, and problem solving skills are important to develop in cooperative learning.

The use of team teaching again emphasizes resolving disagreements harmoniously since teachers here plan objectives, learning opportunities, and appraisal procedures cooperatively. Teachers should not be placed on a team if the chances are great in having conflict. Team teaching does not work if there are continual major disagreements. Minor disagreements will occur and these can be worked out in problem solving situations. In fact, if disagreements occur, then there are opportunities for learning, growth, and development among team members.

In reality, all mathematics teachers should upgrade their classes and adjust instruction to where each pupil is achieving presently. Continuous progress then needs to be in evidence. Ungraded math classes can be emphasized in heterogeneously as well as homogeneously grouped classes.

How classrooms are organized for mathematics instruction and their successes might well depend to a large extent upon how well the needs of pupils have been met. A pupil who has not had physiological needs met such as adequate nutrition, proper clothing, and effective shelter probably will not achieve well in mathematics. If safety and security needs are lacking on the part of a pupil, he/she might feel threatened and cannot do well in school achievement. All pupils desire to have feelings of belonging to a group and have their talents and skills recognized. When these needs have been met, the chances are pupil achievement in mathematics will be at a much higher level than is now in evidence.

There are many other factors needing attention in organizing the mathematics curriculum including developing stimulating bulletin boards, devising laboratory approaches in teaching, as well as connecting the concrete/semiconcrete with abstract numerals and symbols.

Strategies to implement a new lesson or unit of study require the use of stimulating materials of instruction such as using audio-visuall aids, real items and objects, as well as guiding pupils to move to the abstract. The abstract is the goal of all learning in mathematics. However, the abstract such as numerals and other symbols needs to be related to the concrete and the semiconcrete. After the lesson or unit has been a part of the introductory activities, the mathematics teacher needs to stress developmental experience. Here, the mathematics teacher assists pupils to develop facts, concepts, generalizations, and main ideas in greater depth as well as to pursue new objectives. The new objectives are related directly to the old so that the latter provides readiness for the new to be learned. Culminating activities sin a lesson or unit end the class session in an interesting and challenging way for pupils. Curiosity and further interest in learning are paramount on the part of pupils to achieve, develop, and learn.

Marks, Hiatt, and Neufeld wrote:

Under what conditions can pupils learn most effectively?

> How can the teacher provide these conditions? Classroom teachers, as well as experts in learning theory have studied these and similar questions for many years. One important fact that has emerged is that learning conditions must be related to desired outcomes. If information and simple mastery of operations are all that are desired from the mathematics class, then the mechanical learning process of memorize, drill, and test is wholly satisfactory.

The outcomes sought in mathematics classes today are much broader and more significant than is mere mechanical mastery. An important new responsibility of the mathematics teacher is to encourage creativity by helping pupils discover the basic ideas, laws, and principles of mathematics. As a result of this focus on understanding as well as mastery of skills, many pupils discover that the most interesting thing in the study of mathematics is mathematics itself. One of the most striking features in the teaching of mathematics today is thus the increasing attention given to development of ability to discover, verify, and generalize in the systematic study of mathematics. If pupils are to acquire these abilities, they must devote more attention to the development of concepts and gain a precision in vocabulary without which they cannot refine the concepts.

Selected References

Ediger, Marlow (1996). "The School Principal with New Responsibilities," *Education,* 116: 381.

Ediger. Marlow (1988). *The Elementary Curriculum.* Simpson Publishing Company, 130.

Marks, John L., Arthur Hiatt, and Evelyn M. Neufeld (1985). *Teaching Elementary School Mathematics for Understanding.* Fifth Edition. New York: McGraw Hill Book Company.

Kennedy, Leonard. M., and Steve Tipps (1991). *Guiding Children's Learning of Mathematics,* Sixth Edition. Belmont, California: Wadsworth Publishing Company, 65-66.

Reys, Robert E., Marilyn N. Suydam, and Mary Montgomery Lindquist (1995). *Helping Children Learn Mathematics,* Fourth Edition. Boston: Allyn and Bacon, 45.

Stoddard, George D. (1961). *The Dual Progress Plan.* New York: Harper and Row, Publishers.

18

Sequence in Primary Grade Mathematics

Primary grade teachers need to assist pupils to achieve meaning in ongoing lessons and units of study. With meaning, pupils understand what is being taught. It does little good to teach pupils that which does not make sense and cannot be understood. Time is wasted in teaching mathematics in situations such as these. Time needs to be used wisely by the teacher in guiding pupils to attach meaning and understanding in content learned.

A definite sequence should then be in order for pupils to be successful learners. The primary grade teacher may use a logical mathematics curriculum. Here, he/she designs learning opportunities in which pupils achieve increasingly more complex objectives. Each step along the way in learning provides a scaffold for the next sequential objective to achieve. Achieved objectives by pupils provide criteria for the teacher to gauge his/her teaching effectiveness. Learning opportunities are arranged so that pupils individually and collaboratively might achieve stated objectives. The teacher arranges the order of objectives for pupil attainment as well as the order of learning opportunities for learners to experience. Meaning and understanding need to be in evidence for each objective that is attained as well as each sequential learning opportunity pursued. The teacher then devises a mathematics curriculum in which pupils experience sequence, success, and meaning in mathematics.

A second approach stresses a psychological sequence. Here,

there are broad objectives planned for pupil achievement. However, pupil-teacher planning is involved in determining the order or sequence of specific objectives to be achieved as well as the learning opportunities to be pursued.

We have supervised students and regular teachers for thirty years in the public schools in the teaching of mathematics and other curriculum areas in an integrated, interdisciplinary curriculum. We will describe a team consisting of the student teacher and the regular teacher teaching meaningfully using first a logical mathematics curriculum followed by a different student teacher and regular teacher using a psychological curriculum.

Student teachers we supervised generally worked as a team with the regular teacher. Team teaching was then in evidence. There are state mandated objectives which provide constraints in planning the mathematics curriculum. These are measurably stated objectives for pupils to achieve in mathematics. Criterion referenced tests are developed by the state to measure pupil achievement at selected intervals.

The National Council Teachers of Mathematics in 1989 completed *Curriculum and Evaluation Standards for School Mathematics*. This excellent volume provided a framework for the voluntary selection of objectives for pupil attainment. Ouality sequence may then be in the offing for pupils in ongoing lessons and units of study in mathematics.

Achieving Logical Sequence in Mathematics

The following situation emphasizes sequential learning opportunities that the student teacher and the regular teacher, we supervised, attempted to provide. First grade pupils are to achieve the objective pertaining to "adding 5 + 4 = ." A variety of learning opportunities were provided for pupils. The student teacher and the regular teacher showed five sticks to pupils and asked how many there were in the set. If a pupil responded incorrectly, the teaching team asked for another response without any ridiculing the person or answer that was not correct. Correct answers were rewarded with verbal praise. After receiving the right answer, the teaching team hold up four sticks. The first pupil gave the correct response with four members being in the set. Next, the teaching team held all nine sticks up and asked for the correct number of sticks in the new set. The number sentence "5 + 4 = 9" was printed on the chalkboard as well as typed into the computer as each value was given by pupils when responding to the number of sticks in each set as well as the total number with sets combined. A printout of the number sentence was provided to pupils. Meaning theory was emphasized by the student and regular teacher in starting with concrete materials of instruction which were sticks in this case. If pupils responded incorrectly, selected learners were asked to provide reasons for their thinking. In this way teachers analyzed reasons for logic used by pupils in thinking mathematically. Reflective thinking is important in reviewing algorithms and methods of reasoning. Reflection by learners is also important in thinking about correct answers that were given. Processes and products are then analyzed in the mathematics curriculum. Improved retention of content should be an end result when pupils reflect upon what has been learned.

Next in sequence, the student teacher and the regular teacher wished for pupils to see the relationship of 5+4=– and 4+5= –. Thus the teaching team held up four sticks and then five sticks with pupils giving a correct answer for the number of members in each set. The commutative property of addition was emphasized by the teacher. Here, pupils built on previously acquired information by realizing that a+b= b+a. "This is one of the most worthwhile ideas that pupils can achieve," according to the regular teacher. "Modern school mathematics of the latter 1950's," she continued, "truly pinpointed the commutative property of addition and multiplication which has value on any grade level be it primary grades or higher education mathematics. This property continues to be as important as ever in teaching mathematics."

Both the student and the regular teacher emphasized that primary grade pupils should experience pictorial materials, following the concrete, in a logical curriculum. The two teachers determined the order of presentation of materials. Here, the teachers had pictures on a chart. The first chart had five cats and pupils were asked to tell how many there were. The teaching team then held up the chart with four illustrated cats. Pupils told how many there were. To develop concepts of addition in depth, the teaching team had pairs of illustrated charts containing dogs, elephants, tigers, lions, and people. The concept of 5+4=......and 4+5=..... has the same answer and was being emphasized in intensive or in = depth teaching. The teaching team determined the order of presenting the learning opportunities in a logical curriculum. As each set of illustrations or pictures was presented, the teaching team wrote the corresponding numerals on the chalkboard as well in the computer.

The transition needs to be made here by pupils in moving from the concrete and pictorial to abstract numerals. In a logical mathematics curriculum, the teacher determines sequence. For a brief review, the teaching team consisting of the student teacher and the regular teacher asked five pupils to come to the front of the classroom. Then four more pupils were asked to come to the front. The student teacher wrote the numeral "5" to indicate the number of pupils in the first set; the numeral "4" was written to show the number of pupils in the second set. Pupils in the two sets were then joined together with a pupil coming forward to write the numeral "9." The abstract concept of 5+4=9 was clearly written so that all learners could see this number sentence. The two sets of pupils were changed in order of presentation so that learners attached meaning to the commutative property of "4+5=9" or inverse operation. The teaching team stressed consistently that primary grade pupils perceive the concrete and the pictorial stages of learning being related to the resulting abstract number sentence. Also, changing the order of the two addends did not change the sum in addition. To stress the abstract only, the teaching team passed a worksheet to pupils stressing basic number pairs. The number pairs included all previously learned addition and subtraction facts, including the newly acquired learnings in addition. The number pairs were written at random on the worksheet to ascertain what pupils had learned and what needed more emphasis. Each pupil was asked to explain how incorrect answers were obtained. With diagnosis, the student and the regular teacher could better determine logically which the next sequential step of teaching should be. The teachers continued to do the sequencing of learning opportunities for pupils in the ongoing lesson plan. A logical approach was used by the teaching team in that human reason and feedback from pupils determined the order of experiences for learners.

Kennedy and Tips (1993) list sequential steps developed by Madeline Hunter and Douglas Russell that stress a logical mathematics curriculum.

1. Setting the stage
2. Statement of objective
3. Instructional input
4. Modelling
5. Checking for understanding
6. Guided practice
7. Independent practice

According to the above lesson plan, the teacher provides readiness or review of what pupils had learned previously in mathematics (setting the stage). He/she then states the objective(s) for pupils to achieve, as well as choosing learning opportunities so that pupils may achieve the stated objective. In these learning opportunities, the teacher models by showing pupils how to proceed or giving examples of how to work a problem or secure an answer to a question in mathematics. The teacher makes certain that pupils are working problems correctly before providing guided or supervised activities to pupils. Independent practice is the last kind of learning opportunity for pupils. Within these steps of learning, the teacher in a logical order sequences experiences for learners.

A Psychological Mathematics Curriculum

We have also supervised student and regular teachers who believed strongly in a psychological mathematics curriculum. Here, the teaching team made up of the two teachers assisted pupils to develop their very own sequence in learning. These teachers felt that sequence resides within the learner, not textbooks nor teachers. It is the pupil that needs to determine what comes first, second, third, and so on in learning. Thus the psychological curriculum is more open-ended as compared to the logical mathematics curriculum. The mathematics teacher then needs to motivate pupils to pursue what is sequential in their very own minds. The objectives, the learning opportunities, and evaluation procedures in their determination need considerable input from pupils. How might a psychological sequence work in guiding pupils to use what has been learned? Here, pupils with student teacher and regular teacher guidance developed a miniature supermarket with empty fruit and vegetable containers as well as cereal boxes, among other objects. The 'food products' were placed on different shelves in the classroom. Prices on each item harmonized with numerical values being studied in class. Pupils were told that the marked prices of each commodity might not be the real prices found in supermarkets. Toy money was used by pupils to buy different items from the "supermarket shelves." Thus pupils might buy a box of cereal for five cents, as marked, and a can of peaches for four cents. Pupils would then determine what 5+4=....... They could use hand held calculators, if desired. Each pupil had adequate opportunities to buy from the miniature supermarket and use what had been learned previously in mathematics. Learners individually and collaborativelly sequenced their very own experiences in a psychological mathematics curriculum. The teaching team believed very strongly on pupils using what had been learned so that forgetting might less likely occur; the sequential review was determined by pupils, not the teaching team. Pupils together with the teaching team planned and implemented the use of the miniature supermarket; a psychological sequence was involved in experiencing the integrated concrete, pictorial, and abstract facets of learning.

A second approach in guiding pupils to sequence their very own learning activities is to use learning stations. Here, the pupils and their teachers planned the title for each station as well as the materials for instruction that should be at each station. Learning experiences in using the materials were also planned by pupils with the assistance of the student teacher and the regular teacher. There were an ample number of tasks so that pupils might choose which to pursue and which to omit. Pupils selected sequential tasks to pursue and complete; they were motivated and interested in choices made since learners themselves made the selection.

There are excellent ways for teachers to use in guiding pupils to sequence personal learning opportunities. In a philosophy of constructivism pupils need to find meaning in a contextual situation. Learners then construct their very own knowledge as activities and experiences accrue. Knowledge as a result of learning opportunities pursued is made by the self or selves in a constructivist mathematics curriculum.

Needed is Quality Sequence in Learning

With quality sequence, be it logical or psychological, new content acquired is based upon that which had been achieved. The new is related directly to the old. There is a definite relationship here between what is being learned and what has been learned. Feelings of success, very often, come about due to experiencing quality sequence. Jackson and Canada (1995) wrote the following pertaining to their research:

This study explored the relationship between self-concept as measured by the Tennessee Self Concept Scale and mathematics achievement as measured by the California Test of Achievement in a population of 133 students ranging in ages from 13 to 16 and designated at risk of not graduating from high school. Results were based on pre/post test data with the intervening treatment consisting of an eight-week residential summer program with strong social service, counseling, and work components. Significant correlations indicated the student's total mathematics scores increased; so did their self acceptance, feelings of worth and adequacy as well as their sense of capacity in distinctions between right and wrong in their conduct.

From the above study, it is important to notice that as mathematics scores from tests go higher, the self-concept of the learner also increases. A carefully planned program of sequential progress for pupils, be it a logical or psychological sequence, might well improve how pupils feel and think about themselves.

An adequate number of workshops for inservice education and staff development need to stress the importance of emphasizing quality sequence for pupils in mathematics. Columbia and Dologos (1993) wrote the following in teacher education programs:

In the preparation of classroom teachers we must model our commitment to good teaching to enable future teachers of mathematics to present lessons that reflect the vision of the

Curriculum and Evaluation Standards for School Mathematics and its companion document *Professional Standards for Teaching Mathematics*. In addition to adopting the modeled strategies, continual reflection on tasks, discourse, environment, and analysis will enable future teachers to integrate the goals of both documents into their evolving instructional philosophy in order to become effective teachers of mathematics. Finally, we must remember that our goal in connecting teacher preparation to the vision set by the National Council Teachers of Mathematics is to ensure that an environment is created in the classroom where students can be successful and confident in mathematics.

The National Council Teachers of Mathematics (NCTM) is the leading organization in the world for mathematics teachers interested in improving the curriculum in mathematics. Much time and attention have been given by the NCTM in developing objectives for teachers to use in teaching. The objectives are voluntary to use and do provide an excellent framework for determining what should be taught in mathematics, kindergarten through secondary school. Objectives chosen for implementation by teachers (Ediger, 1994) should be emphasized so that learners experience:

1. Meaningful lessons and units of study. With meaning, pupils understand and comprehend that which was contained in ongoing learning opportunities.
2. Interesting content and skills in the curriculum. With interest, the pupil and the curriculum become one, not separate entities. Pupils attend and achieve from ongoing lessons and units of study.
3. Purpose in learning. With purpose for learning, pupils accept reasons for attaining relevant facts, concepts, and generalizations presented....
4. Sequence in learning. With quality sequence, pupils relate newly acquired content with that achieved previously. Previous knowledge obtained provides readiness for the new objectives to be attained. Pupils need guidance to perceive relationship of knowledge in teaching-learning situations.
5.

skills, and attitudes–three kinds of objectives need to be achieved by students. These objectives interact and are not in isolation from each other. For example, if pupils possess positive attitudes, they should achieve needed knowledge and skills more readily.

David Ausubel, a cognitive based educational psychologist, believes that quality sequence is the most important ingredient to emphasize in teaching and learning situations. Thus the mathematics teacher needs to start pupils with where they are presently in achievement and stress continuous progress. Previous learning then provides an advance organizer or readiness for the new objectives to be achieved by pupils (see Shepherd and Ragan, 1982).

In addition to stressing a cognitive psychology in teaching and learning, there are personal characteristics of the teacher that assist pupils to achieve more adequately in mathematics. Lampert and Eshelman (1995) advocate teachers exhibit patience, curiosity, generosity in listening to and caring about people, confidence, trust, and imagination. These characteristics strongly stress the affective dimension of teachers in the instructional arena. Such traits of the ideal teacher, I believe, must be emphasized in mathematics programs which improve quality sequence in pupil learning. Patient, curious, generous, confident, trustful, and imaginative mathematics teachers will be concerned about each pupil making continual optimal progress.

In Closing

Schifter (1996) stresses that constructivism philosophy of teaching mathematics does not emphasize a finished point but rather there is further growth and change in pupil development. In a constructivist philosophy of instruction, pupils are doers, not hearers only. When actively involved in ongoing lessons and units of study, pupils reflect or think about what has transpired previously. Teachers and pupils both have attitudes of inquiry when trying out new ideas. Pupils' ideas are analyzed; there is room then for growth and change. We believe this change brings an improved *sequence* for growth in the mathematics curriculum.

Selected References

Columbia, Lynn, and Kathleen Dologos (1993). "Professional Development for Teachers of Mathematics," *Education,* 114, 32-36.

Ediger, Marlow (1994). "Early Field Experiences in Teacher Education," *College Student Journal,* 28: 302-306.

Jackson. Mary H., and Richard Canada (1995). "Self Concept and Math Among Potential School Dropouts," *Journal of Instructional Psychology,* 22: 234-237.

Kennedy, Leonard M., and Steve Tipps (1993). *Guiding Children's Learning of Mathematics.* Belmont, California: Wadsworth Publishing Company, Pages 47-55.

Lampert, Magdalene, and Angie S. Eshelman (1995). "Using Technology to Support Effective and Responsible Teacher Education: The Case of Interactive Multimedia in Mathematics Methods Courses," paper presented at the annual meeting of the American Educational Research Association, San Francisco, April, 1995.

Shepherd, Gene and William Ragan (1982). *Modern Elementary Curriculum.* New York: The Macmillan Company, pages 22, 23, 39, 309, 342, and 346.

Shifter, Deborah (1996). "A Constructivist Perspective on Teaching and Learning Mathematics, *Phi Delta Kappan* 77: 492-499.

19

Appraising Student Achievement in Mathematics

In an era of accountability for teachers, it is vital that quality procedures in evaluation of learner progress in the mathematics curriculum be in evidence. Which techniques of appraisal then need to be emphasized?

Using Checklists and Rating Scales

A checklist may be utilized if progress can be recorded on an either/or basis. For example, a student who correctly finds the area of a square, rectangle, or triangle can receive a checkmark on his/her checklist to indicate that the following objective has been attained: Given the dimensions of each side of a square, rectangle, or triangle, the pupil can compute the area correctly.

The name of the involved pupil needs to appear on the checklist. The date for achieving the objective needs to be recorded next to the objective on the checklist. Relevant sequential objectives only should appear on the checklist.

The rating scale should be used when general objectives are utilized in ongoing units. It is difficult to state selected objectives in measurable terms. And yet, the following are indeed worthwhile in any unit of study in mathematics: being able to think critically, creatively, and solve problems. Thus, a student's proficiency in each of these higher cognitive level skills may be evaluated on a five-point scale, such as doing excellent, very good, average, below average, and poor in thinking critically, creatively, and being able to solve problems.

No doubt, the checklist and its use appraises students objectively, independent of the evaluator, whereas the rating scale stresses subjectivity, in degrees. Interscorer reliability in utilizing the rating scale can be emphasized by having a colleague assist in developing the ratings on a five-point scale. If the two raters of student achievement in critical thinking, creative thinking, and problem solving agree, the chances are reliability with its consistency of results is in evidence.

Using Standardized Tests

In using standardized tests to appraise student progress, teachers of mathematics in a school system need to notice validity correlation coefficients, as well as reliability values. Certainly, the test used to measure pupil achievement must appraise student progress in terms of what it purports to measure and in this situation achievement in mathematics. Validity in the measurement instrument is then inherent. Consistency of results is also wanted if a test, for example, were taken over again by the student. Otherwise, what worth would a test have if the same pupil taking it two times would rank on the 70th and 25th percentile respectively? Inconsistent results are then in evidence. Ranking on the 70th percentile is high since out of every 100 taking the test, thirty would be above and seventy below. Being on the 25th percentile is low. Thus, out of every 100 students taking the test, seventy-five would be above and twenty-five below for the person taking the test and ranking on the 25th percentile.

Standardized achievement tests are norm referenced. When viewing the results from standardized achievement tests in mathematics, pupils' scores are spread out from high to low. This is typical of norm referenced testing. Thus, a student's results can be compared with others in a classroom or schools. The range in percentile ranks could be from 99th to the first percentile. Or, if grade equivalents are given for each student, the range could be from twelve to grade three, as examples, for a seventh grade student.

Norm referenced tests have been standardized on a set of students which should possess similiar traits and characteristitics, as the general population in society. Otherwise, the concept of external validity would be lacking. For example, if one's present classroom of students were all gifted by definition and the norm group on which the achievement test was standardized were heterogenous (mixed achievement levels), it would mean that the two sets would be highly incongruous. Results of the gifted students can be compared to the norm group. However, the chances are that the standardized test will not measure as accurately as one would wish the results to be for the gifted students. Why? There would be relatively few students in the norm group who were gifted, compared to average achievers. In the norm group, most students will have measured close to the mean or arithmetical average. One standard deviation (34% of the norm group) below the mean and one standard deviation above the mean (another 34% of the norm group) make for 68% of the students in the norm group. These students represent a range of percentiles from the 16th percentile to the 84th percentile. Thus, most of the students in the norm group have been taken into consideration with the ± one standard deviation above the mean. Gifted students in our classroom would tend to score above or well above the 84th percentile. Just sixteen per cent of the students in the norm group scored higher than one standard deviation above the mean. Add another standard deviation above the 84th percentile (one standard deviation above the mean is the 84th percentile approximately) and a student is on the 98th percentile. Thus, two standard deviations above the mean and two standard deviations below the mean account for 96 per cent of the norm group, leaving two per cent three standard deviations above the mean and two per cent three standard deviations below the mean. Thus, one's own gifted class of students in comparison with the gifted on the norm group would find few in number of the latter. Most students in the norm group would cluster more so toward the mean. Thus, an inadequate number of students three standard deviations above the mean are available to compare results with the teacher's own gifted class. Better comparisons can be made with average and talented students in the norm group if students in the teachers classroom are also of similar abilities. An adequate number of any category of pupils be they high, average, or slow learners need to be in any norm group so that students in classrooms who come in any one of these categories may have adequate numbers for making comparisons.

Criterion Referenced Tests (CRTs)

Norm referenced test results provide for a range of achivement among students. Thus, a spread of scores are involved from high to low. On the other hand, CRTs may not provide for much of a spread of scores among students. CRT philosophy is much different from norm referenced generalizations. In CRTs, whether teacher, school, or commercially developed, measurably stated objectives are emphasized. The objectives exist prior to instruction of pupils. Either students attain or do not attain the chosen ends. No guesswork is involved in these testing situations.

The teacher can announce to students at the beginning of a class session which objective(s) a student is to attain. The mathematics teacher may then teach to the stated objective. The learning activity or activities are valid in that they harmonize directly with the objective. Finally, the instructor appraises to see if each student has or has not achieved the specific objective. The teacher then stresses a similar sequence, announce the measurable objective to learners prior to instruction, teach so that students are on course to directly attain the precise end, and measure to notice which pupils have been successful in goal attainment. If a student did not achieve a measurable objective, additional learning activities need to be provided so that the involved learner can be successful in attaining the chosen end(s).

Time is the variable in CRT. Thus, slow learners will need more time as compared to average and gifted students to achieve worthwhile objectives. A computer printout of sequential objectives may be sent home with the pupil to parents. Along with each objective on the printout are the textbook, workbook, and/or worksheet pages so that the parent might know exactly which learning activities assist students to attain an end. On the elementary school level, in most cases, it is possible in homework for parents to help their offspring achieve objectives.

Thus, slow, average, and fast learners can achieve the same sequential objectives. More time and assistance must be given to the slower achiever to attain sequential ends.

From CRT results, there might well be a spread of scores in achievement from high to low. However, that is not the point. The goal in CRT is to assist each student to achieve as many specific objectives as is reasonably possible. Absolute standards are then emphasized. Either a student has or has not achieved a sequential objective.

Anecdotal Records

Teachers of mathematics need to take time to record representative behavior of each student. Unless behaviors are recorded, they can be forgotten by the teacher. Representative behavior of each student needs to be recorded. Biased statements written for any pupil should be omitted. Loaded words also should be left out of written anecdotal statements. If a teacher records observed behavior for two students each school day, it does not take long before the rounds have been made one time. For example, with twenty-four students in a classroom, it should take the teacher twelve school days to complete writing the acecdotal statements for involved learners. The teacher needs to continue writing the anecdotal statements throughout the school year to notice patterns of behavior for each student.

Which statement(s) might be written as an example for a student?

September 7, Lois completed her assignments with no errors in the completed work.

This anecdotal statement is factual and verifiable. No loaded terms were used. The statement indicated the kind of behavior exhibited by Lois.

Another example of an anecdotal statement would be the following:

September 8, Albert looked around the room for five minutes before starting on his mathematics assignment. He missed fifteen out of the thirty addition computations.

Again, a factual statement of Albert's achievement has been recorded. Other observers should be able to verify or refute Albert's observed behavior.

Student Products

Homework and schoolwork assignments provide an adequate supply of student products in terms of completed work. Pupils with teacher guidance may diagnose and remediate errors made by the former. From learner products in mathematics, the teacher may notice the kinds of mistakes students make in ongoing units. The errors may be due to:

1. human factors in that perfection does not reside within the individual.
2. carelessness on the part of the student.
3. computational errors.
4. not understanding an operation or process in mathematics.
5. a lack of readiness within the pupil.
6. not perceiving purpose or reasons for learning.
7. poor sequence in instruction.
8. not perceiving interest in learning.

By diagnosing student progress in mathematics, the teacher can make appropriate judgments in terms of which objective should come next in sequence. Feedback from student products provides teachers with needed information on which learning activities in mathematics need to be provided to learners. Success in learning is basic for students to achieve optimally in the mathematics curriculum.

Teacher Written Tests

Periodically, the teacher will wish to appraise student progress through testing. Test results from learners can provide excellent information to the teacher as to which goals need to be emphasized within diverse units of study.

One kind of teacher written test item appropriate for measuring mathematics achievement is the multiple choice item. The following is an example:

The formula for finding the area of a circle is

(a) $r^2\pi$ (b) ½bh (c) lw (d) s^2.

Criteria to emphasize in writing multiple choice items include the following:

1. Content needs to be clearly written so that either a, b, c, or d is the correct response. Sometimes more than a single response

is correct in a multiple choice item. In the directions for taking the test, clarity is important in the printed content. Students should know precisely how to take the test as a result of having read the directions.

2. The distractors should be plausable. Too frequently, teachers have written ridiculous distractors whereby students need minimal knowledge to eliminate the bizarre, such as

The formula for finding the area of a circle is (a) 13 + 7.

3. No clues should be given as to which response is correct or incorrect. The following violates this standard:

The Pythagorean Theory, in finding the diagonal of a right triangle was developed by

(a) Pythagoras (b) Plato (c) Aristotle

4. Unnecessary words should be eliminated in any test item. The following is an example of useless wording:

The formula $r^2 \pi$ is used

(a) to determine the area of a square.

(b) to determine the area of a circle.

(c) to determine the area of a triangle.

(d) to determine the area of a rectangle.

To eliminate excess words, the multiple choice item should be rewritten in the following way:

The formula $r^2\pi$ is used to determine the area of a

(a) square (b) circle (c) triangle (d) rectangle.

5. The determiners "a" and "an" need to be carefully used in written multiple choice items. For example, in the following test item the article "an" provides the clue as to which is the correct answer:

The formula "a=lw" is not applicable in finding the area of an

(a) square (b) rectangle (c) ellipse

The only correct answer would be an ellipse.

True-false items can be used to evaluate pupil achievement in mathematics, such as in the following clearly written test item:

The formula for finding the circumference of a circle is $d\ \pi$.

The answer to the above true-false item is clearly true. If a true-false item is false, the student could be asked to correct the part that is false. For example, supposing the following item is on the test:

The formula for finding the area of a square is bh÷2. The underlined part if false may then be corrected by students so that it reads s^2.

A matching test can be developed by the teacher to measure factual learnings acquired by students. It is significant to follow the following criteria when developing matching tests:

1. have more items in one column compared to the second column to match. Thus, the process of elimination cannot be used extensively to complete the matching test.
2. have phrases or single concepts in one column to match with the second column. Column two may also contain phrases or single concepts. However, if both columns contain lengthy sentences, the matching test may be complex indeed. One column may have sentences of reasonable length.
3. develop a test of moderate length so that fatigue does not set in on the part of the student taking the test. The mathematics teacher is attempting to measure conceptual learning and not necessarily endurance in taking the matching test.
4. use a single topic when developing test items. If items pertain to diverse topics, it may be relatively easy for a pupil to match selected items in column A with column B. Thus, a matching test may deal with the topic of formulas to determine areas of diverse geometrical figures. A single topic is then utilized in developing the matching test. If a simple addition problem were added to the test involving the above named formulas, it would be relatively easy for the learner to notice that only one possible matching could be made in relating column A with column B of the test items, e.g. a numeral plus a numeral equals a numeral.

Short answer or completion items may be utilized in testing. The following is an example of a short answer test item:

A+B=B+A emphasizes the property of addition. There are relevant criteria to follow in writing short answer test items.

1. Adequate information must be provided in the short answer test item so that students know what is wanted in

terms of responses. The following short answer item lacks needed subject matter in terms of responses wanted:
________and________are the________ of________.

2. The blanks in short answer test items should be of equal length so that clues are not given to the test taker as to which the correct answer is.
3. The blank spaces should be numbered sequentially to make for ease of scoring.
4. It is important to write subject matter clearly so that the involved test taker interprets the short answer test items accurately.
5. Learners need to have an adequately developed writing vocabulary to respond correctly to the blanks in short answer test items.
6. The teacher needs to give credit to correct responses even though they differ from the right answer written on the teachers' own originally developed key.

Essay items as a fifth type of teacher written test item may be utilized to appraise student progress. Thus, an essay item might be written to have students clarify and explain thinking involved in solving a word problem. The following is an example:

Mr. and Mrs. Brown and their two children, aged seven and ten, took a vacation trip in which 1,500 kilometers were traveled. The car averaged ten kilometers traveled for each liter of gasoline used on the excursion. The price of the gasoline was $26 per liter. The total cost for lodging was $280 for the vacation trip which lasted seven days. The average cost per day for meals for each of the four family members was $12. How much did the total vacation trip cost? In your answer, give reasons for using each numeral and/or number name used.

Here students need to analyze their thinking in terms of how each numeral and number name is to be utilized. In the analyzation, selected values will not be used in solving the problem. The cognitive level of analysis may then be appraised by the teacher.

The mathematics teacher may also appraise if pupils can apply that which had been learned previously. Thus, are students able to utilize the cognitive level of application within the framework of problem solving? If a pupil cannot use what has been acquired previously, perhaps meaning and purpose were omitted on the learner's part in learning experiences prior to the essay test item that needs its required responses.

In any essay response, the teacher can notice the quality of spelling, handwriting, punctuation, usage, capitalization, and sequence of ideas. The mechanics of writing described above should be appraised separately from content or subject matter needed to solve the problem.

In writing essay tests to appraise student progress in mathematics, the teacher must

1. write adequately delimited test items. The following essay item is too broad: Discuss mathematics.

Volumes have been written and will continue to be written on mathematics.

The following essay item is adequately delimited:

Describe the meaning of each symbol in the formula A=½bh.

2 . write essay items which are not too factual in terms of needed student responses, such as:

"What is the formula for finding the area of a parallelogram?"

A quality true-false, multiple choice, matching, or completion (short answer) test item can deal in a more effective way with factual content, as compared with the essay test. Thus, instead of the essay item

"What is the formula for finding the area of a parallelogram?" the following completion item would suffice:

"The formula for finding the area of a parallelogram is Conferences with Students,

The mathematics teacher can assist student achievement with the use of conferences. The teacher may meet with one or more (a small group) students to discuss common errors made in ongoing learning activities. Diagnosis is an important concept to emphasize in the conference setting. Which specific errors did one or more learners make? The following are examples of common mistakes:

1. Not copying a problem correctly from a textbook or workbook.

2. A lack of understanding of the terms carrying and borrowing. Another name for the same kinds of errors would be

regrouping and renaming.

3. inability to recall answers to basic addition, subtraction, multiplication, and division number pairs.

4. Not being able to apply formulas in mathematics to concrete situations in life.

5. A lack of proficiency in reading content, such as story problems in mathematics. If a student cannot identify, approximately, ninety per cent of the words in word problems, comprehension will tend to go downhill.

6. inability to analyze in terms of needed content as compared to the unneeded in solving word problems.

7. lacking the desire to evaluate personal achievement in ongoing lessons and units in mathematics.

Thus, the conference method in an atmosphere of respect can assist individual students to achieve at a more optimal rate of progress.

Parent-Teacher Conferences

An adequate number of parent-teachcr (PT) conferences should be held in any given school year. Mathmatics teachers need to inform parents of their son's or daughter's progress in a face-to-face situation. Too frequently, report cards alone are utilized to report pupil progress to parents. However, report card results are a one-way street of communication. Parents, no doubt, have questions pertaining to items on a report card. Sometimes PT conferences are held right after the report card has been issued the first time to a pupil in a given school year.

To achieve readiness in having a PT conference, the teacher needs to:

1. have work samples pertaining to completed daily assignments of the involved student. The parents need to see the quality of work done by their offspring. Seeing directly products of a student is better than merely attempting to describe how well a pupil is achieving in mathematics.
2. be knowledgeable about the capacity and general achievement level of the student in the area of mathematics.

3. understand attitudes possessed by the learner toward mathematics.

In a PT conference, the teacher must:

1. accept parents as human beings having a sincere desire in wanting their son or daughter to achieve well in the mathematics curriculum.
2. respect the thinking of parents. Nothing is gained by exhibiting feelings of hostility and mistrust.
3. work together with the involved parents in guiding each pupil to achieve optimally in mathematics.

Certainly, PT conferences are vital in improving the mathematics curriculum!

Oral Tests

For blind or partially sighted students, oral tests may be utilized to appraise progress. The normal learner, in, selected instances, may also benefit from oral testing. The use of oral tests can eliminate the reading factor in measuring student achievement. Sometimes, a mathematics test appraises reading skills, such as in word or story problems. However, teachers should attempt to ascertain students' progress in computation, concepts, and problem solving. Oral tests can be valid and reliable to measure achievement in mathematics.

Content validity is involved in selected oral items to utilize in appraising student progress in mathematics. Each item selected should relate directly to the precise, measurable objectives emphasized in teaching and learning. Thus, the effectiveness of the teacher's proficiency in the teaching of mathematics is being appraised. Did the involved student attain the precise ends? It is an either or situation. Either the pupil was or was not successful in goal attainment. If a learner has not been successful in achieving an objective diagnosis of the situation is necessary to determine causes and remediation methods.

Test items, orally administered, that relate directly to the statement of precise objectives should be valid. Thus, learning activities have been provided by the teacher which guided students to achieve the specific ends. After instructions the teacher measured the involved pupil's achievement to notice if the stated objectives had been attained. In situations such as these, the test is valid, if items are clearly stated orally, since the learning experiences guided students to achieve the precise objectives, and the measurement procedures harmonized directly with the statement of objectives.

Consistency of results from students who have been administered an oral test in mathematics is important. One way of ascertaining internal consistency in administering a test is to compare odd versus even numbered items. Did those learners who scored high on the even numbered items also score high on the odd numbered items? The teacher may wish to rank each pupil in the class from high to low in the even numbered items on the oral test. The same also needs to be done for the odd numbered items. A reliability coefficient can then be computed for internal consistency. In any teacher determined test be it oral or written, internal consistency reliability can be computed when comparing students in class with responses correct to even versus odd numbered items.

Sociometric Devices

Periodically, the mathematics teacher will wish to have pupils work cooperatively within committees. To determine committee membership, the teacher may want to utilize the sociometric device. Sociometric devices attempt to evaluate social, not academic growth.

The teacher may have students list on paper their first, second, and third choices in working on a committee. Learners need to be assured that their responses will be kept strictly confidential. Also, the mathematics teacher needs to mention to students that the results of the sociometric device will be utilized to determine committee membership.

What might the teacher appraise from the responses given by students as to whom they would prefer to work with on a committee?

1. Students that are chosen frequently by others.
2. Learners who are on the fringe area in that they are chosen, perhaps, only once and that being a third choice.
3. Individuals who are complete isolates.

Guidance can be provided by the mathematics teacher in assisting isolates to becoming increasingly accepted by others. Changes here generally will take place slowly. Students who are isolates can be placed in committees in which other learners are highly accepting of others. Certainly an isolate should not be placed in a committee or small group of cliques.

The goal for any committee to attain is to achieve as much or more using this method of teaching as compared to other procedures.

In Closing

There are numerous means available to acertain learner progress in the mathematics curriculum.

These include using:

1. checklists and rating scales.
2. standardized tests.
3. criterion referenced tests (CRT).
4. anecdotal records.
5. student products.
6. teacher written tests.
7. conferences with students.
8. parent-teacher conferences.
9. oral tests.
10. sociometric devices.

Each evaluation technique has its strengths with selected limitations also. The mathematics teacher needs to utilize a variety of procedures to appraise student progrress. With quality evaluation results from students, the teacher may truly develop a sequential mathematics curriculum from which all students might benefit optimally.

Selected Referemes

Ediger, Marlow & D. Bhaskara Rao (2000). *Teaching Mathematics Successfully. New Delhi:* Discovery Publishing House.

Ediger, Marlow & D. Bhaskara Rao (2003). *Elementary Curriculum.* New Delhi, India: Discovery Publishing House.

Additional Reading

Bhaskara Rao, Digumarti (1994). *Scientific Aptitude.* New Delhi: Ashish Publishing House.

Bhaskara Rao, Digumarti (1995). *Animal Kingdom.* New Delhi: Discovery Publishing House.

Bhaskara Rao, Digumarti (1995). *Batracology.* New Delhi: Discovery Publishing House.

Bhaskara Rao, Digumarti (1996). *Scientific Attitude vis-a-vis Scientfic Aptitude.* New Delhi: Discovery Publishing House.

Bhaskara Rao, Digumarti, ed. (1996). *Encyclopaedia of Education for All,* 5 vols. New Delhi: APH Publishing Corporation.

Vol.I Education for All: The World Conference

Vol.II Education for All: The EPA-9 Summit.

Vol.III Education For All: Quality Education for All.

Vol.IV Education For All: Planning and Monitoring.

Vol. V Education For All: The Indian Scenario.

Bhaskara Rao, Digumarti, ed. (1996). *Global Perception on Peace Education,* 3 Vols. New Delhi: Discovery Publishing House.

Bhaskara Rao, Digumarti, ed. (1996). *National Policy on Education,* 2 Vols. New Delhi: Anmol Publications Pvt. Ltd.

Bhaskara Rao, Digumarti, ed. (1997). *Care the Child,* 2 Vols New Delhi: Discovery Publishing House.

Bhaskara Rao, Digumarti, ed. (1997). *Education for the 21st Century.* New Delhi: Discovery Publishing House.

Bhaskara Rao, Digumarti, ed. (1997). *Reflections on Scientific Attitude.* New Delhi: Discovery Publishing House.

Bhaskara Rao, Digumarti (1997) *Scientific Attitude.* New Delhi:

Discovery Publishing House.

Bhaskara Rao, Digumarti, ed. (1997). *Success Story of a Primary Education Project.* New Delhi: APH Publishing Corporation.

Bhaskara Rao, Digumarti, ed. (1997). *World Food Summit.* New Delhi: Discovery Publishing House.

Bhaskara Rao, Digumarti, ed. (1998). *Adolescence Education.* New Delhi: Discovery Publishing House.

Bhaskara Rao, Digumarti, ed. (1998). *Community and School Nutrition Education.* New Delhi: Discovery Publishing House.

Bhaskara Rao, Digumarti, ed. (1998). *District Primary Education Programme.* New Delhi: Discovery Publishing House.

Bhaskara Rao, Digumarti, ed. (1998). *Earth Summit,* 2 Vols. New Delhi: Discovery Publishing House.

Bhaskara Rao, Digumarti, ed. (1998). *National Policy on Education: Towards an Enlightened and Humane Society.* New Delhi: Discovery Publishing House.

Bhaskara Rao, Digumarti, ed. (1998). *Reforming School Education.* New Delhi: Discovery Publishing House.

Bhaskara Rao, Digumarti, ed. (1998). *Teacher Education in India.* New Delhi: Discovery Publishing House.

Bhaskara Rao, Digumarti, ed. (1998). *World Summit for Social Development.* New Delhi: Discovery Publishing House.

Bhaskara Rao, Digumarti, ed. (2000). *Education for All: Achieving* The Goal. 3 Vols. New Delhi: APH Publishing Corporation.

Vol. I The Global Consensus.

Vol. II Mid-decade Review Reports of Regional Seminars.

Vol. III Issues and Tends.

Bhaskara Rao, Digumarti, ed. (2000). *International Encyclopaedia of AIDS,* 11 Vols in 13 Parts. New Delhi: Discovery Publishing House.

Vol. 1 Introduction to HIV/AIDS.

Vol. 2 HIV/AIDS–Issues and Challenges, 2 parts.

Vol. 3 HIV/AIDS–Socio Economic Realities

Vol. 4 HIV/AIDS Law Ethics and Human Rights, 2 parts.

Vol. 5 AIDS and NGOs.

Vol. 6 AIDS and Home Care.

Vol. 7 STD Case Management.

Vol. 8 HIV Prevention and Care–Teaching Modules for Nurses and Midwives.

Vol. 9 HIV/AIDS Prevention Education for Educational Institutions.

Vol. 10 Instructional Modules for AIDS Education.

Vol. 11 School Health Education to Prevent AIDS and STD A Package for Curriculum Planners.

Bhaskara Rao, Dugumarti, ed. (2000). *International Encyclopaedia of Science and Technology Education.* 11 Volumes. New Delhi:

Discovery Publishing House.

Vol. 1 Science and Technology Education.

Vol. 2 Science Education in Developing Countries.

Vol. 3 Organisational Structure of Science.

Vol. 4 Science Education in Asia and the Pacific.

Vol. 5 Science and Technology Education for All.

Vol. 6 Values, Ethics, Talent and Girls in Science and Technology Education.

Vol. 7 Popularization of Science and Technology Education.

Vol. 8 Science, Power and Society.

Vol. 9 Information Technology.

Vol. 10 Teacher Training in Science and Technology Education.

Vol. 11 Science, Technology and Society: A Curriculum Framework.

Bhaskara Rao, Digumarti, ed. (2001) *Distance Education in Different Countries.* New Delhi : APH Publishing Corporation.

Bhaskara Rao, Digumarti, ed. (2001). *Decentralised Management of Education (Management of Education in Panchayati Raj and Municipal Bodies).* New Delhi: Discovery Publishing House.

Bhaskara Rao, Digumarti, ed. (2001). *Electrochemistry for Environmental Protection.* New Delhi : Discovery Publishing

House.

Bhaskara Rao, Digumarti, ed. (2001). *Global Educational Studies.* New Delhi: Discovery Publishing House.

Bhaskara Rao, Digumarti, ed. (2001) *Global Synthesis of Educational Assessment.* New Delhi: Discovery Publishing House.

Bhaskara Road, Digumarti,ed. (2001) *International Encyclopaedia of Human Rights,* 7 Volumes in 13 parts. New Delhi: Discovery Publishing House.

Vol. 1 International Instruments of Human Rights, 2 parts

Vol. 2 Regional Instruments of Human Rights.

Vol. 3 Humam Rights and the United Nations, 2 parts.

Vol. 4 Fact Files of Human Rights, 2 parts

Vol. 5 Study Stories of Human Rights, 3 parts.

Vol. 6 International Meetings on Human Rights, 2 parts.

Vol. 7 Professional Training in Human Rights.

Bhaskara Rao, Digumarti, ed. (2001) *Jomtein Decade of Education.* New Delhi: Discovery Publishing House.

Bhaskara Rao, Digumarti, ed. (2001). *Nuclear Materials: Issues and Concerns,* 2 vols. New Delhi: Discovery Publishing House.

Bhaskara Rao, Digumarti, ed. (2001). *World Conference on Education for All.* New Delhi: APH Pubishing Corporation.

Bhaskara Rao, Digumarti, ed. (2001). *World Conference in Higher Education.* New Delhi: Discovery Publishing House.

Bhaskara Rao, Digumarti, ed. (2001). *World Conference on Science.* New Delhi: Discovery Publishing House.

Bhaskara Rao, Digumarti ed.(2003). *Inspiring Experiences in Teacher Education.* New Delhi: Discovery Publishing House.

Bhaskara Rao, Digumarti, ed. (2003). *International Studies in Education.* New Delhi: Discovery Publishing House.

Bhaskara Rao. Digumarti, ed. (2003). *Military Conversion: Impact on Science and Technology.* New Delhi: Discovery Publishing House.

Bhaskara Rao, Digumarti ed. (2003). *United Nations Millennium Summit.* New Delhi: Discovery Publishing House.

Bhaskara Rao, Digumarti ed. (2003). *World Assembly on Aging.* New Delhi: Discovery Publishing House.

Bhaskara Rao, Digumarti ed. (2003). *World Conference on Human Rights.* New Delhi: Discovery Publishing House.

Bhaskara Rao, Digumarti ed. (2003). *World Education Forum.* New Delhi: Discovery Publishing House.

Bhaskara Rao, Digumarti, ed. (2003). *Education, Employment and Human Resource Development.* New Delhi: Discovery Publishing House.

Bhaskara Rao, Digumarti, ed. (2003). *Teachers in a Changing World.* New Delhi: Discovery Publishing House.

Bhaskara Rao, Digumarti, ed. (2003). *European Education and Teachers.* New Delhi: Discovery Publishing House.

Bhaskara Rao, Digumarti, ed. (2003). *Successful Schooling.* New Delhi: Discovery Publishing House.

Bhaskara Rao, Digumarti, ed. (2003). *Learning to Live Together.* New Delhi: Discovery Publishing House.

Bhaskara Rao, Digumarti, C.A.P. Swamy & B.S.V. Dutt (1997). *Self Evaluation in Student Teaching.* New Delhi: Discovery Publishing House.

Bhaskara Rao, Digumarti, C. Sridevi & K. Vijaya (1995). *Achievement in Social Studies.* New Delhi: Discovery Publishing House.

Bhaskara Rao, Digumarti & Digumarti Pushpa Latha (1994). *Achievement in Biology.* New Delhi: Discovery Publishing House.

Bhaskara Rao, Digumarti & Digumarti Pushpa Latha (1995). *Achievement in English.* New Delhi: Discovery Publishing House.

Bhaskara Rao, Digumarti & Digumarti Pushpa Latha (1995). *Achievement in Science.* New Delhi: Discovery Publishing House.

Bhaskara Rao, Digumarti & Digumarti Pushpa Latha (1995). *Achievement in Mathematics.* New Delhi: Discovery Publishing House.

Bhaskara Rao, Digumarti & Digumarti Pushpa Latha, eds. (1998). *International Encyclopaedia of Women,* 5 Vols. New Delhi:

Discovery Publishing House.

Vol. 1 Status of World's Women.

Vol. 2 Women, Education amd Empowerment.

Vol. 3 Women Challenges and Advancement.

Vol. 4 Women and Family Heath.

Vol. 5 Women and International Action.

Bhaskara Rao, Digumarti, Digumarti Pushpa Latha & Digumarti Harshitha, eds. (2001). *Biological Warfare*. New Delhi: Discovery Publishing House.

Bhaskara Rao, Digumarti, Digumarti Pushpa Latha & Digumarti Harshitha, eds. (2001). *Women as Educators*. New Delhi: Discovery Publishing House.

Bhaskara Rao, Digumarti & Digumarti Harshitha (2000). *Education in India*. New Delhi: APH Publishing Corporation.

Bhaskara Rao, Digumarti & Digumarti Harshitha eds. (2001). *Assessing Learning Achievement*. New Delhi: Discovery Publishing House.

Bhaskara Rao, Digumarti & Digumarti Harshitha, eds. (2001). *Energy Security*. New Delhi: Discovery Publishing House.

Bhaskara Rao, Digumarti, D. Harshitha and K.R.S.S. Rao, eds. (1999). *Advanced Biotechnology*. New Delhi: Discovery Publishing House.

Bhaskara Rao, Digumarti & D. Sridhar (2002). *Job Satisfaction of School Teachers*. New Delhi: Discovery Publishing House.

Bhaskara Rao, Digumarti & K.R.S. Sambasiva Rao, eds. (1996). *Current Trends in Indian Education*. New Delhi: Discovery Publishing House.

Bhaskara Rao, Digumarti and K. Vijaya (1995). *A Text Book Evaluation*. Ambala Cantt: The Associated Publishers. pp:100. Rs. 160.

Bhaskara Rao, Digumarti and N.V.M. Mohana Rao (2003). *Problems of Mentally Handicapped*. New Delhi: Discovery Publishing House.

Bhaskara Rao, Digumarti, V.V.Rao, V.V. Lakshmi and V.V. Krishna, eds. (2000). *Status and Advancement of Women*. New

Delhi: APH Publishing Corporation.

Babu, P.C. and Digumarti Bhaskara Rao, ed. (2003) *Flowers of Wisdom*. New Delhi: Discovery Publishing House.

Bhagya Lakshmi, Lingineni and Digumarti Bhaskara Rao, ed. (2000). *Reading and Comprehension*. New Delhi: Discovery Publishing House.

Bhuvaneswara Lakshmi, G. & Digumarti Bhaskara Rao, ed. (2000). *Attitude Towards Science*. New Delhi: Discovery Publishing House.

Devraj, T.A.S. & Digumarti Bhaskara Rao, ed. (1997). *Trace Analysis of Uranium and Thorum*. New Delhi: Discovery Publishing House.

Durga Rani, K. & Digumarti Bhaskara Rao, ed. (2000). *Educational Aspirations and Scientific Attitudes*. New Delhi: Discovery Publishing House.

Dutt, B.S.V. & Digumarti Bhaskara Rao, (2001). *Empowering Primary Teachers*. New Delhi: Discovery Publishing House.

Ediger, Marlow & Digumarti Bhaskara Rao (1996). *Science Curriculum*. New Delhi: Discovery Publishing House.

Ediger, Marlow & Digumarti Bhaskara Rao (2000). *Teaching Mathematics Successfully*. New Delhi: Discovery Publishing House.

Ediger, Marlow & Digumarti Bhaskara Rao (2000). *Teaching Reading Successfully*. New Delhi: Discovery Publishing House.

Ediger Marlow & Digumarti Bhaskara Rao (2001). *Teaching Science Successfully*. New Delhi: Discovery Publishing House.

Ediger, Marlow & Digumarti Bhaskara Rao (2001). *Teaching Social Studies Successfully*. New Delhi: Discovery Publishing House.

Ediger, Marlow & Digumarti Bhaskara Rao (2003). *Philosophy and Curriculm*. New Delhi: Discovery Publishing House.

Ediger, Marlow & Digumarti Bhaskara Rao (2003). *Improving School Administaration*. New Delhi: Discovery Publishing House.

Ediger, Marlow & Digumarti Bhaskara Rao (2003). *Elementry Curriculum*. New Delhi: Discovery Publishing House.

Ediger, Marlow & Digumarti Bhsakara Rao (2003). *Language Arts*

Curriculum. New Delhi: Discovery Publishing House.

Ediger, Marlow & Digumarti Bhaskara Rao (2003). *Teaching Language Arts Successfully*. New Delhi: Discovery Publishing House.

Ediger, Marlow & Digumarti Bhaskara Rao (2003). *Teaching Science in elementary Schools*. New Delhi: Discovery Publishing House.

Ediger, Marlow & Digumarti Bhaskara Rao (2003). *Teaching Social Studies in Elementary Schools*. New Delhi: Discovery Publishing House.

Jayasree, Kamdi & Digumarti Bhaskara Rao, ed. (1999). *Correlates of Socialisation*. New Delhi: Discovery Publishing House.

Jyothi, Nirmala & Digumarti Bhaskara Rao, ed (2002) . *Non-detention System in Education*. New Delhi : Discovery Publishing House .

Marja, Talvi & Digumarti Bhaskara Rao, eds. (1996). *Educational Leadership and Social Changes*. New Delhi : Discovery Publishing House.

Prabhakaram, K.S. & Digumarti Bhaskara Rao, ed. (1998) . *Concept Attainment Model in Mathematics Teaching*. New Delhi : Discovery publishing House.

Prasanth Kumar, J. & Digumarti Bhaskara Rao, ed. (1988). *Effectiveness of Distance Educational System*, New Delhi : Discovery Publishing House.

Prasanth Kumar, J. & Digumarti Bhaskara Rao and G. Sundara Rao, eds. (2000). *Open University Support Services*. New Delhi : Discovery Publishng House.

Ramatulasamma K. & Digumarti Bhaskara Rao, ed. (2002) . *Job Satisfaction of Teacher Educators*. New Delhi : Discovery Publishing House.

Rama Krishnaiah, D. & Digumarti Bhaskara Rao, ed. (1998). *Job Statisfaction of College Teachers*. New Delhi : Discovery Publishing House.

Ramkumar Ratnam & Digumarti Bhaskara Rao, ed. (2003). *Dukkha : Suffering in Early Buddhism* . New Delhi: Discovery Publishing House.

Ramesh, Ganta & Digumarti Bhaskara Rao, eds. (1998).

Environmental Education: Problems and Prospects. New Delhi: Discovery Publishing House.

Rathaiah, L. and Digumarti Bhaskara Rao, eds. (1997). *International Innovation in Education*. New Delhi: Discovery Publishing House.

Rathaiah, Lavu, Digumarti Bhaskara Rao and Paturi Koteswara Rao (1997). *Achievement Correlates*. New Delhi: Discovery Publishing House.

Reddy, Sudhakar & Digumarti Bhaskara Rao, ed. (2003). *Creativity in Adolescents*. New Delhi: Discovery Publishing House.

Sanjeeva Rao, P.C. & Digumarti Bhaskara Rao, ed. (1996). *A Text Book of Geology*. New Delhi: Discovery Publishing House.

Satya Narayana, V. & Digumarti Bhaskara Rao, ed. (2001). *Physical Education, Social Attitudes and Leadership Qualities*. New Delhi:

Srinivasulu Reddy, M., K.R.S. Sambasiva Rao & Digumarti Bhaskara Rao, ed. (1999). *A Text Book of Aquaculture*. New Delhi: Discovery Publishing House.

Vanaja, M. & Digumarti Bhaskara Rao, ed. (1999). *Inquiry Training Model*. New Delhi: Discovery Publishing House.

Valeri V. Koustiouk & Digumarti Bhaskara Rao, ed. (2003). *A Text Book of Cryogenics*. New Delhi: Discovery Publishing House.

Veena Kumari, Balusu & Digumarti Bhaskara Rao ed. (1996). *Operation Black Board*. New Delhi: A.P.H. Publishing Corporation.

Veena Kumari, B. & Digumarti Bhaskara Rao, ed. (2000). *Psycho Social Correlates of Achievement*. New Delhi : Discovery Publishing House.

Venkata Rao, P. & Digumarti Bhaskara Rao (1989). *A Text Book of Zoology–Junior Intermediate*. Guntur: Vignan Publishers.

Venkata Rao, P. & Digumarti Bhaskara Rao (1989). *A Text Book of Zoology–Senior Intermediate*. Guntur: Vignan Publishers.

Venugopala Rao, K. & Digumarti Bhaskara Rao, ed. (2000). *Teacher Morale in Secondary Schools*. New Delhi: Discovery Publishing House.

Vidya, C. & Digumarti Bhaskara Rao, ed. (1996). *A Text Book of Nutrition*. New Delhi: Discovery Publishing House.

Vijaya Bharathi, D. & Digumarti Bhaskara Rao, ed. (2000).

Educational Philosophies of Swami Vivekanand and John Dewey. New Delhi: APH Publishing Corporation.

Bhaskara Rao, Digumarti (1986). *Dhrushya Sravana Bodhanapakaranalu* (Audio Visual Teaching Aids). Guntur: Nagarjuna Publishers.

Bhaskara Rao, Digumarti (1993). *Jeevasashtra Bodhana* (Teaching of Biology). Guntur: Nagarjuna Publishers.

Bhaskara Rao, Digumarti (1995). *Vignanasasthra Bodhana.* (Teaching of Science). Guntur: Nagarjuna Publishers.

Bhaskara Rao, Digumarti (1997). *Vidya Manovignana Sashtram.* (Educational Psychology). Guntur: Creative Press.

Bhaskara Rao, Digumarti (1998). *DSC Study Material.* Guntur: Nagarjuna Publishers.

Bhaskara Rao, Digumarti (1998). *Upadhyayudu Vidya* (Teacher and Education). Guntur: Nagarjuna Publishers.

Bhaskara Rao, Digumarti (1998). *Vidya Dhrukpadhalu* (Perspectives of Education). Guntur: Nagarjuna Publishers.

Bhaskara Rao, Digumarti (1999).*EdCET Teaching Aptitude.* Guntur: Nagarjuna Publishers.

Bhaskara Rao, Digumarti (2001). *Bharata Samajamulo Upadhayagudu Vidya* (Teacher and Education in Emerging Indian Society). Guntur: Nagarjuna Publishers.

Bhaskara Rao, Digumarti (2001). *Bhoutika Sastra Bodhana Padatula* (Methods of Teaching Physical Science). Guntur: Nagarjuna Publishers.

Bhaskara Rao, Digumarti (2001). *Jeeva Sastra Bodhana Padhatulu* (Methods of Teaching Biological Science). Guntur : Nagarjuna Publishers.

Bhaskara Rao, Digumarti (2001). *Vidya Manovignana Sastram* (Educational Psychology). Guntur: Nagarjuna Publishers.

Bhaskara Rao, Digumarti (2003). *Vidya Sanketika Sastram.* (Educational Technology). Guntur : Nagarjuna Publishers.

Bhaskara Ra, Digumarti (2003). *Pathasala Paripalana & Virvahana* (School Administration and Management). Guntur: Nagarjuna Publishers.

❑

Index